The Summa Theologiæ ranks among the greatest documents of the Christian Church, and is a landmark of medieval western thought. It provides the framework for Catholic studies in systematic theology and for a classical Christian philosophy, and is regularly consulted by scholars of all faiths and none, across a range of academic disciplines. This paperback reissue of the classic Latin/English edition first published by the English Dominicans in the 1960s and 1970s, in the wake of the Second Vatican Council, has been undertaken in response to regular requests from readers and librarians around the world for the entire series of 61 volumes to be made available again. The original text is unchanged, except for the correction of a small number of typographical errors.

The original aim of this edition was not narrowly ecclesiastical. It sought to make this treasure of the Christian intellectual heritage available to theologians and philosophers of all backgrounds, including those who, without claiming to be believers themselves, appreciate a religious integrity which embodies hardbitten rationalism and who recognise in Thomas Aquinas a master of that perennial philosophy which forms the bedrock of European civilisation. Because of this the editors worked under specific instructions to bear in mind not only the professional theologian, but also the general reader with an interest in the 'reason' in Christianity. The parallel English and Latin texts can be used successfully by anybody with a basic knowledge of Latin, while the presence of the Latin text has allowed the translators a degree of freedom in adapting their English version for modern readers. Each volume contains a glossary of technical terms and is designed to be complete in itself to serve for private study or as a course text.

NIHIL OBSTAT

KENELMUS FOSTER O.P.

EDOUARDUS BOOTH O.P.

IMPRIMI POTEST

JONATHAS FLEETWOOD O.P.
Prior Provincialis Angliæ

die 21 Januarii 1975

NIHIL OBSTAT

R. J. CUMING. D.D.
Censor

IMPRIMATUR

DAVID NORRIS
Vic. Gen.

Westminster 24 January 1975

ST THOMAS AQUINAS

SUMMA THEOLOGIÆ

ST THOMAS AQUINAS

SUMMA THEOLOGIÆ

Latin text and English translation,
Introductions, Notes, Appendices
and Glossaries

NON NISI TE

PIÆ MEMORIÆ

JOANNIS

PP. XXIII

DICATUM

IN AN AUDIENCE, 13 December 1963, to a group representing the Dominican Editors and the combined Publishers of the New English *Summa*, His Holiness Pope Paul VI warmly welcomed and encouraged their undertaking. A letter from His Eminence Cardinal Cicognani, Cardinal Secretary of State, 6 February 1968, expressed the continued interest of the Holy Father in the progress of the work, 'which does honour to the Dominican Order, and the Publishers, and is to be considered without doubt as greatly contributing to the growth and spread of a genuinely Catholic culture', and communicated his particular Apostolic Blessing. The assurance was repeated in a letter, 5 February 1973, from the present Secretary of State, His Eminence Cardinal Villot.

ST THOMAS AQUINAS

SUMMA THEOLOGIÆ

VOLUME 59

HOLY COMMUNION

(3a.79–83)

Latin text, English translation, Introduction, Notes & Glossary

THOMAS GILBY O.P.

CAMBRIDGE UNIVERSITY PRESS
Cambridge, New York, Melbourne, Madrid, Cape Town, Singapore, São Paulo

Cambridge University Press
The Edinburgh Building, Cambridge CB2 2RU, UK

Published in the United States of America by Cambridge University Press, New York

www.cambridge.org
Information on this title: www.cambridge.org/9780521394062

This digitally printed first paperback version 2006

A catalogue record for this publication is available from the British Library

ISBN-13 978-0-521-39406-2 hardback
ISBN-10 0-521-39406-6 hardback

ISBN-13 978-0-521-02967-4 paperback
ISBN-10 0-521-02967-8 paperback

CONTENTS

CONTENTS

EDITORIAL NOTES

VARIATIONS of text between the Piana and Leonine are of little importance; a few have been noted in this edition. The punctuation has been tidied, and some of the paragraphing has been changed for the sake of clearness. The translation follows the order of sentences in the original.

FOOTNOTES

Those signified by a superior number are usually the references given by St Thomas and tracked down by the Leonine Commission, with the exception of no. 1 to each article which refers to parallel texts in his writings. Those signified alphabetically are editorial references and explanatory remarks.

REFERENCES

Biblical references are to the Vulgate; Patristic references to Migne (PG, Greek Fathers; PL, Latin Fathers). Titles of St Thomas's works are abbreviated as follows:

Summa Theologiæ, without title. Part, question, article, reply; e.g. 1a. 70, 1 ad 2, 2a2æ. 25, 4.

Summa Contra Gentiles, *CG*. Book, chapter; e.g. CG II, 14.

Scriptum in IV Libros Sententiarum, *Sent*. Book, distinction, question, article, solution, or *quæstiuncula*, reply; e.g. II *Sent*. 15, 1, 1, ii ad 3.

Compendium Theologiæ, *Compend. theol.*

Scriptural commentaries (*lecturæ*, *expositiones*, *reportata*): Job, *In Job*; Psalms, *In Psal.*; Isaiah, *In Isa.*; Jeremiah, *In Jerem.*; St Matthew, *In Matt.*; St John, *In Joan.*; Epistles of St Paul, e.g. *In* 1 *Cor*. Chapter, verse, *lectio* as required.

Philosophical commentaries: Aristotle, *Peri Hermeneias*, *In Periherm.*; Posterior Analytics, *In Post. Anal.*; Physics, *In Phys.*; *De Cælo et Mundo*, *In de Cæl.*; *De Generatione et Corruptione*, *In de Gen. et Corr.*; *De Anima*, *In de Anima*; Metaphysics, *In Meta.*; Nichomachean Ethics, *In Ethic.*; Politics, *In Pol.* Book, chapter, *lectio* as required. Also for references to Dionysius, *De divinis Nominibus*, *In de Div. Nom.* References to Aristotle include the Bekker numbering.

Quæstiones quodlibetæ, *Quodl.*

Mansi = J. D. Mansi, *Sacrorum Conciliorum Nova et Amplissima Collectio*, 54 vols. Paris & Leipzig, 1901–27.

RF = E. L. Richter & E. Freidberg, *Corpus Juris Canonici*, 2 vols. Leipzig, 1922.

INTRODUCTION

THIS is the second and concluding part of the treatise on the Eucharist. The first part[1] is a classical and definitive explanation of the doctrine of the Real Presence, which, together with his liturgical offices for Corpus Christi, establishes St Thomas's fame and authority as a theologian and poet of the Blessed Sacrament. On a superficial reading much of the present set of inquiries seems to peter out into relatively unimportant and passing points of ritual observance and rubrics. Their very length may serve to dim the flashes of insight and detract from the more concise discourses on pure theology, so that we may have to remind ourselves of St Augustine's saying, *In his quæ non mole magna sunt idem est esse majus quod melius.*[2]

Yet there is more to it than that. True, St Thomas was wont to take his time over topics that engaged his contemporaries in a manner that may tax the patience of a student set on questions of more lasting and perennial importance. But even here, and especially in this volume, there is a reason for his delaying on them. He is not separating the sacrifice and the sacrament, and is considering the Eucharist in the whole setting of the Church's worship in a given period and region, not in the isolated and dramatic moments of consecration and communion. No matter that the ritual acts and languages have been so changed in recent years that many of the details he dwelt on are now mainly pieces of the past, as, too, is much of their devout allegorization. Though the weak sense of liturgical history will be regretted, a strength should not pass unnoticed.

That is the regard for the empirical here and now which runs throughout his philosophy and is taken up into his theology. Given a historical imagination, sympathetic and informed, this no more imprisons the doctrine than the Old Testament chronicle of the battles of the children of Israel does the revelation of God. The more profound of his Aristotelean convictions may make him a man for all seasons, yet he was not an unearthly prodigy who could, even had he wanted to, shake off his medieval and Neapolitan culture and temper.

So then it is from an assemblage of concretely realized items, of the words, gestures, and things which went to make up Eucharistic worship as he knew it, that the theological principles stand out clear, strong, and lasting. The sacrament-sacrifice is a sign wholly derivative from and relative to Christ, who is not changed by it and whose offering is not

---

[1] 3a. 73–78. Vol. 58 of this series, ed. W. Barden, *The Eucharistic Presence*
[2] *De Trinitate* VI, 8

added to or repeated in himself, but presented and continued in those who join in it. Yet it differs from the other sacraments in that it holds Christ himself in person.[1] St Thomas's idiom, perhaps too blunt at times to be inoffensive to polite ears, matches his conviction that the Eucharist is not just a symbol, but also an embodiment of God.

The treatise is the last but one of the *Summa* which was left incomplete in 1273: it may be remarked that in the present section Aristotle is invoked only four times, and that on minor points. In December of that year St Thomas fell into a trance, after which he confessed that compared to what he had seen his writings now seemed to him like so much straw. He died in the following March, in a hurry for heaven, according to an early biographer, from love more than illness.

---

[1]cf 3a. 65, 3; 73, 1 ad 3

Quæstio 79. de effectibus sacramenti eucharistiæ

DEINDE CONSIDERANDUM EST de effectibus hujus sacramenti. Et circa hoc quæruntur octo:

1. utrum hoc sacramentum conferat gratiam;
2. utrum effectus hujus sacramenti sit adeptio gloriæ;
3. utrum effectus hujus sacramenti sit remissio peccati mortalis;
4. utrum per hoc sacramentum remittatur peccatum veniale;
5. utrum per hoc sacramentum tota pœna peccati remittatur;
6. utrum hoc sacramentum homines præservet a peccatis futuris;
7. utrum hoc sacramentum prosit aliis quam sumentibus;
8. de impedimento effectus hujus sacramenti.

articulus I. *utrum per hoc sacramentum conferatur gratia*

AD PRIMUM sic proceditur:[1] I. Videtur quod per hoc sacramentum non conferatur gratia. Hoc enim sacramentum est nutrimentum spirituale. Nutrimentum autem non datur nisi viventi. Cum ergo vita spiritualis sit per gratiam, non competit hoc sacramentum nisi habenti gratiam. Non ergo per hoc sacramentum confertur gratia ut primo habeatur; similiter etiam nec ad hoc quod augeatur, quia augmentum spirituale pertinet ad sacramentum confirmationis, ut dictum est.[2] Non ergo per hoc sacramentum gratia confertur.

2. Præterea, hoc sacramentum assumitur ut quædam spiritualis refectio. Sed refectio spiritualis magis videtur pertinere ad usum gratiæ quam ad gratiæ collationem.* Ergo videtur quod per hoc sacramentum gratia non conferatur.

3. Præterea, sicut supra dictum est,[3] in hoc sacramento corpus Christi offertur pro salute corporis, sanguis autem pro salute animæ. Sed corpus non est subjectum gratiæ, sed anima, ut in *Secunda Parte* habitum est.[4] Ergo ad minus quantum ad corpus per hoc sacramentum gratia non confertur.

SED CONTRA est quod Dominus dicit, *Panis quem ego dabo, caro mea est pro mundi vita.*[5] Sed vita spiritualis est per gratiam. Ergo per hoc sacramentum gratia confertur.

---

*Leonine: *consecutionem*, the gaining of grace

[1]cf IV *Sent.* 12, 2, 1, i; 2, i ad 2

[2]3a. 65, 1; 72, 1

Question 79. effects of the Eucharist

NEXT WE COME TO CONSIDER the effects of this sacrament. And here there are eight points of inquiry:

1. whether the Eucharist brings grace;
2. whether its effect is the attainment of heaven;
3. whether its effect is to forgive mortal sin;
4. and venial sin;
5. and the pardon of all punishment due to sin;
6. whether the sacrament safeguards us from future sins;
7. whether it benefits others besides the recipient;
8. of obstacles to its effect.

article 1. does the sacrament give grace?

THE FIRST POINT:[1a] 1. It seems not. For this sacrament is spiritual nourishment. Now nourishment is given only to the living. Since spiritual life is through grace, this sacrament is only for a person living in grace. Not then that he should receive it in the first instance. Nor, likewise, that he should have it for spiritual growth, since that is the fruit of the sacrament of confirmation, as we have seen.[2] Therefore grace is not conferred by this sacrament.

2. Besides, this sacrament is taken as spiritual refreshment. But its purpose seems to be for the using rather than the granting of grace. And so apparently the sacrament does not bestow grace.

3. Then also, it has been said[3] that in this sacrifice the body of Christ is offered for bodily health, the blood of Christ for spiritual health. It is in the soul, not the body, that grace is seated, as was shown in the *Secunda Pars*.[4] So then at least so far as the body is concerned grace is not bestowed through this sacrament.

ON THE OTHER HAND our Lord says, *The bread which I will give is my flesh for the life of the world.*[5] But the life of the spirit comes from grace. Therefore grace is conferred through this sacrament.

---

[3]3a. 74, 1
[4]2a2æ. 110, 4
[5]*John* 6, 52
[a]How grace is the chief effect of the sacraments of the New Law has been treated in 3a. 62, and the difference noted between their causality in this respect and that of the sacraments of the Old Law.

RESPONSIO: Dicendum quod effectus hujus sacramenti debet considerari primo quidem et principaliter ex eo quod in hoc sacramento continetur, quod est Christus; qui sicut in mundum visibiliter veniens contulit mundo vitam gratiæ, secundum illud *Joan.*, *Gratia et veritas per Jesum Christum facta est*,[6] ita in hominem sacramentaliter veniens vitam gratiæ operatur, secundum illud *Joan.*, *Qui manducat me, vivet propter me.*[7] Unde et Cyrillus dicit, *Vivificativum Dei Verbum uniens seipsum propriæ carni, fecit ipsam vivificativam. Decebat enim eum nostris quodammodo uniri corporibus per sacram ejus carnem et pretiosum sanguinem, quæ accipimus in benedictionem vivificativam in pane et in vino.*[8]

Secundo consideratur ex eo quod per hoc sacramentum repræsentatur, quod est passio Christi, sicut supra dictum est.[9] Et ideo effectum quem passio Christi fecit in mundo hoc sacramentum facit in homine. Unde super illud *Joan.*, *Continuo exivit sanguis et aqua*,[10] dicit Chrysostomus, *Quia hinc suscipiunt principium sacra mysteria, cum accesseris ad tremendum calicem, ut ab ipsa bibiturus Christi costa ita accedas.*[11] Unde et ipse Dominus dicit *Matt.*, *Hic est sanguis meus qui pro vobis effundetur in remissionem peccatorum.*[12]

Tertio consideratur effectus hujus sacramenti ex modo quo traditur hoc sacramentum, quod traditur per modum cibi et potus. Et ideo omnem effectum quem cibus et potus materialis facit quantum ad vitam corporalem, quod scilicet sustentat, auget, reparat et delectat, hoc totum facit hoc sacramentum quantum ad vitam spiritualem. Unde Ambrosius dicit, *Iste panis est vitæ æternæ, qui animæ nostræ substantiam fulcit.*[13] Et Chrysostomus dicit, *Præstat se nobis desiderantibus et palpare, et comedere, et amplecti.*[14] Unde et ipse Dominus dicit, *Caro mea vere est cibus, et sanguis meus vere est potus.*[15]

Quarto consideratur effectus hujus sacramenti ex speciebus in quibus traditur hoc sacramentum. Unde Augustinus ibidem dicit, *Dominus noster corpus et sanguinem suum in eis rebus commendavit quæ ad unum aliquid rediguntur ex multis; namque aliud*, scilicet panis, *ex multis granis in unum constat; aliud*, scilicet vinum, *in unum ex multis acinis confluit.*[16] Et ideo ipse alibi dicit, *O sacramentum pietatis, o signum unitatis, o vinculum caritatis!*[17]

---

[6] *John* 1, 17
[7] *John* 6, 58
[8] *In Luc.* 22, 19. PG 72, 92. *Catena Aurea*
[9] 3a. 74, 1; 76, 2 ad 1
[10] *John* 19, 34
[11] *In Joan.* LXXXV. PG 59, 463
[12] *Matthew* 26, 28
[13] *De Sacramentis* V, 4. PL 16, 471. Gratian, *Decretum* III, 2, 56. RF I, 1335
[14] *Hom.* XLVI. PG 59, 260. *Catena Aurea. Luke* 22, 19
[15] *John* 6, 56

REPLY:[b] The effect of this sacrament should be looked at first and foremost from what the sacrament holds, and this is Christ. Just as by coming visibly into the world he brought the life of grace into it, according to *John, Grace and truth came through Jesus Christ,*[6] so by coming to men sacramentally he causes the life of grace; *He who eats me also shall live because of me.*[7] Accordingly Cyril[c] writes, *The life-giving Word of God by uniting himself with his own flesh made it also life-giving. And so it was right that he should be united with our bodies through his sacred flesh and precious blood, which we receive as a life-giving blessing in the bread and wine.*[8]

Secondly, consider what is represented by this sacrament, namely Christ's Passion, as we have recalled.[9] Accordingly the effect his Passion wrought in the world the sacrament works in a man. Hence on the words, *At once there came out blood and water,*[10] Chrysostom[d] tells us, *Because from that source flow the sacred mysteries, when you approach the awesome chalice so approach as if you were about to drink from Christ's own side.*[11] For so our Lord himself declares, *This is my blood,*[e] *which is shed for many for the forgiveness of sins.*[12]

Third, consider the effect of this sacrament in the manner of its giving, namely of food and drink. And so this sacrament does for the life of the spirit all that material food and drink does for the life of the body, by sustaining, building up, restoring, and contenting. Thus Ambrose[f] writes, *This is the bread of eternal life, which supports the substance of our soul.*[13] And Chrysostom, *He gives himself to us who desire to feel and feed and embrace.*[14] And our Lord himself says, *My flesh is food indeed and my blood is drink indeed.*[15]

Fourth, consider the species under which the sacrament is given. Augustine[g] says, *Our Lord entrusted his body and blood to those things where a single whole is rendered from many particles, for out of many grains is one thing made*, namely bread, *and from many grapes flows one thing*, namely wine.[16] And so he cries, *O sacrament of piety, O sign of unity, O bond of charity.*[17]

---

[16]*In Joan.* XXVI. On 6, 56. PL 35, 1614

[17]op cit. On 6, 41. PL 35, 1613

[b]Bear in mind, for this and the following discussions, the distinction between *ipsum sacramentum* and *res sacramenti*, the outward sign and the inward grace of union with Christ, 3a. 73, 3.

[c]St Cyril of Alexandria, d. 444.

[d]St John Chrysostom, d. *c.* 407. Bishop of Constantinople.

[e]*tēs kainēs diathēkēs*; Vulgate, *novi testamenti*; Douay, *of the new testament*; RSV, *of the covenant.*

[f]St Ambrose, d. 397, Bishop of Milan.

[g]St Augustine of Hippo, d. 430.

Et quia Christus et ejus passio est causa gratiæ et spiritualis refectio, et caritas sine gratia esse non potest, ex omnibus præmissis manifestum est quod hoc sacramentum gratiam confert.

1. Ad primum ergo dicendum quod hoc sacramentum ex seipso virtutem habet gratiam conferendi; nec aliquis habet gratiam ante susceptionem hujus sacramenti, nisi ex aliquo voto ipsius, vel per seipsum, sicut adulti, vel voto Ecclesiæ, sicut parvuli, sicut supra dictum est.[18] Unde ex efficacia virtutis ipsius est quod etiam ex voto ipsius aliquis gratiam consequatur, per quam spiritualiter vivificetur. Restat igitur ut cum sacramentum realiter sumitur, gratia augeatur et vita spiritualis perficiatur; aliter tamen quam per sacramentum confirmationis, in quo augetur et perficitur gratia ad persistendum contra exteriores impugnationes inimicorum Christi; per hoc autem sacramentum augetur gratia et perficitur spiritualis vita, ad hoc quod homo in seipso perfectus existat per conjunctionem ad Deum.

2. Ad secundum dicendum quod hoc sacramentum confert gratiam spiritualiter cum virtute caritatis. Unde Damascenus comparat hoc sacramentum carboni quem Isaias vidit,[19] *Carbo enim lignum simplex non est, sed unitum igni; ita et panis communionis non simplex panis est, sed unitus divinitati.*[20] Sicut autem Gregorius dicit, *amor Dei non est otiosus: magna enim operatur, si est.*[21] Et ideo per hoc sacramentum, quantum est ex sui virtute, non solum habitus gratiæ et virtutis confertur sed etiam excitatur in actum, secundum illud II *Cor.*, *Caritas Christi urget nos.*[22] Et inde est quod ex virtute hujus sacramenti anima spiritualiter reficitur, per hoc quod anima spiritualiter delectatur, et quodammodo inebriatur dulcedine bonitatis divinæ, secundum illud *Cantic.*, *Comedite, amici, et bibite, et inebriamini, carissimi.*[23]

3. Ad tertium dicendum quod quia sacramenta operantur salutem quam significant, ideo per quandam assimilationem dicitur quod in hoc sacramento corpus offertur pro salute corporis, et sanguis pro salute animæ, quamvis utrumque ad salutem utriusque operetur, cum sub utroque totus sit Christus, ut supra dictum est.[24] Et licet corpus non sit immediatum subjectum gratiæ, ex anima tamen redundat effectus gratiæ ad corpus dum in præsenti membra nostra exhibemus *arma justitiæ Deo*, ut habetur *Rom.*,[25] et in futuro corpus nostrum sortietur incorruptionem et gloriam animæ.

---

[18] 3a. 73, 3
[19] *Isaiah* 6, 6
[20] *De Fide Orthodoxa* IV, 13. PG 94, 1149
[21] *In Evang.* II, 30. Homily for Pentecost. PL 76, 1221
[22] II *Corinthians* 5, 14
[23] *Song of Solomon* 5, 1
[24] 3a. 76, 2
[25] *Romans* 6, 13
[h] St John of Damascus, d. 749.
[i] St Gregory I, the Great, Pope, d. 604.

And since Christ and his Passion are the cause of grace and spiritual refreshment and charity cannot be without grace, it is clear from what has been set forth that through this sacrament grace is bestowed.

Hence: 1: Of itself this sacrament has grace-giving virtue, nor does anyone have grace before receiving it except from the longing for it, whether his own, as with an adult, or the Church's, as with babies, as has been stated.[18] Accordingly it is from the effectiveness of its power that even by desiring it a person obtains grace whereby he is spiritually alive. Still it is true that when the sacrament itself is really received grace is increased and the life of the spirit perfected. Nevertheless in a different manner, from the working of the sacrament of confirmation: there grace is increased and the life of the spirit perfected so as to remain staunch before the outward onslaughts of Christ's enemies. In this sacrament, however, grace is increased and the life of the spirit perfected and made whole by union with God.

2. This sacrament spiritually confers grace together with the virtue of charity. And so Damascene[h] compares it to the burning coal in *Isaiah*;[19] *For a live ember is not simply wood, but wood united with fire; so also the bread of communion is not simple bread, but bread united with divinity.*[20] Now as Gregory[i] says, *God's love is never idle, for wherever it is it works mightily.*[21] And consequently with regard to its power this sacrament confers not only the habits of grace and virtue, but furthermore they are aroused to activity, according to St Paul, *The charity of Christ presseth us.*[22] Hence it is that through its power the soul is spiritually nourished, by being spiritually gladdened and as it were inebriated with the sweetness of divine goodness, according to the *Song of Songs*, *Eat, O friends, and drink, drink deep, O lovers.*[23j]

3. Because the sacraments effect the blessing they signify, there are some grounds for the comparison, and saying that in this sacrament the body is offered for the salvation of our body and the blood for that of our soul,[k] though in fact each works for the salvation of both body and soul, since the whole Christ is under each, as we have shown.[24] Though grace is not immediately seated in our body, its effect flows over into the body when in the present life we yield our members *to God as instruments of righteousness*;[25] and in the life to come the body will share in the incorruption and glory of the soul.

---

[j]'Spiritual', as contrasted with material or physical: cf 3a. 62, 4 ad 1; *De Veritate* XXVII, 7.

[k]The thought may be traced to Ambrosiaster. *In* 1 *Cor.* 11, 20. PL 17, 256. Ambrosiaster, the name given by Erasmus to the author of Scriptural commentaries ascribed to Ambrose by medieval writers.

articulus 2. utrum effectus hujus sacramenti sit adeptio gloriæ

AD SECUNDUM sic proceditur:[1] 1. Videtur quod effectus hujus sacramenti non sit adeptio gloriæ. Effectus enim proportionatur suæ causæ. Sed hoc sacramentum competit viatoribus, unde et viaticum dicitur. Cum igitur viatores nondum sint capaces gloriæ, videtur quod hoc sacramentum non causet adeptionem gloriæ.

2. Præterea, posita causa sufficienti, ponitur effectus. Sed multi accipiunt hoc sacramentum qui nunquam pervenient ad gloriam, ut patet per Augustinum.[2] Non ergo hoc sacramentum est causa adeptionis gloriæ.

3. Præterea, majus non efficitur a minori, quia nihil agit ultra suam speciem. Sed minus est accipere Christum sub specie aliena, quod fit in hoc sacramento, quam frui eo in specie propria, quod pertinet ad gloriam. Ergo hoc sacramentum non causat adeptionem gloriæ.

SED CONTRA est quod dicitur *Joan.*, *Si quis manducaverit ex hoc pane, vivet in æternum.*[3] Sed vita æterna est vita gloriæ. Ergo effectus hujus sacramenti est adeptio gloriæ.

RESPONSIO: Dicendum quod in hoc sacramento potest considerari et id ex quo habet effectum, scilicet ipse Christus contentus et passio ejus repræsentata, et id per quod habet effectum, scilicet usus sacramenti et species ejus. Et quantum ad utrumque competit huic sacramento quod causet adeptionem vitæ æternæ. Nam ipse Christus per suam passionem aperuit nobis aditum vitæ æternæ, secundum illud *Hebr.*, *Novi Testamenti mediator est; ut, morte intercedente, qui vocati sunt accipiant repromissionem æternæ hæreditatis.*[4] Unde et in forma hujus sacramenti dicitur, *Hic est calix sanguinis mei, novi et æterni Testamenti.*[5] Similiter etiam refectio cibi spiritualis et unitas significata per species panis et vini habentur quidem in præsenti, sed imperfecte, perfecte autem in statu gloriæ. Unde Augustinus dicit super illud *Joan.*, *Caro mea vere est cibus*,[6] *Cum cibo et potu id appetant homines ut non esuriant neque sitiant, hoc veraciter non præstat nisi iste cibus et potus qui eos a quibus sumitur immortales et incorruptibiles facit in societate sanctorum, ubi pax erit, et unitas plena atque perfecta.*[7]

1. Ad primum ergo dicendum quod sicut passio Christi, in* cujus virtute hoc sacramentum operatur, est quidem causa sufficiens gloriæ, non

---

*Leonine: *ex*

[1]cf *In Joan.* 6, *lect.* 7
[2]*De Civitate Dei* XXI, 25. PL 41, 742
[3]*John* 6, 52
[4]*Hebrews* 9, 15
[5]Roman Canon
[6]*John* 6, 56
[7]*In Joan.* XXVI. PL 35, 1614

article 2. is the attaining of heaven an effect of this sacrament?

THE SECOND POINT:[1a] 1. Apparently not. For an effect is proportionate to its cause. Now this sacrament is for wayfarers and hence is called *viaticum*, provision for a journey. Since wayfarers[b] are not yet ready for glory, it seems that this sacrament does not cause them to attain it.

2. Moreover, given a sufficient cause an effect follows. But many who take this sacrament will never come to glory, as Augustine makes clear.[2] Consequently it is not the cause of coming to heaven.

3. Further, the greater is not brought about by the lesser, for nothing acts beyond its nature. Now it is lesser to receive Christ under a strange guise, which is the case in this sacrament, than to be happy with him in his proper form, which is the case in heaven. Therefore this sacrament does not cause the attaining of glory.

ON THE OTHER HAND it is written, *If any man eat of this bread he shall live for ever.*[3] But eternal life is the life of heaven. Therefore an effect of this sacrament is the attainment of heaven.

REPLY: In this sacrament may be considered that from which it has its effect, namely Christ there present and his Passion there represented, and that through which it works its effect, namely the receiving of the sacrament and the sacramental elements. On both counts it is proper for this sacrament to cause the attainment of eternal life. Because it was by his Passion that Christ opened for us the entry to eternal life, according to *Hebrews*, *He is the mediator of a new covenant, that through his death, those who are called may receive the promised eternal inheritance.*[4] Accordingly in the form of this sacrament are the words, *This is the cup of my blood, of the new and eternal covenant.*[5] Likewise also the refreshment of spiritual food and the oneness signified by the elements of bread and wine are realized albeit partially in the present life, wholly, however, in the state of heaven. And so on the words in *John*, *My flesh is food indeed*,[6] Augustine writes, *Since men desire food and drink so that they may not hunger and thirst, and this in truth is provided by the food and drink which makes those who take it deathless and incorruptible in the companionship of the saints, where there will be peace and full and perfect unity.*[7]

Hence: 1. Christ's Passion, in virtue of which this sacrament works, is indeed the sufficient cause, not, nevertheless, that we are at once brought

---

[a]The eschatological setting. cf 3a. 49, 5, Christ's Passion has opened the gates of heaven. 3a. 69, 7, Baptism opens the gates of heaven.

[b]*Viator*, one in the company in the pilgrim Church. Contrasted with *comprehensor*, one who holds heavenly bliss.

tamen ita quod statim per ipsam introducamur in gloriam, sed oportet ut prius simul compatiamur, ut postea simul glorificemur, sicut dicitur *Rom.*,[8] ita hoc sacramentum non statim nos in gloriam introducit, sed dat nobis virtutem perveniendi ad gloriam, et ideo viaticum dicitur, in cujus figuram legitur *Reg.* quod *Elias comedit et bibit, et ambulavit in fortitudine cibi illius quadraginta diebus et quadraginta noctibus usque ad montem Dei Oreb.*[9]

2. Ad secundum dicendum quod sicut passio Christi non habet suum effectum in his qui se ad eam non habent ut debent, ita et per hoc sacramentum non adipiscuntur gloriam qui indecenter ipsum suscipiunt. Unde Augustinus dicit super *Joan.*, exponens illa verba loci cit., *Aliud est sacramentum et aliud virtus sacramenti. Multi de altari accipiunt, et accipiendo moriuntur. Panem ergo cœlestem spiritualiter manducate, innocentiam ad altare apportate.*[10] Unde non est mirum si illi qui innocentiam non servant effectum hujus sacramenti non consequuntur.

3. Ad tertium dicendum quod hoc quod Christus sub aliena specie sumitur pertinet ad rationem sacramenti, quod instrumentaliter agit. Nihil autem prohibet causam instrumentalem producere potiorem effectum, ut ex supra dictis patet.[11]

articulus 3. utrum effectus hujus sacramenti sit remissio peccati mortalis

AD TERTIUM sic proceditur:[1] 1. Videtur quod effectus hujus sacramenti sit remissio peccati mortalis. Dicitur enim in quadam collecta, *Sit hoc sacramentum ablutio scelerum.*[2] Sed scelera dicuntur peccata mortalia. Ergo per hoc sacramentum peccata mortalia abluuntur.

2. Præterea, hoc sacramentum agit in virtute passionis Christi, sicut et baptismus. Sed per baptismum dimittuntur peccata mortalia, ut supra dictum est.[3] Ergo et per hoc sacramentum, præsertim cum in forma hujus sacramenti dicatur, *Qui pro multis effundetur in remissionem peccatorum.*[4]

3. Præterea, per hoc sacramentum gratia confertur, ut dictum est.[5] Sed per gratiam justificatur homo a peccatis mortalibus, secundum illud *Rom.*, *Justificati gratis per gratiam ipsius.*[6] Ergo per hoc sacramentum remittuntur peccata mortalia.

SED CONTRA est quod dicitur 1 *Cor.*, *Qui manducat et bibit indigne, judicium sibi manducat et bibit;*[7] dicit autem glossa ibidem quod *ille manducat et bibit indigne, qui in crimine est, vel irreverenter tractat; et talis manducat, et bibit sibi judicium, idest damnationem.*[8] Ergo ille qui est in peccato mortali, per

---

[8] *Romans* 8, 17
[9] 1 *Kings* 19, 8
[10] loc cit notes 6 & 7
[11] 3a. 77, 3 ad 3
[1] cf IV *Sent.* 9, 3, ii; 12, 2, 2, ii

thereby into heaven, for beforehand we must, as St Paul states, *suffer with him* that afterwards we may be *glorified with him.*[8] And so the sacrament does not immediately usher us in, but gives us the strength to journey to heaven. That is why it is called the viaticum. It was foreshadowed by Elijah who *ate and drank and walked in the strength of that food for forty days and forty nights as far as Mount Horeb.*[9]

2. As Christ's Passion does not produce its effect on those who do not hold him as they should, so also those do not attain heaven through this sacrament who receive him unworthily. Accordingly Augustine writes, *The sacrament is one thing, its virtue another. Many receive from the altar and, receiving it, are dead. Eat therefore heavenly bread, carry innocence to the altar.*[10] So then it is not surprising that those who do not keep a pure heart fail to gain the effect of the sacrament.

3. That Christ is received under appearances not his own is bound up with the nature of a sacrament, which works as an instrumental cause. There is no reason, as we have explained,[11] why such a cause should not produce an effect higher than itself.

article 3. is an effect of this sacrament the forgiveness of mortal sin?

THE THIRD POINT:[1] It would seem so. For in a collect we read, *May this sacrament be the cleansing of crimes.*[2] Now crimes mean mortal sins. Therefore it cleanses from mortal sin.

2. Further, this sacrament acts in virtue of Christ's Passion, as does Baptism. Yet, as we have agreed,[3] through Baptism mortal sins are forgiven. Also, therefore, by this sacrament, especially since the form of consecration says, *shed for many for the remission of sins.*[4]

3. Again, it has been shown[5] that grace is given through this sacrament. But grace makes a person righteous and free from mortal sin, according to *Romans, Freely justified by his grace as a gift.*[6] Therefore mortal sins are forgiven through this sacrament.

ON THE OTHER HAND is the text, *Who eats and drinks unworthily eats and drinks a judgement on himself.*[7] On it a gloss comments, *He who eats and drinks unworthily is he who is in crime, or he who eats irreverently: such a one eats and drinks on himself judgement, that is condemnation.*[8] Therefore a person

---

[2]Postcommunion in Mass for living and dead
[3]3a. 69, 1
[4]Roman Canon
[5]art. 1 above
[6]*Romans* 3, 24
[7]1 *Corinthians* 11, 29
[8]Interlinear & Lombard. PL 191, 1646

hoc quod accipit hoc sacramentum, magis accumulat sibi peccatum quam remissionem sui peccati consequatur.

RESPONSIO: Dicendum quod virtus hujus sacramenti potest considerari dupliciter. Uno modo secundum se; et sic hoc sacramentum habet virtutem ad remittendum quæcumque peccata ex passione Christi, quæ est fons et causa remissionis peccatorum. Alio modo potest considerari per comparationem ad eum qui recipit hoc sacramentum, prout in eo invenitur impedimentum percipiendi hujus sacramenti effectum. Quicumque autem habet conscientiam peccati mortalis habet in se impedimentum percipiendi effectum hujus sacramenti, eo quod non est conveniens susceptor hujus sacramenti, tum quia non vivit spiritualiter, et ita non debet spirituale nutrimentum suscipere, quod non est nisi viventis, tum quia non potest uniri Christo (quod fit per hoc sacramentum), dum est in affectu peccandi mortaliter. Et ideo, ut dicitur in libro *de Eccles. Dogm.*, *si mens in affectu peccandi est, gravatur magis Eucharistiæ perceptione quam purificetur.*[9] Unde hoc sacramentum in eo qui ipsum percipit in conscientia peccati mortalis non operatur remissionem peccati.

Potest tamen hoc sacramentum operari remissionem peccati dupliciter. Uno modo non perceptum actu, sed voto, sicut cum quis prius justificatur a peccato. Alio modo etiam perceptum ab eo qui est in peccato mortali, cujus conscientiam et affectum non habet: forte enim primo non fuit sufficienter contritus, sed devote et reverenter accedens consequetur per hoc sacramentum gratiam caritatis, quæ contritionem perficiet, et remissionem peccati.

1. Ad primum ergo dicendum quod petimus ut hoc sacramentum sit ablutio scelerum, vel eorum quorum conscientiam non habemus, secundum illud *Psalmi*, *Ab occultis meis munda me, Domine;*[10] vel ut contritio in nobis perficiatur ad scelerum remissionem; vel etiam ut nobis robur detur ad scelera vitanda.

2. Ad secundum dicendum quod baptismus est spiritualis generatio, quæ est mutatio de non esse spirituali in esse spirituale, et datur per modum ablutionis; et ideo, quantum ad utrumque, non inconvenienter accedit ad baptismum qui habet conscientiam peccati mortalis. Sed per hoc sacramentum homo sumit in se Christum per modum spiritualis nutrimenti, quod non competit mortuo in peccatis. Et ideo non est similis ratio.

---

[9]Gennadius, *De Ecclesiasticis Dogmatibus* 53. PL 58, 994

[10]*Psalms* 18, 13

[a]A well-founded tradition in the East and West, expressed in many liturgical texts, holds that the Eucharist is a remedy for sin. This appears, with respect to the sacri-

in mortal sin rather heaps on himself a sin by receiving this sacrament instead of receiving forgiveness.

REPLY:[a] The power of this sacrament can be considered on two points. The first, in itself: and thus the power is there of forgiving any sin whatever from Christ's Passion, who is the font and cause of our being forgiven. The second, in relation to the recipient, inasmuch as he is or is not blocked from reaching the effect of this sacrament. For whoever is wedded to mortal sin is thereby hindered in himself from obtaining the sacramental effect. He is not a fit recipient; both because he is not spiritually alive, and to receive spiritual nourishment is only for the living, and because while he has an affection for mortal sin he cannot be one with Christ, which is effected by this sacrament. And so it is written in the book, *De Ecclesiasticis Dogmatibus*,[b] *If the affection for sin is heightened, the soul is more burdened than purified by receiving the Eucharist.*[9] Consequently the sacrament does not effect forgiveness of sin in one who receives it while being conscious of mortal sin.

Nevertheless this sacrament can effect the forgiveness of sins in two ways. One by its reception, not in fact, but in promise,[c] as when a person is first justified from sin. The other when it is received by a person who is in mortal sin though he is not conscious of it or attached to it; though beforehand perhaps not sufficiently contrite, yet by approaching the sacrament reverently and devoutly he receives the grace of charity which makes contrition complete and brings forgiveness of sin.

Hence: 1. We pray that the sacrament may be a cleansing from crime, or from sins of which we are not conscious, according to the verse, *Wash me from my secret sins, O Lord*,[10] or that our contrition may be perfect for forgiveness, or also that we be given the strength to avoid wrongdoing.

2. Baptism is a spiritual birth, a passing from spiritual non-being to spiritual being, and is given in the manner of washing. On neither count is to approach it unfitting to one who is conscious of mortal sin. But in this sacrament a person takes Christ to himself by way of spiritual food, which is not proper to one who is dead in sin. And so there is no parallel.

---

fice, in the words of the consecration of the chalice, *it shall be shed for you and many others, so that sins may be forgiven*; and, with respect to the sacrament, in this and the following arts.

Mortal and venial sin; 1a2æ. 88, 1 & 2

[b]By Gennadius of Marseilles, *fl.* 470.

[c]*perceptum voto*, by committed longing or firm purpose to accept the implications of justification; like baptism by desire this does not require an explicit recognition of the sacramental fact.

3. Ad tertium dicendum quod gratia est sufficiens causa remissionis peccati mortalis; non tamen actu remittit peccatum mortale, nisi cum primo datur peccatori. Sic autem non datur in hoc sacramento. Unde ratio non sequitur.

articulus 4. *utrum per hoc sacramentum remittantur peccata venialia*

AD QUARTUM sic proceditur:[1] 1. Videtur quod per hoc sacramentum non remittantur peccata venialia. Hoc enim sacramentum, ut Augustiuns dicit, est *sacramentum caritatis.*[2] Sed venialia peccata non contrariantur caritati, ut in *Secunda Parte* habitum est.[3] Cum ergo contrarium tollatur per suum contrarium, videtur quod peccata venialia per hoc sacramentum non remittantur.

2. Præterea, si peccata venialia per hoc sacramentum remittantur, qua ratione remittitur unum, remittuntur et omnia. Sed non videtur quod omnia remittantur, quia sic frequenter aliquis esset absque omni peccato veniali, contra id quod dicitur 1 *Joan.*, Si *dixerimus quia peccatum non habemus, ipsi nos seducimus.*[4] Non ergo per hoc sacramentum remittitur aliquod peccatum veniale.

3. Præterea, contraria mutuo se expellunt. Sed peccata venialia non prohibent a perceptione hujus sacramenti: dicit enim Augustinus super illud *Joan.*, *Si quis ex ipso manducaverit non morietur in æternum,*[5] *Innocentiam ad altare apportate: peccata, etsi sunt quotidiana, non sint mortifera.*[6] Ergo neque peccata venialia per hoc sacramentum tolluntur.

SED CONTRA est quod Innocentius III dicit quod hoc sacramentum *venialia delet et cavet mortalia.*[7]

RESPONSIO: Dicendum quod in hoc sacramento duo possunt considerari, scilicet ipsum sacramentum et res sacramenti. Et ex utroque apparet quod hoc sacramentum habet virtutem ad remissionem venialium peccatorum.

Nam hoc sacramentum sumitur sub specie cibi nutrientis. Nutrimentum autem cibi est necessarium corpori ad restaurandum id quod quotidie deperditur per actionem caloris naturalis. Spiritualiter autem quotidie aliquid in nobis deperditur ex calore concupiscentiæ per peccata venialia, quæ diminuunt fervorem caritatis, ut in *Secunda Parte* habitum est.[8] Et ideo competit huic sacramento ut remittat peccata venialia. Unde et

---

[1]cf 3a. 87, 3. IV *Sent.* 12, 2, 1, i; 2, i
[2]*Super Joan.* XXVI. On 6, 41. PL 35, 1613
[3]1a2æ. 88, 1 & 2. 2a2æ. 24, 8 ad 2; 10
[4]1 *John* 1, 8 [5]*John* 6, 50 [6]*Super Joan.* xxvi. PL 35, 1611

3. Grace is the sufficient cause of forgiveness for mortal sin, yet it is not actually forgiving except when newly given to a sinner.[d] Not so is it given in this sacrament. Consequently the objection is a *non sequitur*.

article 4. are venial sins forgiven through this sacrament?

THE FOURTH POINT:[1a] 1. It seems not. For this sacrament is, as Augustine says, *the sacrament of charity*.[2] Now venial sins are not contrary to charity, so it has been held.[3] Since one contrary is taken away by its opposite contrary, it would appear that venial sins are not forgiven through this sacrament.

2. Further, if venial sins were forgiven, the reason for forgiving one would clearly apply to all. Yet apparently all are not forgiven, for otherwise a person would often be without any venial sin, which is against *St John*, *If we say we have no sin we deceive ourselves*.[4] Any venial sin, then, is not forgiven through this sacrament.

3. Moreover, contraries are mutually exclusive. But venial sin does not forbid reception of this sacrament; on the text, *If anyone eats of this he shall not die for ever*,[5] Augustine comments, *Bring innocence with you to the altar, let sins even though everyday be not deadly*.[6] Therefore neither are venial sins taken away by this sacrament.

ON THE OTHER HAND there is Innocent III[b] who writes that the sacrament *deletes venial sins and wards off mortal sins*.[7]

REPLY: These two can be considered, namely both the sacrament itself and the reality therein.[c] From both it is clear that the virtue of forgiving sins is present.

For the sacrament itself is received under the species of nourishing food. The body needs nourishment to restore what is lost daily through the action of natural heat. In the life of the spirit, too, something is lost in us every day through venial sin by the fever of concupiscence, which lessens the warmth of charity, as we have shown in the *Secunda Pars*.[8] And so to

---

[7] *De Sacro Altaris Mysterio* IV, 44. PL 217, 885

[8] 2a2æ. 24, 10; 54, 3

[d] As in the *justificatio impii*, the justification of the unrighteous; 1a2æ. 113, 1.

[a] Sin taken simply and without qualification means for St Thomas mortal sin; venial sin is not sin in the full sense of the term; 1a2æ, 88, 1 & 2. It conflicts with the activity rather than the habit of charity. But cf 1a2æ, 88 & 89. Vol. 27 of this series, ed. T. C. O'Brien, Appendix 3, *Venial Sin*.

[b] Pope Innocent III, d. 1216.

[c] *Ipsum sacramentum* and *res sacramenti*; 3a. 73, 3.

Ambrosius dicit quod *iste panis quotidianus sumitur in remedium quotidianæ infirmitatis.*[9]

Res autem hujus sacramenti est caritas, non solum quantum ad habitum, sed etiam quantum ad actum, qui excitatur in hoc sacramento, per quem peccata venialia solvuntur. Unde manifestum est quod virtute hujus sacramenti remittuntur peccata venialia.

1. Ad primum ergo dicendum quod peccata venialia etsi non contrariantur caritati quantum ad habitum, contrariantur tamen ei quantum ad fervorem actus, qui excitatur per hoc sacramentum, ratione cujus peccata venialia tolluntur.

2. Ad secundum dicendum quod illud verbum non est intelligendum quin aliqua hora possit homo esse absque omni reatu peccati venialis, sed quia vitam istam sancti non ducunt sine peccatis venialibus.

3. Ad tertium dicendum quod major est virtus caritatis, cujus est hoc sacramentum, quam venialium peccatorum. Nam caritas tollit per suum actum peccata venialia, quæ tamen non possunt totaliter impedire actum caritatis. Et eadem ratio est de hoc sacramento.

articulus 5. utrum per hoc sacramentum tota pœna peccati remittatur

AD QUINTUM sic proceditur:[1] 1. Videtur quod per hoc sacramentum tota pœna peccati remittatur. Homo enim per hoc sacramentum suscipit in se effectum passionis Christi, ut dictum est,[2] sicut et per baptismum: sed per baptismum percipit homo remissionem omnis pœnæ virtute passionis Christi, quæ sufficienter satisfecit pro omnibus peccatis, ut ex supra dictis patet.[3] Ergo videtur quod per hoc sacramentum homini remittatur totus reatus pœnæ.

2. Præterea, Alexander Papa dicit, *Nihil in sacrificiis majus esse potest quam corpus et sanguis Christi.*[4] Sed per sacrificia veteris legis homo satisfaciebat pro peccatis suis; dicitur enim *Levit.*, *Si peccaverit homo, offeret* hoc vel illud *pro peccato suo, et remittetur ei.*[5] Ergo multo magis hoc sacramentum valet ad remissionem omnis pœnæ.

---

[9] *De Sacram.* v, 4. PL 16, 472. cf Peter Lombard, *Sentences* iv, 12, 6

[1] cf iv *Sent.* 4, 2, 1, ii ad 3; 12, 2, 2, iii

[2] arts 1 & 2 above

[3] 3a. 69, 2

[4] Pseudo-Alexander, *Epist.* 1 *ad omnes orthod.* 4. Mansi 1, 639. Gratian, *Decretum*, iii, 2, 8. RF 1, 1317

[5] *Leviticus* 4 & 5

[d] A venial sin is not incompatible with our being in love with God, but with our acting from that love then and there. The devout reception of the Eucharist offsets this in proportion to the intensity of love present. Analogies in human friendship are not far to seek. Yet venial sin hinders the effect of the Eucharist, cf art. 8 below.

[a] The heart of sin lies in the fault, *culpa*: this is forgiven by contrition. Two effects, however, may remain; the first is metaphorically called the stain of sin, cf 1a2æ. 86,

forgive venial sins fits this sacrament. Hence Ambrose writes that *this our daily bread is taken as a remedy against daily infirmity.*[9]

The reality in this sacrament is charity, not merely in habit, but also in act: this is aroused in this sacrament, and so venial sin is shaken off. Clearly, then, venial sins are forgiven in virtue of this sacrament.

Hence: 1. Though not contrary to the habit of charity, venial sins are contrary to the fervour of its activity, which is kindled by this sacrament, and is the reason why venial sins are taken away.[d]

2. The passage quoted is not to be understood as if at some time a person could not be quite guiltless of venial sin, but that God's friends do not pass through this life without committing venial sins.

3. This is the sacrament of charity, and charity is more powerful than venial sins, which are taken away by its activity, and this they cannot entirely hinder. And the same holds good of this sacrament.

article 5. is the entire punishment for sin pardoned through this sacrament?

THE FIFTH POINT:[1a] 1. So it would seem. For through this sacrament a person receives within himself the effect of Christ's Passion, as we have agreed,[2] just as he does through Baptism. Now through Baptism he receives the pardon of all punishment due to sin in virtue of Christ's Passion, which was sufficient satisfaction for all sins, as we have also agreed.[3] So then it seems through this sacrament the entire debt of punishment is pardoned.

2. Besides, Pope Alexander[b] writes, *No sacrifice is greater than the body and blood of Christ.*[4] In the sacrifices of the Old Law, men rendered satisfaction for their sins: it is written, *If a man shall have sinned let him offer such and such and it will be forgiven him.*[5] Much more then does this sacrament avail for the pardon of all punishment.

---

1 & 2; the other the *reatus pœnæ*, the charge of having to expiate by punishment or by satisfaction, cf 1a2æ. 87, 1 & 6. So, in human relations, the distinction between a heartfelt—and accepted—apology and making amends. There is a double movement in sin, the turning away from God, *aversio a bono incommutabili*, and the turning to something else, *conversio ad bonum commutabile* (1a2æ. 87, 4): the first is taken away by God's forgiveness and man's repentance, but the effects of the second may still last. It is in this turning to what in the situation is a false good, *bonum tantum apparens*, that we have to look for the cause of evil and sin; cf 1a. 49, 1 & 1a2æ. 75, 1.

[b]Allegedly in many printed texts, including Leonine, Alexander I, d. *c.* 117, the 5th successor of St Peter. Alexander III, Roland Bandinelli, is a likelier connection. He wrote a commentary on Gratian's *Decretum*. Gratian, the father of canon law, author of the *Concordantia Discordantium Canonum*, commonly known as the *Decretum*, which appeared about 1150 and became the first part of the *Corpus Juris Canonici*. It will be often cited in the following discussions.

3. Præterea, constat quod per hoc sacramentum aliquid de reatu pœnæ dimittitur; unde et in satisfactionem aliquibus injungitur quod pro se missas faciant celebrari. Sed qua ratione una pars pœnæ dimittitur, eadem ratione et alia, cum virtus Christi, quæ in hoc sacramento continetur, sit infinita. Ergo videtur quod per hoc sacramentum tota pœna tollatur.

SED CONTRA est quod secundum hoc non esset homini alia pœna injungenda, sicut nec baptizato injungitur.

RESPONSIO: Dicendum quod hoc sacramentum simul est sacrificium et sacramentum; sed rationem sacrificii habet inquantum offertur, rationem autem sacramenti inquantum sumitur. Et ideo effectum sacramenti habet in eo qui sumit, effectum autem sacrificii in eo qui offert, vel in his pro quibus offertur.

Si igitur consideretur ut sacramentum, habet effectum dupliciter: uno modo directe ex vi sacramenti; alio modo quasi ex quadam concomitantia, sicut et circa continentiam sacramenti dictum est.[6] Ex vi quidem sacramenti directe habet illum effectum ad quem est institutum. Non est autem institutum ad satisfaciendum, sed ad spiritualiter nutriendum per unionem ad Christum et ad membra ejus, sicut et nutrimentum unitur nutrito. Sed quia hæc unitas fit per caritatem, ex cujus fervore aliquis consequitur remissionem non solum culpæ, sed etiam pœnæ, inde est quod ex consequenti per quamdam concomitantiam ad principalem effectum homo consequitur remissionem pœnæ, non quidem totius, sed secundum modum suæ devotionis et fervoris.

Inquantum vero est sacrificium, habet vim satisfactivam. Sed in satisfactione magis attenditur affectus offerentis quam quantitas oblationis. Unde et Dominus dicit *Luc.*[7] de vidua quæ obtulit duo æra quod *plus omnibus misit.*[7] Quamvis ergo hæc oblatio ex sui quantitate sufficiat ad satisfaciendum pro omni pœna, tamen fit satisfactoria illis pro quibus offertur, vel etiam offerentibus secundum quantitatem suæ devotionis, et non pro tota pœna.

1. Ad primum ergo dicendum quod sacramentum baptismi directe ordinatur ad remissionem pœnæ et culpæ, non autem Eucharistia, quia baptismus datur homini quasi commorienti Christo, Eucharistia autem quasi nutriendo et perficiendo per Christum. Unde non est similis ratio.

2. Ad secundum dicendum quod illa sacrificia et oblationes non operabantur remissionem totius pœnæ neque quantum ad quantitatem oblati, sicut hoc sacrificium, neque quantum ad devotionem hominis, ex qua contingit quod etiam hic non tollitur tota pœna.

---

[6] 3a. 76, 1 & 2

[7] *Luke* 21, 4. *Mark* 12, 43

[c] cf art. 7 below.

3. Again, it is evident that some part of the debt of punishment is pardoned by this sacrament: hence the practice of enjoining on some by way of satisfaction to have masses offered on their behalf. But the reason why one part of punishment is pardoned holds for another part, is because Christ's power contained in this sacrament is infinite. So therefore it seems that through it the whole punishment is taken away.

ON THE OTHER HAND in that case it would follow that no further penance would have to be enjoined as satisfaction, as with the newly baptized.

REPLY: The Eucharist is at once a sacrifice and a sacrament:[c] it has the nature of a sacrifice in that it is offered, and of a sacrament in that it is received. Therefore, its effect as a sacrament is in the recipient, its effect as a sacrifice is in the offerer or in those for whom it is offered.

Considered as a sacrament its effect is wrought in two ways, first, directly through the power of the sacrament, secondly, by a certain concomitance, as we have explained in treating of the content of the sacrament.[6] Through the power of the sacrament it produces directly that effect for which it was instituted. Now this was not for the satisfaction of sins but for spiritual nourishment through union with Christ and his members, as food becomes one with the person fed. However, because this union is through charity, from the fervour of which comes forgiveness, not only of fault, but also of penalty, it follows as a consequence and by way of concomitance to the principal effect that a person obtains pardon of the penalty of sin, not indeed of all of it, but proportionately to the measure of his devotion and fervour.

Considered as a sacrifice, however, it has the power of rendering satisfaction. In this the affection of the offerer is counted more than the size of the offering, as our Lord said of the widow who offered two coins that *she has put in more than all.*[7] Although the offering of the Eucharist suffices of its own quantity to satisfy for all punishment, nevertheless it renders satisfaction for those for whom it is offered, and also for those who offer it, according to the amount of their devotion, and not for the whole penalty.

Hence: 1. The sacrament of Baptism, not however of the Eucharist, is directly ordained for the remission of punishment and fault, for Baptism is given to a man as dying with Christ, whereas the Eucharist is given him as being nourished and fulfilled by Christ. And so the analogy fails.

2. Those Old Law sacrifices and oblations did not effect the pardon of the whole of punishment, either in view of the size of the offering, as the Eucharistic sacrifice does, or in view of the personal devotion which may not take away the entire penalty.

3. Ad tertium dicendum quod hoc quod tollitur pars pœnæ, et non tota pœna per hoc sacramentum, non contingit ex defectu virtutis Christi, sed ex defectu devotionis humanæ.

articulus 6. *utrum per hoc sacramentum præservetur homo a peccatis futuris*

AD SEXTUM sic proceditur:[1] 1. Videtur quod per hoc sacramentum non præservetur homo a peccatis futuris. Multi enim digne sumentes hoc sacramentum postea in peccatum cadunt; quod non accideret si hoc sacramentum præservaret a peccatis futuris. Non ergo effectus hujus sacramenti est a peccatis futuris præservare.

2. Præterea, Eucharistia est sacramentum caritatis, ut supra dictum est.[2] Sed caritas non videtur præservare a peccatis futuris, quia semel habita potest amitti per peccatum, ut in *Secunda Parte* habitum est.[3] Ergo videtur quod nec hoc sacramentum præservet hominem a peccato.

3. Præterea, origo peccati in nobis est *lex peccati, quæ est in membris nostris*, ut patet per Apostolum.[4] Sed mitigatio fomitis, qui est lex peccati, non ponitur effectus hujus sacramenti, sed magis baptismi. Ergo præservare a peccatis futuris non est effectus hujus sacramenti.

SED CONTRA est quod Dominus dicit, *Hic panis de cœlo descendens, ut si quis ex ipso manducaverit, non moriatur*;[5] quod quidem manifestum est non intelligi de morte corporali. Ergo intelligitur quod hoc sacramentum præservet a morte spirituali, quæ est per peccatum.

RESPONSIO: Dicendum quod peccatum est quædam spiritualis mors animæ. Unde hoc modo præservatur aliquis a peccato futuro quo præservatur corpus a morte futura, quod quidem fit dupliciter: uno modo inquantum natura hominis interius roboratur contra interiora corruptiva, et sic præservatur a morte per cibum et medicinam; alio modo per hoc quod munitur contra exteriores impugnationes, et sic præservatur per arma quibus munitur corpus.

Utroque autem modo hoc sacramentum præservat a peccato. Nam primo quidem per hoc quod Christo conjungit per gratiam roborat spiritualem vitam hominis, tanquam spiritualis cibus et spiritualis medicina, secundum illud *Psal.*, *Panis cor hominis confirmat*.[6] Et Augustinus dicit, *Securus accede; panis est, non venenum*.[7] Alio modo inquantum est quoddam signum passionis Christi, per quam victi sunt dæmones, repellit omnem

---

[1] cf IV *Sent.* 12, 2, 2, ii ad 1
[2] art. 4 above. 3a. 78, 3 ad 3; 74, 4 ad 3; 78, 3 ad 6
[3] 2a2æ. 24, 2

3. That part and not the whole of punishment is pardoned comes about from a defect of human devotion, not of Christ's power.

article 6. is a person through this sacrament preserved from future sins?

THE SIXTH POINT:[1] 1. It seems not. For there are many who receive the sacrament worthily yet who afterwards fall into sin. This would not happen were the sacrament to preserve them. Consequently to preserve from future sin is not an effect of this sacrament.

2. Also, we have agreed[2] that the Eucharist is the sacrament of charity. Yet charity does not seem to preserve us from sin, for, as we have seen,[3] it can be lost through sin after having been once possessed. Nor, so it seems, does the sacrament preserve from sin.

3. Besides, a source of sin is within us, *the law of sin, which is in our members*,[4] as St Paul declares.[a] But the damping down of concupiscence, the law of sin, is set down as an effect of Baptism—not of the Eucharist. Accordingly being safeguarded from sin is not the effect of this sacrament.

ON THE OTHER HAND there are the words of our Lord, *This is the bread which comes down from heaven, that man may eat of it and not die.*[5] Manifestly this does not mean death of the body, but that this sacrament preserves from the death of the spirit, which is sin.

REPLY: Sin is for the soul a sort of spiritual death. Accordingly a person is preserved from future sin much as he is preserved from future death of the body. This is done in two ways, first by strengthening his constitution against inner forces of decay, and thus he is preserved from death by nourishment and medicine. Second, by being protected against attack from outside and thus is safeguarded by bodily weapons of defence.

In both ways the sacrament safeguards a person against sin. First, by joining him to Christ through grace it strengthens his spiritual life, as spiritual food and spiritual medicine according to the *Psalm, That bread strengthens man's heart.*[6] And Augustine says, *Approach without fear; it is bread, not poison.*[7] Second, as a sign of Christ's Passion, whereby devils are conquered, it repels all their assaults. Accordingly, Chrysostom says,

---

[4]*Romans* 7, 23

[5]*John* 6, 50

[6]*Psalms* 103, 15

[7]*Super Joan.* XXVI. On 6, 49. PL 35, 1617

[a]*Lex peccati* or *lex fomitis*, the tinder or kindling for sin, not a law properly speaking, but by divine ordinance a penal consequence of original sin; 1a2æ. 91, 6.

dæmonum impugnationem. Unde Chrysostomus dicit, *Ut leones flammam spirantes, sic ab illa mensa discedimus terribiles effecti diabolo.*[8]

1. Ad primum ergo dicendum quod effectus hujus sacramenti recipitur in homine secundum hominis conditionem, sicut contingit de qualibet causa activa, quod ejus effectus recipitur in materia secundum modum materiæ. Homo autem in statu viæ est hujus conditionis, quod liberum arbitrium ejus potest flecti in bonum et malum. Unde licet hoc sacramentum, quantum est de se, habeat virtutem præservativam a peccato, non tamen aufert homini possibilitatem peccandi.

2. Ad secundum dicendum quod etiam caritas, quantum est in se, præservat hominem a peccato, secundum illud *Rom.*, *Dilectio proximi malum non operatur*;[9] sed ex mutabilitate liberi arbitrii contingit quod aliquis post habitam caritatem peccat, sicut post susceptionem hujus sacramenti.

3. Ad tertium dicendum quod licet hoc sacramentum non directe ordinetur ad diminutionem fomitis, diminuit tamen fomitem ex quadam consequentia, inquantum auget caritatem, quia, sicut Augustinus dicit, *augmentum caritatis est diminutio cupiditatis.*[10] Directe autem confirmat cor hominis in bono. Per quod etiam præservatur homo a peccato.

articulus 7. utrum hoc sacramentum prosit aliis quam sumentibus

AD SEPTIMUM sic proceditur:[1] 1. Videtur quod hoc sacramentum non prosit nisi sumenti. Hoc enim sacramentum est unius generis cum aliis sacramentis, utpote aliis condivisum. Sed alia sacramenta non prosunt nisi sumentibus, sicut effectum baptismi non suscipit nisi baptizatus. Ergo nec hoc sacramentum prodest aliis nisi sumenti.

2. Præterea, effectus hujus sacramenti est adeptio gratiæ et gloriæ, et remissio culpæ, ad minus venialis. Si ergo hoc sacramentum haberet effectum in aliis quam in sumentibus, posset contingere quod aliquis adipisceretur et gratiam, et gloriam, et remissionem culpæ, absque actione et passione propria, alio sumente vel offerente hoc sacramentum.

3. Præterea, multiplicata causa, multiplicatur effectus. Si ergo hoc sacramentum prodesset aliis quam sumentibus, sequeretur quod magis prodesset alicui si multi sumerent hoc sacramentum, multis hostiis in una missa consecratis, quod non habet Ecclesiæ consuetudo, ut scilicet multi

---

[8] *Super Joan.* XLVI. PL 59, 261

[9] *Romans* 13, 10

[10] *lxxxiii Quæst.* 36. PL 40, 25

[1] cf art. 5 above. 3a. 78, 3 ad 8. IV *Sent.* 12, 2, 2, ii ad 4; 15, 2, 3, i ad 3. *In* I *Cor.* 11, *lect.* 6. *In Joan.* 6, *lect.* 6

Like lions breathing fire, thus do we leave that table, made redoubtable to the devil.[8]

Hence: 1. A person receives the effect of this sacrament according to his condition, as happens with any active cause, the effect of which is received in the subject according to the condition of the material. While a pilgrim man's condition is such that his free will can be turned to good and evil. Hence, although of itself this sacrament has the power of safeguarding against sin, it does not remove from a person the possibility of sinning.

2. Even charity of itself keeps man from sin, according to *Romans*, *Love does no wrong to a neighbour.*[9] Nevertheless, it is from the mutability of free will that a person happens to sin after having had charity; so also after having received this sacrament.[b]

3. Although not directly designed to damp down concupiscence, yet that is a consequence of this sacrament in that it increases charity: Augustine says that *the growth of charity is the lessening of cupidity.*[10] But its direct purpose is to confirm man's heart to good. And thereby it keeps him from sin.

article 7. does this sacrament benefit others besides the recipients?

THE SEVENTH POINT:[1a] 1. It would seem not. For this sacrament is of the same class with the other sacraments as being a condivision together with them. Yet other sacraments benefit only the recipients; thus the effect of Baptism is received only by the one who is baptized. Consequently neither does this sacrament benefit others than the recipients.

2. Besides, the effect of this sacrament is the laying hold of grace and glory together with the forgiveness of sin, at least of venial sin. Were this sacrament to have an effect on others apart from those who receive it, it would happen that a person could reach grace and glory and forgiveness without doing or undergoing anything on his part, through another receiving or offering the Eucharist for him.

3. Then, also, multiply the cause and you multiply the effect. If this sacrament were to benefit others besides the recipients, it would follow that it would benefit someone more were many to take communion by many hosts consecrated at one mass. Whereas this is not the Church's custom for

---

[b]cf 2a2æ. 24, 11; the fragility of our charity.

[a]It is a devout practice to offer one's Holy Communion for the welfare and intentions of another. It is based on the theology of the communication of grace between the members of the Church's mystical body under the headship of Christ; cf 3a. 8, 3.

communicent pro alicujus salute. Non ergo videtur quod hoc sacramentum prosit nisi sumenti.

SED CONTRA est quod in celebratione hujus sacramenti fit pro multis aliis deprecatio; quod frustra fieret nisi hoc sacramentum aliis prodesset. Hoc ergo sacramentum non solum sumentibus prodest.

RESPONSIO: Dicendum quod, sicut prius dictum est,[2] hoc sacramentum non solum est sacramentum, sed etiam est sacrificium. Inquantum enim in hoc sacramento repræsentatur passio Christi, qua Christus *obtulit se hostiam Deo*,[3] ut dicitur *Ephes.*, habet rationem sacrificii; inquantum vero in hoc sacramento traditur invisibilis gratia sub visibili specie, habet rationem sacramenti.

Sic ergo hoc sacramentum sumentibus quidem prodest, et per modum sacramenti et per modum sacrificii, quia pro omnibus sumentibus offertur. Dicitur enim in canone missæ, *Quotquot ex hac altaris participatione sacrosanctum Filii tui corpus et sanguinem sumpserimus, omni benedictione cœlesti et gratia repleamur.*[4] Sed aliis qui non sumunt prodest per modum sacrificii, inquantum pro salute eorum offertur. Unde et in canone missæ dicitur, *Memento, Domine, famulorum famularumque tuarum, pro quibus tibi offerimus vel qui tibi offerunt hoc sacrificium laudis pro se suisque omnibus, pro redemptione animarum suarum, pro spe salutis et incolumitatis suæ.*[5] Et utrumque modum proficiendi Dominus expressit, dicens, *Qui pro vobis*, scilicet sumentibus, *et pro multis*, scilicet aliis, *effundetur in remissionem peccatorum.*[6]

1. Ad primum ergo dicendum quod hoc sacramentum præ aliis habet quod est sacrificium; et ideo non est similis ratio.

2. Ad secundum dicendum quod sicut passio Christi prodest quidem omnibus quantum ad sufficientiam, ad remissionem culpæ et adeptionem gratiæ et gloriæ, sed effectum non habet nisi in illis qui passioni Christi conjunguntur per fidem et caritatem, ita et hoc sacrificium, quod est memoriale dominicæ passionis, non habet effectum nisi in illis qui conjunguntur huic sacramento per fidem et caritatem. Unde et Augustinus dicit, *Quis offerat corpus Christi nisi pro his qui sunt membra Christi?*[7] Unde et in canone missæ non oratur pro his qui sunt extra Ecclesiam. Illis tamen prodest plus vel minus secundum modum devotionis eorum.

3. Ad tertium dicendum quod sumptio pertinet ad rationem sacramenti, sed oblatio pertinet ad rationem sacrificii. Et ideo ex hoc quod aliquis sumit corpus Christi, vel etiam plures, non accrescit aliis aliquod

---

[2]art. 5 above
[3]*Ephesians* 5, 2
[4]Roman Canon
[5]ibid

many to receive communion for the welfare of one. So then it seems that the sacrament benefits only the recipient.

ON THE OTHER HAND intercession for others is offered in the celebration of this sacrament. This would seem to no purpose were it not to profit them. The sacrament, therefore, is profitable not only to them who receive it.

REPLY: As we have shown[2] already, the Eucharist is a sacrament and also a sacrifice. For it has the nature of a sacrifice inasmuch as it makes present Christ's Passion, whereby, according to *Ephesians*, *he gave himself as a victim to God.*[3] And it has the nature of a sacrament inasmuch as under visible species invisible grace is bestowed.

So then it benefits recipients both as sacrament and sacrifice, for it is offered for them all, according to the words of the Canon of the Mass: *May as many of us as, by participation at this altar, shall receive the sacred body and blood of your Son, be filled with all heavenly blessing and grace.*[4] To others, who do not receive it, it is salutary as a sacrifice because it is offered for their salvation. Thus the words of the Canon, *Be mindful of your servants, men and women, for whom we offer, or who offer up to you, this sacrifice of praise for themselves and all theirs, for the redemption of their souls, for the hope of their safety and salvation.*[5] Our Lord spoke of both when he said, *Which for you*, namely who receive communion, *and for many*, namely others, *shall be shed unto remission of sins.*[6b]

Hence: 1. This sacrament adds this to the other sacraments, the character of being a sacrifice. And so the comparison fails.

2. As Christ's Passion benefits all, being sufficient for the forgiving of sins and the attaining of grace and glory, though it produces no effect save in those who are united to his Passion through faith and charity, so likewise this sacrifice, which is a memorial of the Lord's Passion, has no effect save on those who are united to the sacrament through faith and charity. Accordingly Augustine writes, *Who may offer Christ's body except for those who are his members?*[7] And so the Canon of the Mass makes no prayer for those who are outside the pale of the Church. Others, however, are helped, some more, some less, according to the measure of their devotion.

3. Receiving is of the nature of a sacrament: offering, however, of the nature of a sacrifice. Hence the fact of one or many receiving the body of Christ gives no increase of help to others, and likewise the fact that the

---

[6]*Matthew* 26, 28. *Luke* 22, 20
[7]*De Anima et ejus Orig.* I. 9, *Ad Renatum*. PL 44, 480
[b]Christ's Passion is instrumental for our salvation by way of merit, of satisfaction, of redemption, and of sacrifice; 3a. 48, 6 ad 3.

juvamentum. Similiter etiam ex hoc quod sacerdos plures hostias consecrat in una missa non multiplicatur effectus hujus sacramenti, quia non est nisi unum sacrificium; nihil enim plus est virtutis in multis hostiis consecratis quam in una, cum sub omnibus et sub una non sit nisi totus Christus. Unde nec si aliquis simul in una missa multas hostias consecratas sumat, participabit majorem effectum sacramenti. In pluribus vero missis multiplicatur sacrificii oblatio, et ideo multiplicatur effectus sacrificii et sacramenti.

articulus 8. *utrum per veniale peccatum impediatur effectus hujus sacramenti*

AD OCTAVUM sic proceditur:[1] 1. Videtur quod per veniale peccatum non impediatur effectus hujus sacramenti. Dicit enim Augustinus super illud *Joan.*, *Si quis ex ipso manducaverit*,[2] *Panem cœlestem spiritualiter manducate; innocentiam ad altare apportate; peccata, etsi sunt quotidiana, non sint mortifera.*[3] Ex quo patet quod venialia peccata, quæ quotidiana dicuntur, spiritualem manducationem non impediunt. Sed spiritualiter manducantes effectum hujus sacramenti percipiunt. Ergo peccata venialia non impediunt effectum hujus sacramenti.

2. Præterea, hoc sacramentum non est minoris virtutis quam baptismus. Sed effectum baptismi, sicut supra dictum est,[4] impedit sola fictio, ad quam non pertinent peccata venialia, quia, sicut *Sap.* dicitur, *Spiritus Sanctus disciplinæ effugiet fictum*,[5] qui tamen per peccata venialia non fugatur. Ergo neque effectum hujus sacramenti impediunt peccata venialia.

3. Præterea, nihil quod removetur per actionem alicujus causæ potest impedire ejus effectum. Sed peccata venialia tolluntur per hoc sacramentum. Ergo non impediunt ejus effectum.

SED CONTRA est quod Damascenus dicit, *Ignis ejus, quod in nobis est desiderii, assumens eam, quæ ex carbone*, idest ex hoc sacramento, *ignitionem, comburat nostra peccata, et illuminet corda nostra, ut participatione divini ignis igniamur et deificemur.*[6] Sed ignis nostri desiderii vel amoris impeditur per peccata venialia, quæ impediunt fervorem caritatis, ut in *Secunda Parte* habitum est.[7] Ergo peccata venialia impediunt effectum hujus sacramenti.

RESPONSIO: Dicendum quod peccata venialia dupliciter accipi possunt: uno modo prout sunt præterita; alio modo prout sunt actu exercita. Primo quidem modo peccata venialia nullo modo impediunt effectum hujus sacramenti. Potest enim contingere quod aliquis post multa peccata

---

[1]cf IV *Sent.* 12, 2, 1, iii; 2, i ad 2
[2]*John* 6, 50
[3]*In Joan.* XXVI. PL 35, 1611
[4]3a. 69, 9 & 10
[5]*Wisdom* 1, 5
[6]*De Fide Orth.* VI, 13. PG 94, 1149

priest consecrates many hosts at one mass does not multiply the effect of the sacrament, since there is but a single sacrifice: there is no more virtue in several consecrated hosts than in one, since under one and under many the whole Christ is present. Accordingly a person will not more fully share in the sacrament's effect by taking many consecrated hosts at one mass. As for the offering of sacrifice, however, that is multiplied in many masses, and so the sacramental and sacrificial effect is increased.

article 8. *does venial sin hinder the effect of this sacrament?*

THE EIGHTH POINT:[1a] 1. It seems not. For on the text, *If any man eat of this bread*,[2] Augustine comments, *Eat the heavenly bread spiritually; bring innocence to the altar; your sins though they may be daily, let them not be deadly.*[3] It is clear from this that venial sins, which are called daily, are no bar to spiritual eating. Now those who eat spiritually receive the effect of this sacrament. Therefore venial sins do not hinder it.

2. Moreover, this sacrament is not less powerful than Baptism. But, as we have agreed,[4] only pretence blocks the effect of Baptism, and that is not to the point when venial sin is being considered, since, according to *Wisdom, the Holy Spirit of discipline will flee from the deceitful*;[5] yet he is not put to flight by venial sins. Neither, therefore, do they stop the effect of this sacrament.

3. Further, nothing which is removed by the action of a cause can hinder its effect. Now venial sins are taken away by this sacrament. Consequently they do not hamper its effectiveness.

ON THE OTHER HAND is Damascene, *The fire of that desire within us which is kindled by the burning coal*, namely the sacrament, *will consume our sins and enlighten our hearts, so that we shall be enflamed and made godlike.*[6] That fire of desire or love is checked by venial sins, which damp down its glow, as we have seen in the *Secunda Pars*.[7] Therefore venial sins hamper this sacrament's effect.

REPLY: Venial sins can be regarded in two ways, first, as past events, second, as being actually present.[b] In the first way they do not at all hinder the effect of this sacrament. For it may well come to pass that a person

---

[7]2a2æ. 24, 10; 54, 3

[a]cf art. 4 above.

[b]Actually present: this does not mean that venial sin is then being committed, but that an affection for it remains; Billuart glosses, *peccata venialia actu placentia vel exercita.*

venialia commissa devote accedat ad hoc sacramentum, et plenarie hujus sacramenti consequatur effectum. Secundo autem modo peccata venialia non ex toto impediunt hujus sacramenti effectum, sed in parte. Dictum est enim[8] quod effectus hujus sacramenti non solum est adeptio habitualis gratiæ vel caritatis, sed etiam quædam actualis refectio spiritualis dulcedinis, quæ quidem impeditur, si aliquis accedat ad hoc sacramentum per peccata venialia mente distractus; non autem tollitur augmentum habitualis gratiæ vel caritatis.

1. Ad primum ergo dicendum quod ille qui cum actu venialis peccati ad hoc sacramentum accedit habitualiter quidem manducat spiritualiter, sed non actualiter; et ideo habitualem effectum hujus sacramenti percipit, non autem actualem.

2. Ad secundum dicendum quod baptismus non ita ordinatur ad actualem effectum, idest fervorem caritatis, sicut hoc sacramentum. Nam baptismus est spiritualis regeneratio, per quam acquiritur prima perfectio, quæ est habitus vel forma; hoc autem sacramentum est spiritualis manducatio, quæ habet actualem delectationem.

3. Ad tertium dicendum quod illa ratio procedit de venialibus præteritis, quæ per hoc sacramentum tolluntur.

---

[8]arts 1 & 2 above

after having committed many venial sins approaches this sacrament devoutly and fully attains its effect. In the second way venial sins do not utterly stop its effect, but do so in part.[c] We have said[8] that the effect is to receive not only habitual grace and charity but also a certain actual refreshment of spiritual sweetness. This indeed is prevented if one approaches this sacrament with a mind distracted by venial sins. However, growth in habitual grace and charity is not arrested.

Hence: 1. He who comes to communion with actual venial sins eats spiritually indeed by his habitual disposition, but not actually. And so he is in a condition to gather the fruit of the sacrament, but does not do so actively.

2. Unlike this sacrament, Baptism is not ordained to produce a warmth of charity as its active effort. For it is a spiritual rebirth, which establishes a disposition or quality of being,[d] whereas this sacrament is a spiritual feeding which carries active enjoyment.

3. This argument fixes on past venial sins, which are taken away by this sacrament.

---

[c]A more severe teaching based on IV *Sent.* 12, 2, 1, iii seems to take the text out of context. Cajetan and Contenson.

[d]The indelible form of sacramental character; 3a. 63, 1, 5 & 6. Here taken as a *prima perfectio*, a settled quality of being, rather than a *secunda perfectio*, a quality of acting on occasion.

Quæstio 80. de usu sacramenti in communi

DEINDE CONSIDERANDUM EST de usu sive sumptione hujus sacramenti, et primo quidem in communi; secundo quomodo Christus est usus hoc sacramento. Circa primum quæruntur duodecim:

1. utrum sint duo modi manducandi hoc sacramentum, scilicet sacramentaliter et spiritualiter;
2. utrum soli homini conveniat manducare spiritualiter hoc sacramentum;
3. utrum solius hominis justi sit manducare sacramentaliter;
4. utrum peccator manducans sacramentaliter peccet;
5. de quantitate hujus peccati;
6. utrum peccator accedens ad hoc sacramentum sit repellendus;
7. utrum nocturna pollutio impediat hominem a sumptione hujus sacramenti;
8. utrum sit solum a jejunis sumendum;
9. utrum sit exhibendum non habentibus usum rationis;
10. utrum sit quotidie sumendum;
11. utrum liceat omnino obstinere;
12. utrum liceat percipere corpus sine sanguine.

articulus 1. utrum distingui debeant duo modi manducandi corpus Christi

AD PRIMUM sic proceditur:[1] 1. Videtur quod non debeant distingui duo modi manducandi corpus Christi, scilicet sacramentaliter et spiritualiter. Sicut enim baptismus est spiritualis regeneratio, secundum illud *Joan.*,

[1]cf IV *Sent.* 9, 1, iii. *In* 1 *Cor.* 11, *lect.* 7. *In Joan.* 6, *lect.* 6 & 7

[a]*Usus*, the employment, execution, application, *chrēsis*, even the enjoyment (thus the juridical term *ususfructus*), and so the sense here is not that of *uti* as opposed to *frui*; see 1a2æ. 11 & 15. Vol. 16, ed. T. Gilby.

[b]Arts 1–5 are of sacramental theology, 6–12 rather of sacramental discipline.

[c]*Sacramental and spiritual Communion.* A devout practice has led to 'spiritual Communion' being defined as an active union with our Lord effected by the desire of receiving him apart from his sacramental reception. This, though touched on (art. 1 ad 3 & art. 2 below), and certainly not deprecated, is not what is meant by spiritual reception, *spiritualis manducatio*, in this Question. The two terms, 'sacramental' and 'spiritual', are formally distinguished, not as corresponding to alternative situations, but as parts of a single process in which the first leads to the second (art. 1 ad 2 below). The first, the *sacramentum*, is divinely designed to bring about by its being done, *ex opere operato*, the spiritual reality, *res sacramenti*, the grace of union with Christ really present and with his mystical body. The sacramental

Question 80. holy communion

NOW TO BE DISCUSSED is the sacramental usage or reception of the Eucharist.[a] First, in general, and second, its application by Christ at the Last Supper (81). Here there are twelve points of inquiry:

1. whether there are two ways of communicating, namely sacramentally and spiritually;
2. whether it is for man alone to make a spiritual communion;
3. whether it is only for the righteous to make a sacramental communion;
4. whether a sinner sins by taking the sacrament;
5. on the gravity of this sin;
6. whether the sacrament should be refused to a sinner;
7. whether a nocturnal pollution prevents a man from receiving it;
8. whether it is to be received only when fasting;
9. whether it is to be offered to those not having the use of reason;
10. whether it is to be received daily;
11. whether it is lawful to refrain from it altogether;
12. whether it is lawful to receive the body without the blood.[b]

article 1. should we draw a distinction between the two manners of eating Christ's body?

THE FIRST POINT:[1c] 1. The distinction between the two manners, namely, sacramental and spiritual communion, should not, it seems, be drawn. For as Baptism is a spiritual rebirth, *Unless a man be born again of water*

---

without the spiritual, the outward sign without the inward grace, is a sinful anomaly; the spiritual without the sacramental is for angels (art. 2 below) and for the many human beings outside the economy of the visible Christian Church who do not know about or cannot receive Holy Communion. Their position is that of people who may receive it *in voto*, as they may receive Baptism by desire (ad 3 below). The eating of a consecrated host by an animal, or by a person who does not know it is consecrated is not a sacramental communion (art. 3 ad 3 below). Accidents are allowed for by St Thomas with no gasp of shock, for instance mishaps occurring in the mass (83, 6 below). Christ cannot be injured in himself: his body is not displaced by the transportation of the sacramental species or divided by the breaking of the bread. We cannot defile his body and blood, and sacrilege merely redounds on the person or persons dishonouring. Though quite firm and concrete on the Real Presence, St Thomas is far from materializing it in such a way as to countenance the sentiment of our Lord being abased or imprisoned in the sacrament, or that he could be lonely there, or at the mercy of human perversion and practices of satanism.

Nisi quis renatus fuerit ex aqua et Spiritu Sancto, etc.,[2] ita etiam hoc sacramentum est spiritualis cibus; unde Dominus de hoc sacramento loquens dicit, *Joan.*, *Verba quæ ego locutus sum vobis, spiritus et vita sunt.*[3] Sed circa baptismum non distinguitur duplex modus sumendi, scilicet sacramentalis et spiritualis. Ergo neque circa hoc sacramentum debet hæc distinctio adhiberi.

2. Præterea, ea quorum unum est propter alterum non debent ab invicem dividi, quia unum ab alio speciem trahit. Sed sacramentalis manducatio ordinatur ad spiritualem sicut ad finem. Non ergo debet sacramentalis manducatio contra spiritualem dividi.

3. Præterea, ea quorum unum non potest esse sine altero non debent contra se dividi. Sed videtur quod nullus possit manducare spiritualiter nisi etiam sacramentaliter manducet; alioquin antiqui patres hoc sacramentum spiritualiter manducassent: frustra etiam esset sacramentalis manducatio si sine ea spiritualis esse posset. Non igitur convenienter distinguitur circa hoc sacramentum duplex manducatio, scilicet sacramentalis et spiritualis.

SED CONTRA est quod super illud 1 *Cor.*, *Qui manducat et bibit indigne*, etc.,[4] dicit Glossa, *Duos dicimus esse modos manducandi, unum sacramentalem, et alium spiritualem.*[5]

RESPONSIO: Dicendum quod in sumptione hujus sacramenti duo sunt consideranda, scilicet ipsum sacramentum et effectus ipsius; de quorum utroque jam supra dictum est.[6] Perfectus igitur modus sumendi hoc sacramentum est quando aliquis ita hoc sacramentum suscipit quod percipit ejus effectum. Contingit autem quandoque, sicut supra dictum est,[7] quod aliquis impeditur a percipiendo effectu hujus sacramenti; et talis sumptio hujus sacramenti est imperfecta. Sicut igitur perfectum contra imperfectum dividitur, ita sacramentalis manducatio, per quam sumitur solum sacramentum sine effectu ipsius, dividitur contra spiritualem manducationem, per quam quis percipit effectum hujus sacramenti, quo spiritualiter homo Christo conjungitur per fidem et caritatem.

1. Ad primum ergo dicendum quod etiam circa baptisma et alia hujusmodi sacramenta similis distinctio adhibetur. Nam quidam suscipiunt tantum sacramentum, quidam vero sacramentum et rem sacramenti. Hic tamen differt quia cum alia perficiantur in usu materiæ, percipere sacramentum est ipsa perfectio sacramenti, hoc autem sacramentum perficitur in consecratione materiæ, et ideo uterque usus est consequens

---

[2] *John* 3, 5
[3] *John* 6, 64

and the Holy Ghost, etc.,[2] so is this sacrament *spiritual food*: hence our Lord speaking of it says, *The words that I have spoken to you are spirit and life.*[3] Now there are not two distinct manners of receiving Baptism, sacramentally and spiritually. Neither, then, should the distinction be applied to this sacrament.

2. Besides, when one of two is subordinate to the other they should not be condivided, for the one derives its nature from the other. But sacramental is subordinate to spiritual eating which is its fulfilment. Therefore the two should not be set in contradistinction.

3. Moreover, when one of two cannot exist without the other, they should not be set in contradistinction. But it seems no one can eat spiritually without eating sacramentally, otherwise the Old Testament patriarchs would have eaten this sacrament spiritually. Also sacramental eating would be pointless if without it there could be spiritual eating. Therefore it is not right to distinguish the two, namely sacramental and spiritual reception.

ON THE OTHER HAND, on the text, *He who eats and drinks unworthily*, etc.[4] the Gloss comments, *We hold that there are two manners of eating, the one sacramental, and the other spiritual.*[5]

REPLY: These two, namely the sacrament itself and its effects, are to be considered in receiving the sacrament: we have spoken of them both already.[6] The perfect manner is so to receive the sacrament as to partake also of its effect. Now, as we have noticed,[7] sometimes it happens that a person is hindered from gathering its effect; and such a receiving is imperfect. Since then the embryonic and the full-grown are contrasted, so the sacramental eating, in which the sacrament is received without its effect, is contrasted with the spiritual eating in which is received the sacramental effect whereby a person is spiritually joined to Christ in faith and charity.

Hence: 1. A like distinction also is employed with Baptism and the other sacraments, for some receive the outward sign only while some receive this and the inward reality of the sacrament too. However, there is this difference, for other sacraments are accomplished in the application of their matter and are thus achieved in being received, but this sacrament is achieved in the consecration of the matter, and hence its being received

---

[4] 1 *Corinthians* 11, 29

[5] Ordinaria. Lombard. PL 191, 1647

[6] 3a. 73–79.

[7] 3a. 79, 3 & 8

hoc sacramentum. In baptismo etiam et in aliis sacramentis characterem imprimentibus illi qui accipiunt sacramentum recipiunt aliquem spiritualem effectum, scilicet characterem, quod non accidit in hoc sacramento. Et ideo magis in hoc sacramento distinguitur usus sacramentalis a spirituali quam in baptismo.

2. Ad secundum dicendum quod sacramentalis manducatio, quæ pertingit ad spiritualem, non dividitur contra spiritualem, sed includitur ab ea; sed illa sacramentalis manducatio contra spiritualem dividitur quæ effectum non consequitur; sicut imperfectum, quod non pertingit ad perfectionem speciei, dividitur contra perfectum.

3. Ad tertium dicendum quod, sicut supra dictum est,[8] effectus sacramenti potest ab aliquo percipi, si sacramentum habeatur in voto quamvis non habeatur in re. Et ideo sicut aliqui baptizantur baptismo flaminis propter desiderium baptismi antequam baptizentur baptismo aquæ, ita etiam aliqui manducant spiritualiter hoc sacramentum antequam sacramentaliter sumant. Sed hoc contingit dupliciter. Uno modo propter desiderium sumendi ipsum sacramentum, et hoc modo dicuntur baptizari et manducare spiritualiter et non sacramentaliter illi qui desiderant sumere hæc sacramenta jam instituta. Alio modo propter figuram sicut dicit Apostolus I *Cor.*, quod antiqui patres *baptizati sunt in nube et in mari*, et quod *spiritualem escam manducaverunt, et spiritualem potum biberunt.*[9] Nec tamen frustra adhibetur sacramentalis manducatio, quia plenius inducit sacramenti effectum ipsa sacramenti susceptio quam solum desiderium, sicut supra circa baptismum dictum est.[10]

articulus 2. utrum solius hominis sit hoc sacramentum spiritualiter sumere

AD SECUNDUM sic proceditur:[1] 1. Videtur quod non solius hominis sit hoc sacramentum spiritualiter sumere, sed etiam angelorum, quia super illud *Psalmi*, *Panem angelorum manducavit homo*,[2] dicit Glossa, *idest corpus Christi, qui est vere cibus angelorum.*[3] Sed hoc non esset, si angeli spiritualiter Christum non manducarent. Ergo angeli spiritualiter Christum manducant.

2. Præterea, Augustinus dicit, *Hunc cibum et potum societatem vult*

---

[8] 3a. 68, 2; 73, 3
[9] I *Corinthians* 10, 2
[10] 3a. 69, 4 ad 2
[1] cf IV *Sent.* 9, 2, iv & v
[2] *Psalms* 77, 25
[3] Ordinaria. Lombard. PL 191, 732
[d] Sacramental character; 3a. 63, 1–6.
[e] As an acorn and an oak-tree.
[f] By desire, the customary English term. The Latin, *in voto*, is stronger; a promise and commitment, perhaps even an earnest. Commentators qualify it as a *votum*

whether sacramentally or spiritually is consequential to the sacrament. Furthermore in Baptism and other sacraments that imprint a character,[d] they who receive a sacrament receive also a spiritual effect, namely the sacramental character, which is not the case with this sacrament. And so, rather than with Baptism, the distinction is drawn between sacramental and spiritual reception.

2. The sacramental eating which reaches to the spiritual eating is not apart from it, but is included under it. But that sacramental taking that does not secure the sacramental effect is contrasted with spiritual taking, rather as that which is embryonic and does not attain the full nature of its species is contrasted with a developed being.[e]

3. As we have stated already,[8] the effect of a sacrament can be secured if it is received by desire,[f] and not in fact. Consequently just as some are baptized with the baptism of desire, through their longing before they are baptized with water, so some take this sacrament spiritually before they eat sacramentally. And this in two ways. First, by desire of receiving the actual sacrament, and thus those are said to be baptized and to communicate spiritually, though not sacramentally, who desire to receive sacraments which have been already instituted.[g] The second is figurative; thus St Paul spoke of the patriarchs being *baptized in the cloud and in the sea*, and also that they *ate the same spiritual food and all drank the same supernatural drink.*[9] All the same, the sacramental eating is not useless, because the actual receiving of the sacrament produces the effect more fully than the desiring of it, as we have noted above about Baptism.[10]

article 2. is it for man alone to eat this sacrament spiritually?

THE SECOND POINT:[1] 1. No; it seems it is for angels as well. Because on the *Psalm, Man ate the bread of angels,*[2] the Gloss says, *that is, the body of Christ, which is truly the food of angels.*[3] It would not be so were the angels not nourished by Christ spiritually. Therefore the angels eat Christ spiritually.

2. Further, Augustine writes, *By this meat and drink, he would have us understand the fellowship of his body and members, which is the Church in the*

---

objectivum, or entailed in the first grace that forgives original sin, not *subjectivum*, a conscious resolve to receive the Eucharist. So also baptism of desire, *flaminis*, is present in the original turning to God even of a person not sacramentally baptized. Cf 1a2æ. 89, 6, an article a child psychologist and catechist may find unacceptable, but which has generous and ecumenical implications beneath its apparent apriorism.

[g]So also a Christian devoutly receiving an invalid sacrament is not to be supposed to receive no Eucharistic graces.

intelligi corporis et membrorum suorum, quod est Ecclesia in prædestinatis.[4] Sed ad istam societatem non solum pertinent homines, sed etiam sancti angeli. Ergo etiam sancti angeli spiritualiter manducant.

3. Præterea, Augustinus dicit, *Spiritualiter manducandus est Christus, quoniam ipse dicit, Qui manducat meam carnem, et bibit meum sanguinem, in me manet, et ego in eo.*[5] Sed hoc convenit non solum hominibus, sed etiam sanctis angelis, in quibus per caritatem est Christus, et ipsi in eo. Ergo videtur quod spiritualiter manducare non solum sit hominum, sed etiam angelorum.

SED CONTRA est quod Augustinus dicit, *Panem de altari spiritualiter manducate; innocentiam ad altare apportate.*[6] Sed angelorum non est accedere ad altare tanquam aliquid sint inde sumpturi. Ergo angelorum non est spiritualiter manducare.

RESPONSIO: Dicendum quod in hoc sacramento continetur ipse Christus, non quidem in specie propria, sed in specie sacramenti. Dupliciter ergo contingit manducare spiritualiter ipsum Christum. Uno modo prout in sua specie consistit; et hoc modo angeli manducant spiritualiter ipsum Christum inquantum ei uniuntur fruitione caritatis perfectæ, et visione manifesta (quem panem expectamus in patria), non per fidem sicut nos ei hic unimur. Alio modo contingit spiritualiter manducare Christum, prout est sub speciebus hujus sacramenti, inquantum scilicet aliquis credit in Christum cum desiderio sumendi hoc sacramentum. Et hoc non solum est spiritualiter manducare Christum, sed etiam spiritualiter manducare hoc sacramentum; quod non competit angelis. Et ideo licet angeli spiritualiter manducent Christum, non tamen convenit eis spiritualiter manducare hoc sacramentum.

1. Ad primum ergo dicendum quod sumptio Christi sub hoc sacramento ordinatur, sicut ad finem, ad fruitionem patriæ, eo modo quo angeli eo fruuntur. Et quia ea quæ sunt ad finem derivantur a fine, inde est quod ista manducatio Christi qua eum suminus sub sacramento quodammodo derivatur ab illa manducatione qua angeli fruuntur Christo in patria. Et ideo dicitur *homo manducare panem angelorum*, quia primo et principaliter est angelorum, qui eo fruuntur in specie propria; secundario autem est hominum, qui Christum sub sacramento accipiunt.

2. Ad secundum dicendum quod ad societatem corporis mystici pertinent quidem et homines et angeli; sed homines per fidem, angeli autem per manifestam visionem. Sacramenta autem proportionantur fidei, per quam veritas videtur *in speculo et in ænigmate.*[7] Et ideo, proprie loquendo,

---

[4] *Super Joan.* XXVI. On 6, 54. PL 35, 1614

predestined.[4] But this belongs not to humans only but to the holy angels as well, who, therefore, also eat spiritually.

3. Again, Augustine writes, *Christ is to be eaten spiritually, as he himself declares, He who eats my flesh and drinks my blood, abides in me, and I in him.*[5] But this is not only for men but for angels as well, in whom Christ abides by charity, and they in him. Consequently it seems that to eat Christ spiritually is not for men alone but for angels also.

ON THE OTHER HAND Augustine says, *Eat the bread of the altar spiritually, take innocence to the altar.*[6] But it is not for angels to approach the altar to receive. Therefore they do not eat spiritually.

REPLY:[a] This sacrament holds Christ himself, not in his proper guise but under the external appearance of the sacrament. So there are two ways of feeding on him spiritually. First under his own appearance, and thus the angels live on Christ himself spiritually by being united to him in clear vision and enjoyment of perfect charity: this is the bread we look for in heaven; not by faith, as we are united to him here. The other way of feeding on Christ spiritually is under the sacramental species, in that a person believes in Christ with a desire of receiving this sacrament. This is not merely to feed on Christ spiritually, but also spiritually to feed on this sacrament. This is not the case with angels. Therefore, though angels feed on Christ spiritually, yet it is not for them to eat this sacrament spiritually.

Hence: 1. The purpose of receiving Christ in this sacrament is designed for the enjoyment of heaven: in this way the angels enjoy him. And since deeds done for an end are charged with that end, so it is that our feeding on Christ in the sacrament flows from that feeding whereby angels enjoy Christ in heaven. That is why men are said to eat the *bread of angels*, for first and foremost it is for angels, who enjoy him under his proper aspect, secondly for men, who receive him under the sacrament.

2. Both men and angels share the fellowship of the mystical body, men by faith, angels by manifest vision. Now sacraments correspond to faith, which sees the truth *through a glass and in a dark manner.*[7] Therefore,

---

[5]*Serm. ad Popul.* CXXXII. PL 38, 735. *John* 6, 57. cf Gratian, *Decretum* III, 2, 46. RF I, 1331

[6]*Super Joan.* XXVI. On 6, 40. PL 35, 1611

[7]I *Corinthians* 13, 12

[a]*Panis angelicus, panis angelorum*: the terms are used in liturgical offices, notably for the feast of Corpus Christi, echoing *Psalms* 77, 24 & 102, 20, which refer to the giving of manna in the desert.

Adoremus in æternum; this implies a relative perpetuity, so long as the sacrament exists, not its reservation for all eternity.

non angelis, sed hominibus convenit manducare spiritualiter hoc sacramentum.

3. Ad tertium dicendum quod Christus manet in hominibus secundum præsentem statum per fidem, sed in angelis beatis est per manifestam visionem. Et ideo non est simile, sicut dictum est.[8]

articulus 3. utrum solus homo justus possit Christum sacramentaliter manducare

AD TERTIUM sic proceditur:[1] 1. Videtur quod nullus possit manducare Christum sacramentaliter, nisi homo justus. Dicit enim Augustinus, *Ut quid paras dentem et ventrem? Crede, et manducasti; credere enim in eum, hoc est panem vivum manducare.*[2] Sed peccator non credit in eum, quia non habet fidem formatam, ad quam pertinet credere in Deum, ut in *Secunda Parte* habitum est.[3] Ergo peccator non potest manducare hoc sacramentum, quod est panis vivus.

2. Præterea, hoc sacramentum maxime dicitur esse sacramentum caritatis, ut supra dictum est.[4] Sed sicut infideles privantur fide, ita omnes peccatores privantur caritate; infideles autem non videntur posse sacramentaliter sumere hoc sacramentum, cum in forma hujus sacramenti dicatur, *mysterium fidei.*[5] Ergo pari ratione neque aliquis peccator potest corpus Christi sacramentaliter manducare.

3. Præterea, peccator magis est abominabilis Deo quam creatura irrationalis; dicitur in *Psal.* de homine peccatore, *Homo, cum in honore esset, non intellexit, comparatus est jumentis insipientibus, et similis factus est illis.*[6] Sed animal brutum, puta mus aut canis, non potest sumere hoc sacramentum, sicut etiam non potest sumere sacramentum baptismi. Ergo videtur quod pari ratione neque peccatores hoc sacramentum manducent.

SED CONTRA est quod super illud *Joan.*, *Si quis manducaverit non moriatur,*[7] dicit Augustinus,[8] *Multi de altari accipiunt et accipiendo moriuntur; unde dicit Apostolus, Judicium sibi manducat et bibit.*[9] Sed non moriuntur sumendo nisi peccatores. Ergo peccatores corpus Christi sacramentaliter manducant, et non solum justi.

RESPONSIO: Dicendum quod circa hoc quidam antiqui erraverunt,[10] dicentes quod corpus Christi nec etiam sacramentaliter a peccatoribus sumitur; sed quam cito labiis peccatoris figitur, tam cito sub speciebus

---

[8]ad 2
[1]cf IV *Sent.* 9, 2, i, ii & iii. *In* I *Cor.* 11, *lect.* 7
[2]Gratian, *Decretum* III, 2, 47. RF I, 1331. cf Augustine, *Super Joan.* XXV, on 6, 28. PL 35, 1602
[3]2a2æ, 2, 2; 4, 5

properly speaking, it is for men, not for angels, to eat this sacrament spiritually.

3. Christ dwells in man according to their present state through faith, but in the blessed angels by open vision. As we have said,[8] the comparison does not hold.

article 3. *can only the upright receive Christ sacramentally?*

THE THIRD POINT:[1a] 1. So it seems. For Augustine writes, *Why make ready tooth and belly? Believe, and thou hast eaten. Believe in him, this is to eat the living bread.*[2] Now the sinner does not believe, because he lacks living faith, which implies believing in God,[b] as we have agreed in the *Secunda Pars.*[3] Therefore the sinner cannot receive this sacrament, which is the living bread.

2. Further, this sacrament is especially called the sacrament of charity, as has been noted.[4] As unbelievers lack faith so also sinners lack charity. Now unbelievers do not seem capable of receiving this sacrament since in the form of consecration it is called the *mystery of faith.*[5] Therefore by like reason neither can a sinner receive the body of Christ sacramentally.

3. Besides, a sinner is more offensive before God than a non-rational creature; it is said of him, *Man when he was in honour did not understand, he hath been compared to senseless beasts, and made like to them.*[6] But a beast, such as a mouse or a dog, can receive this sacrament no more than it can receive Baptism. Equally, then, sinners cannot receive it.

ON THE OTHER HAND on the words *If any man eat of it he may not die,*[7] Augustine writes,[8] *Many receive from the altar, and in receiving die, according to St Paul, 'He eats and drinks judgement on himself'.*[9] Therefore sinners, and not only the just, receive the body of Christ sacramentally.

REPLY: Some theologians[10] in the past have been mistaken on this point by holding that Christ's body is not even sacramentally received by sinners, but that as soon as it touches their mouth it ceases to be under the

---

[4] 3a. 73, 3 ad 3; 78, 3 ad 6

[5] Roman Canon

[6] *Psalms* 48, 21

[7] *John* 6, 50

[8] *Super Joan.* XXVI. PL 35, 1611

[9] 1 *Corinthians* 11, 29

[10] e.g. Honorius of Autun. PL 172, 1131. But cf PL 172, 1255

[a] *Homo justus*, an upright person, one living in grace.

[b] *Credere in Deum, credere Deo, credere Deum*; Augustine's terms. cf 2a2æ. 2, 2. Vol. 31, ed. T. C. O'Brien.

sacramentalibus desinit esse corpus Christi. Sed hoc est erroneum; derogat enim veritati hujus sacramenti, ad quam pertinet, sicut supra dictum est,[11] quod manentibus speciebus, corpus Christi sub eis esse non desinat. Species autem manent quamdiu substantia panis maneret si ibi adesset, ut supra dictum est.[12] Manifestum est autem quod substantia panis assumpta a peccatore non statim esse desinit, sed manet quamdiu per calorem naturalem digeratur: unde tamdiu corpus Christi sub speciebus sacramentalibus manet a peccatoribus sumptis. Unde dicendum est quod peccator sacramentaliter corpus Christi manducare potest, et non solum justus.

1. Ad primum ergo dicendum quod verba illa et similia sunt intelligenda de spirituali manducatione, quæ peccatoribus non convenit. Et ideo ex pravo intellectu horum verborum videtur prædictus error processisse, dum nescierunt distinguere inter corporalem et spiritualem manducationem.

2. Ad secundum dicendum quod etiamsi infidelis sumat species sacramentales, corpus Christi sub sacramento sumit; unde manducat Christum sacramentaliter, si ly[13] *sacramentaliter* determinat verbum ex parte manducati; si autem ex parte manducantis, tunc proprie loquendo non manducat sacramentaliter, quia non utitur eo quod accipit ut sacramento, sed ut simplici cibo. Nisi forte infidelis intenderet recipere illud quod Ecclesia confert, licet non haberet fidem veram circa alios articulos, vel etiam circa hoc sacramentum.

3. Ad tertium dicendum quod etiamsi mus vel canis hostiam consecratam manducet, substantia corporis Christi non desinit esse sub speciebus quamdiu species illæ manent, hoc est quamdiu substantia panis maneret; sicut etiam si projiceretur in lutum. Nec hoc vergit in detrimentum dignitatis corporis Christi, qui voluit a peccatoribus crucifigi absque diminutione suæ dignitatis, præsertim cum mus aut canis non tangat ipsum corpus Christi secundum propriam speciem, sed solum secundum species sacramentales. Quidam autem dixerunt[14] quod statim cum sacramentum tangitur a mure vel cane, desinit ibi esse corpus Christi; quod etiam derogat veritati sacramenti, sicut supra dictum est.[15]

Nec tamen dicendum est quod animal brutum sacramentaliter corpus Christi manducet, quia non est natum uti eo ut sacramento; unde non sacramentaliter, sed per accidens corpus Christi manducat, sicut manducaret ille qui sumeret hostiam consecratam, nesciens eam esse consecratam. Et quia id quod est per accidens non cadit in divisione alicujus

---

[11] 3a. 76, 6 ad 3; 77, 8
[12] 3a. 77, 4
[13] *ly*, transliteration of Arabic article *el*, used as Greek *to*

sacramental species. But this is erroneous, because it detracts from the truth of this sacrament, part of which is that so long as the species last Christ's body does not cease to be under them. This we have explained.[11] Now the species last so long as the substance of bread would remain were it to be present.[12] This when taken by a sinner lasts until digested by natural heat, hence Christ's body remains just as long. Hence it must be said that sinners, and not merely the just, can receive Christ's body sacramentally.

Hence: 1. Such words are to be understood of spiritual receiving, which does not apply to sinners. It is from their being misunderstood that the error seems to have arisen, through ignoring the distinction between bodily and spiritual reception.

2. Should an unbeliever receive the sacramental species he would receive Christ's body under the sacrament, and so would eat Christ sacramentally, if the term[13] 'sacramentally' qualifies the verb as to what is eaten. However, if it qualifies as to the eater, then properly speaking an unbeliever does not eat sacramentally, because he uses what he takes as simple food, not as a sacrament. Unless perhaps he intends to receive what the Church bestows, although without true faith concerning other articles of belief, even those concerning this sacrament.[c]

3. Even were a mouse or dog to eat the consecrated host, the substance of Christ's body would not cease to be under the species so long as the substance of bread remained; it would be the same were it cast into the mire. This does not cast indignity on Christ's body, who willed to be crucified by sinners without loss of his true dignity; more especially since the mouse or dog does not touch Christ under his own species, but only under the sacramental species. Though some have said[14] that Christ's body would cease to be there directly it were touched by a mouse or dog. We repeat,[15] however, that this would derogate from the truth of the sacrament.

All the same, that the animal eats the body of Christ sacramentally should not be held, since it is not of a nature to use it as a sacrament. Hence in point of fact Christ's body is accidentally consumed, not sacramentally, as when one consumes a host not knowing it was consecrated. And since what is accidental does not fall into the division of a class, this

---

[14]Pseudo-Abelard, *Epitome Theol.* 29. PL 178, 1743. cf Alan of Lille. PL 210, 359. Innocent III. PL 210, 359

[15]body of art.

[c]So also a child who goes to Communion without proper instruction or preparation, but wishing to join in with what the Church is doing. The doctrine of *in voto* leaves many things trustfully to God's Providence. For this reply and the next see notes *a* and *f* to art. 1 above.

generis, ideo hic modus manducandi corpus Christi non ponitur tertius præter sacramentalem et spiritualem.

articulus 4. utrum peccator sumens corpus Christi sacramentaliter peccet

AD QUARTUM sic proceditur:[1] 1. Videtur quod peccator sumens corpus Christi sacramentaliter non peccet. Non enim est majoris dignitatis Christus sub specie sacramenti quam sub specie propria. Sed peccatores tangentes corpus Christi sub specie propria non peccabant; quin etiam veniam peccatorum consequebantur, sicut legitur *Luc.* de muliere peccatrice;[2] et *Matt.* dicitur, *Quicumque tetigerunt fimbriam vestimenti ejus, salvi facti sunt.*[3] Ergo non peccant, sed magis salutem consequuntur, sacramentum corporis Christi sumendo.

2. Præterea, hoc sacramentum, sicut et alia, est quædam spiritualis medicina. Sed medicina datur infirmis ad salutem, secundum illud *Matt.*, *Non est opus valentibus medicus, sed male habentibus:*[4] infirmi autem vel male habentes spiritualiter sunt peccatores. Ergo hoc sacramentum absque culpa sumere possunt.

3. Præterea, hoc sacramentum, cum in se Christum contineat, est de maximis bonis. Maxima autem bona, secundum Augustinum, sunt quibus nullus male potest uti.[5] Nullus autem peccat, nisi per abusum alicujus rei. Ergo nullus peccator sumens hoc sacramentum peccat.

4. Præterea, sicut hoc sacramentum sentitur gustu et tactu, ita et visu. Si ergo peccator ex eo quod sumit hoc sacramentum peccet gustu et tactu, videtur etiam quod peccaret videndo, quod patet esse falsum, cum Ecclesia omnibus hoc sacramentum videndum et adorandum proponat. Ergo peccator non peccat ex hoc quod manducat hoc sacramentum.

5. Præterea, contingit quandoque quod aliquis peccator non habet conscientiam sui peccati, nec tamen talis peccare videtur corpus Christi sumendo, quia secundum hoc omnes peccarent qui sumunt, quasi periculo se exponentes, cum Apostolus dicat, *Nihil mihi conscius sum; sed non in hoc justificatus sum.*[6] Non ergo videtur quod peccatori cedat in culpam, si hoc sacramentum sumat.

SED CONTRA est quod Apostolus dicit, *Qui manducat et bibit indigne, judicium sibi manducat et bibit,*[7] idest condemnationem. Dicit autem glossa ibidem quod *indigne manducat et bibit, qui in crimine est, vel irreverenter tractat.*[8] Ergo qui est in peccato mortali, si hoc sacramentum accipiat, damnationem acquirit, mortaliter peccans.

---

[1]cf 3a. 79, 3. IV *Sent.* 9, 3, i & ii. *In* I *Cor.* 11, *lect.* 7
[2]*Luke* 7, 37
[3]*Matthew* 14, 36

manner of eating Christ's body is not set down as a third besides sacramental and spiritual eating.

article 4. does a sinner do wrong by receiving Christ's body sacramentally?

THE FOURTH POINT:[1] 1. It seems not. For Christ has no greater dignity under the sacramental species than under his own. But sinners did not sin by touching Christ's own proper body, instead rather they gained forgiveness of their sins, as we read in *Luke*[2] of the woman who was a sinner; and in *Matthew*, that *as many who touched the hem of his garment were healed.*[3] Therefore they do not sin, but rather obtain salvation by receiving the body of Christ.

2. Further, this sacrament, like the others, is a spiritual medicine. Now medicine is given to the sick for their recovery. *They that are in health need not a physician.*[4] And the spiritually sick or poorly are sinners. Therefore this sacrament can be received by them without fault.

3. Moreover, this sacrament, since it holds Christ, is among the greatest blessings. According to Augustine, these are things *no one can abuse.*[5] No one sins save by abusing something. Therefore no one commits a sin in receiving this sacrament.

4. Again, as this sacrament is received by taste and touch, so also by sight. Well then, were a sinner to do wrong by tasting and touching the sacrament he would also, it seems, do wrong by seeing it. This is clearly false, since the Church exposes the sacrament for all to see and worship. Therefore a sinner does not sin by receiving it.

5. Beside, sometimes, as happens, a sinner is unconscious of his sin, yet such a one does no wrong by receiving the body of Christ: if he did all who receive it would sin as exposing themselves to danger, since St Paul admits, *I am not aware of anything against myself, but I am not thereby justified.*[6] So then it does not seem that a sinner falls into fault by receiving the sacrament.

ON THE OTHER HAND St Paul says, *He that eats and drinks unworthily eats and drinks judgement upon himself.*[7] Now a gloss says, *He eats and drinks unworthily who is in sin or who treats it with irreverence.*[8] Therefore if a person while in mortal sin receives the sacrament he earns condemnation by sinning mortally.

---

[4]*Matthew* 9, 12
[5]*De Libero Arbitrio* II. 19. PL 32, 1268
[6]1 *Corinthians* 4, 4
[7]1 *Corinthians* 11, 29
[8]Lombard. PL 191, 1646

RESPONSIO: Dicendum quod in hoc sacramento, sicut in aliis, id quod est sacramentum est signum ejus quod est res sacramenti. Duplex autem est res hujus sacramenti, sicut supra dictum est:[9] una quidem quæ est significata et contenta, scilicet ipse Christus; alia autem est significata et non contenta, scilicet corpus Christi mysticum, quod est societas sanctorum. Quicumque ergo hoc sacramentum sumit, ex hoc ipso significat se esse Christo unitum, et membris ejus incorporatum; quod quidem fit per fidem formatam, quam nullus habet cum peccato mortali. Et ideo manifestum est quod quicumque cum peccato mortali hoc sacramentum sumit, falsitatem in hoc sacramento committit; et ideo incurrit sacrilegium, tanquam sacramenti violator, et propter hoc mortaliter peccat.

1. Ad primum ergo dicendum quod Christus in propria specie apparens non exhibebat se tangendum hominibus in signum spiritualis unionis ad ipsum, sicut exhibetur sumendus in hoc sacramento. Et ideo peccatores eum in propria specie tangentes non incurrebant crimen falsitatis circa divina, sicut peccatores sumentes hoc sacramentum. Et præterea Christus adhuc gerebat similitudinem carnis peccati; et ideo convenienter se peccatoribus tangendum exhibebat; sed remota similitudine carnis peccati per gloriam resurrectionis, se tangi prohibuit a muliere, quæ defectum fidei circa ipsum patiebatur, secundum illud *Joan.*, *Noli me tangere; nondum enim ascendi ad Patrem meum*,[10] scilicet *in corde tuo*, ut Augustinus exponit.[11] Et ideo peccatores, qui defectum fidei formatæ patiuntur circa Christum, repelluntur a contactu hujus sacramenti.

2. Ad secundum dicendum quod non quælibet medicina competit secundum quemlibet statum infirmitatis; nam medicina quæ datur jam liberatis a febre ad confortationem noceret si daretur adhuc febricitantibus. Ita etiam baptismus et pœnitentia sunt quasi medicinæ purgativæ, quæ dantur ad tollendam febrem peccati; hoc autem sacramentum est medicina confortativa, quæ non debet dari nisi liberatis a peccato.

3. Ad tertium dicendum quod maxima bona intelligit Augustinus virtutes animæ, quibus nullus male utitur quasi principiis mali usus; utitur tamen eis aliquis male quasi objectis mali usus, ut patet in his qui de virtutibus superbiunt. Ita et hoc sacramentum, quantum est ex se, non est principium mali usus, sed objectum. Unde Augustinus dicit, *Multi indigne accipiunt corpus Christi, per quod docemur quam cavendum sit male accipere bonum. Ecce enim per bonum factum est malum, dum male accipitur bonum; sicut e contra Apostolo per malum factum est bonum, cum bene accepit malum*,[12] scilicet cum stimulum Satanæ patienter portavit.

4. Ad quartum dicendum quod per visum non accipitur ipsum corpus

---

[9] 3a. 60, 3; 73, 6

[10] *John* 20, 17

[11] *Super Joan.* CXXI. PL 35, 1957

REPLY: With this sacrament, as with the others, the outward sacrament is a sign of an inward reality. Now the reality of this sacrament is twofold, as we have explained,[9] one which is signified and contained, namely Christ himself, the other which is signified yet not contained, namely Christ's mystical body, which is the fellowship of the saints. Whoever, then, receives the sacrament by that very fact signifies that he is joined with Christ and incorporated in his members. This is done through living faith, which no one possesses who is in mortal sin. Clearly, then, whoever in mortal sin receives this sacrament thereby acts a falsehood, and is guilty of sacrilege as a violation of the sacrament, and accordingly sins mortally.[a]

Hence: 1. When Christ appeared under his proper form, he did not offer himself to be touched as a sign of spiritual union, as he presents himself to be received in this sacrament. And therefore sinners mingling with him did not incur the crime of falsehood about divine things, as sinners do in receiving this sacrament. Furthermore Christ still bore the likeness of the flesh of sin,[b] and so fittingly allowed himself to be touched by sinners. As soon, however, as the likeness of that flesh was taken away by the glory of the Resurrection, he forbade the woman to touch him, *Do not touch me, for I have not yet ascended to the Father,*[10c] that is, comments Augustine, *in your heart.*[11] Sinners, then, who lack living faith in Christ, are turned away from touching this sacrament.

2. Any medicine whatever does not suit every stage of sickness; the tonic given to those recovering from a fever would hurt those still with the high temperature. Baptism and Penance are like purgative medicine, given to take away the fever of sin, whereas this sacrament is fortifying medicine not to be given except to those recovered from sin.

3. The greatest blessings Augustine understands to be the soul's virtues, which nobody uses ill,[d] as though they could be principles of activity badly done. All the same, a person sometimes uses them ill as objects of activity badly done, as is seen in those who preen themselves on their virtues. Likewise this sacrament of itself is not a principle of a sin, though it can be an object. As Augustine says, *Many receive the body of Christ unworthily, which teaches us to beware of receiving a blessing badly. For, look you, from good received badly evil is wrought, as on the other hand in the Apostle's case, good was wrought through evil well received, namely, bearing patiently the thorn in the flesh, the messenger of Satan.*[12]

4. Christ's very body is not taken by being seen, but only its sacrament,

---

[12]*Super Joan.* VI. On 1, 33. PL 35, 1432. II *Corinthians* 12, 7

[a]Sacrilege, 2a2æ. 99, 1–3; falsehood, 2a2æ. 110, 1–4.

[b]Born under the Law, and with a mortal and passible body.

[c]cf 3a. 55, 6 ad 3.

[d]cf 1a2æ. 55, 4. Objection 3 has already been met in 3a. 76, 7.

Christi, sed solum sacramentum ejus, quia scilicet non pertingit visus ad substantiam corporis Christi, sed solum ad species sacramentales, ut supra dictum est.[13] Sed ille qui manducat, non solum sumit species sacramentales, sed etiam ipsum Christum, qui est sub eis. Et ideo a visione corporis Christi nullus prohibetur qui sit sacramentum Christi consecutus, scilicet baptismum. Non baptizati autem non sunt admittendi etiam ad inspectionem hujus sacramenti, ut patet per Dionysium.[14] Sed ad manducationem non sunt admittendi, nisi soli illi qui non solum sacramentaliter, sed etiam realiter, sunt Christo conjuncti.

5. Ad quintum dicendum quod hoc quod non habet aliquis conscientiam sui peccati potest contingere dupliciter. Uno modo per culpam suam, vel quia per ignorantiam juris, quæ non excusat, reputat non esse peccatum quod est peccatum, puta si aliquis fornicator reputaret simplicem fornicationem non esse peccatum mortale; vel quia negligens est in examinatione sui ipsius, contra id quod Apostolus dicit 1 *Cor.*, *Probet autem seipsum homo, et sic de pane illo edat, et de calice bibat.*[15] Et sic nihilominus peccat peccator sumens corpus Christi, licet non habeat conscientiam peccati, quia ipsa ignorantia est ei peccatum.

Alio modo potest contingere sine culpa ipsius, puta cum doluit de peccato, sed non est sufficienter contritus; et in tali casu non peccat sumendo corpus Christi, quia homo per certitudinem scire non potest utrum sit vere contritus; sufficit enim si in se signa contritionis inveniat, puta *si doleat de præteritis, et proponat cavere de futuris.*[16] Si vero ignorat hoc quod fecit esse actum peccati, propter ignorantiam facti quæ excusat, puta si accessit ad non suam quam credebat esse suam, non est ex hoc dicendus peccator; similiter etiam si totaliter est peccatum oblitus, sufficit ad ejus deletionem generalis contritio, ut infra dicetur[17]; unde jam non est dicendus peccator.

articulus 5. utrum accedere ad hoc sacramentum cum conscientia peccati sit gravissimum omnium peccatorum

AD QUINTUM sic proceditur:[1] 1. Videtur quod accedere ad hoc sacramentum cum conscientia peccati sit gravissimum omnium peccatorum. Dicit enim Apostolus, *Quicumque manducaverit panem, et biberit calicem Domini indigne, reus erit corporis et sanguinis Domini*;[2] glossa ibidem, *hoc est, ac si Christum occiderit, punietur.*[3] Sed peccatum Christum occidentium

[13] 3a. 76, 7
[14] *De Ecclesiastica Hierarchia* 3. PG 3, 557
[15] 1 *Corinthians* 11, 28
[16] An echo of the Rule of St Augustine
[17] *Supplementum* 2, 3 ad 2
[1] cf IV *Sent.* 9, 3, iii. *In* 1 *Cor.* 11, *lect.* 7
[2] 1 *Corinthians* 11, 27
[3] Interlinear. Lombard. PL 191, 1646

for sight does not reach to the substance of Christ's body, but merely to the sacramental species, as we have said.[13e] But he who eats receives, not only the sacramental species, but also Christ himself who is under them. Accordingly, no one who has received Christ's sacrament, namely Baptism, is forbidden to behold Christ's body; however, as appears from Dionysius,[14f] the non-baptized are not allowed even to view this sacrament. But only those who are really one with Christ, not just sacramentally, are admitted to partake of it.

5. The fact that a person is unconscious of his sins comes about in two ways.[g] One is through his own fault, when by ignorance of the law, which is not excusable, he takes as no sin something which is a sin, for instance a fornicator who does not count fornication to be a mortal sin. Or again through neglect to examine his conscience, which is against St Paul, *Let a man examine himself, and so eat of the bread and drink of the cup.*[15] And so, though unconscious of sin, a sinner who receives Christ's body commits sin, for his very ignorance is sinful on his part.

The other way comes about without fault on his part, as for instance, when he has sorrowed over his sins, but is not contrite enough; in such a case he does not sin in receiving Christ's body, for who can know for certain whether he be truly contrite? It suffices if he finds in himself the signs of contrition, *if he grieves over past sins* and *proposes to avoid them for the future.*[16] If, however, he be ignorant that what he did was a sinful act, through ignorance of fact which excuses, for instance if a man lay with a woman he believed was his own wife when in fact she was not, he is not called a sinner on that account. Likewise if the sin is utterly forgotten general contrition suffices to blot it out, as we shall see later,[17] and he is no longer to be called a sinner.

article 5. is it the gravest of sins to approach this sacrament while conscious of being in mortal sin?

THE FIFTH POINT:[1] 1. It would seem so. For St Paul says, *Whoever eats the bread or drinks the cup of the Lord unworthily will be guilty of profaning the body and blood of the Lord,*[2] on which a gloss comments, *As though he slew Christ he shall be punished.*[3] But the sin of those who slew Christ seems

---

[e]In effect an implicit criticism of the custom of receiving Communion rarely yet gazing on the body of the Lord every day or week; the ritual elevation of the host was introduced at Paris at the beginning of the 13th century.

[f]Dionysius, the Pseudo-Areopagite, an unknown author, probably Syrian, about 500. His writings, Neo-Platonist and tinged with moderate Monophysitism, were a major influence on medieval theology. See Vol. 14, ed. T. C. O'Brien. Appendix 3.

[g]cf 1a2æ. 6, 8.

videtur fuisse gravissimum. Ergo et hoc peccatum quo aliquis cum conscientia peccati ad mensam Christi accedit videtur esse gravissimum.

2. Præterea, Hieronymus dicit in quadam epistola, *Quid tibi cum feminis, qui ad altare cum Deo fabularis? Dic, sacerdos, dic, clerice, qualiter eisdem labiis Filium Dei oscularis, quibus osculatus es labia meretricis? Cum Juda, osculo Filium hominis tradis?*[4] Et sic videtur fornicator ad mensam Christi accedens peccare, sicut Judas peccavit, cujus peccatum fuit gravissimum. Sed multa alia peccata sunt graviora quam peccatum fornicationis, et præcipue peccatum infidelitatis. Ergo cujuslibet peccatoris ad mensam Christi accedentis peccatum est gravissimum.

3. Præterea, magis est abominabilis Deo immunditia spiritualis quam corporalis. Sed si quis projiceret corpus Christi in lutum vel sterquilinium, gravissimum reputaretur ejus peccatum. Ergo gravius peccat si ipsum sumat cum peccato, quod est immunditia spiritualis. Ergo hoc peccatum est gravissimum.

SED CONTRA est quod super illud *Joan.*, *Si non venissem, et locutus eis non fuissem, peccatum non haberent*,[5] dicit Augustinus, hoc intelligendum esse de peccato infidelitatis, quo tenentur cuncta peccata,[6] et ita videtur hoc peccatum non esse gravissimum, sed magis peccatum infidelitatis.

RESPONSIO: Dicendum quod, sicut in *Secunda Parte* dictum est,[7] dupliciter aliquod peccatum potest dici gravius alio: uno modo per se, alio modo per accidens. Per se quidem, secundum rationem suæ speciei, quæ attenditur ex parte objecti. Et secundum hoc, quanto id contra quod peccatur est majus tanto peccatum est gravius. Et quia divinitas Christi est major humanitate ipsius, et ipsa humanitas est potior quam sacramenta humanitatis, inde est quod gravissima peccata sunt quæ committuntur in ipsam divinitatem, sicut est peccatum infidelitatis et blasphemiæ. Secundario autem sunt gravia peccata quæ committuntur in humanitatem Christi: unde dicitur *Matt.*, *Qui dixerit verbum contra Filium hominis, remittetur ei; qui autem dixerit verbum contra Spiritum Sanctum, non remittetur ei neque in hoc sæculo, neque in futuro.*[8] Tertio autem loco sunt peccata quæ committuntur contra sacramenta, quæ pertinent ad humanitatem Christi; et post hæc sunt alia peccata contra puras creaturas.

Per accidens autem unum peccatum est gravius alio ex parte peccantis; puta peccatum quod est ex ignorantia vel infirmitate est levius peccato quod est ex contemptu, vel ex certa scientia; et eadem ratio est de aliis circumstantiis. Et secundum hoc istud peccatum in quibusdam potest esse

---

[4]Ascribed to Jerome; Alexander of Hales. *Summa Theol.* IV, 46, 5, 5. First sentence authentic. *Ep.* XLII. PL 30, 298

[5]*John* 15, 22

[6]*Super Joan.* LXXXIX. PL 35, 1856

to have been most grave, therefore also the sin of a person approaching Christ's table while conscious of being in sin.

2. Again Jerome says, *What hast thou to do with women, thou that speakest familiarly with God? Say, priest, say, cleric, how dost thou kiss the Son of God with the same lips that have kissed a harlot? O Judas, thou hast betrayed the son of man with a kiss.*[4] Thus it appears that the fornicator who comes to Christ's table sins as Judas did, that is most gravely. Yet there are many sins graver than fornication, especially the sin of unbelief.[a] Accordingly the sin of one approaching Christ's table is the gravest.

3. Besides, spiritual uncleanness is more offensive to God than bodily uncleanness.[b] Now were a person to throw Christ's body into the mire or the midden his sin would be most grave. Much more were he to receive it in sin, which is spiritual uncleanness. Therefore this sin is most grave.

ON THE OTHER HAND on the text, *If I had not come and spoken to them, they would not have sin,*[5] Augustine says the words are to be understood of the sin of unbelief, *in which all sins are comprised.*[6] That, and not the sin we are considering, appears therefore to be the greatest.

REPLY: As we have explained in the *Secunda Pars,*[7] one sin can be called graver than another in two ways, one, directly, the other, indirectly. Directly, or *per se,* according to its essential nature taken from its object. In this respect a sin is greater according as that against which it sins is greater. And since Christ's divinity is greater than his humanity, and his humanity greater than the sacraments of his humanity, hence it is that those are the gravest sins which are committed against the divinity, such as disbelief and blasphemy.[c] In the second place come those committed against his humanity; hence it is written, *Whoever says a word against the Son of Man will be forgiven, whoever speaks against the Holy Spirit will not be forgiven, neither in this age or in the age to come.*[8] In the third place come sins committed against the sacraments of Christ's humanity, and after these come other sins committed against mere creatures.

Indirectly, or accidentally, one sin is graver than another on the sinner's part, for instance a sin which results from ignorance or weakness is lighter than one arising from contempt or sure knowledge of what one is about,

---

[7] 1a2æ. 73, 3 & 6; 2a2æ. 73, 3
[8] *Matthew* 12, 32
[a] The sin of unbelief, 2a2æ. 10.
[b] The stain of sin, 1a2æ. 86, 1 & 2.
[c] cf 2a2æ. 14.

gravius, sicut in his qui ex actuali contemptu, cum conscientia peccati ad hoc sacramentum accedunt in quibusdam vero minus grave; puta in his qui ex quodam timore, ne deprehendantur in peccato, cum conscientia peccati ad hoc sacramentum accedunt.

Sic ergo patet quod hoc peccatum est multis aliis gravius secundum suam speciem, non tamen est omnium gravissimum.

1. Ad primum ergo dicendum quod peccatum indigne sumentium hoc sacramentum comparatur peccato occidentium Christum secundum similitudinem, quia utrumque committitur contra corpus Christi; non tamen secundum criminis quantitatem. Peccatum enim occidentium Christum fuit multo gravius, primo quidem quia illud peccatum fuit contra corpus Christi in specie propria, hoc autem peccatum est contra corpus Christi in specie sacramenti; secundo quia illud peccatum processit ex intentione nocendi Christo, non autem hoc peccatum.

2. Ad secundum dicendum quod fornicator accipiens corpus Christi comparatur Judæ Christum osculanti quantum ad similitudinem criminis, quia uterque ex signo caritatis Christum offendit; non tamen quantum ad criminis quantitatem, sicut etiam prius dictum est.[9] Hæc tamen criminis similitudo non minus competit aliis peccatoribus quam fornicatoribus. Nam et per alia peccata mortalia agitur contra caritatem Christi, cujus signum est hoc sacramentum; et tanto magis quanto peccata sunt graviora. Secundum quid tamen peccatum fornicationis magis reddit hominem ineptum ad perceptionem hujus sacramenti, inquantum scilicet per hoc peccatum spiritus maxime carni subjicitur, et ita impeditur fervor dilectionis, qui requiritur in hoc sacramento.

Plus tamen ponderat impedimentum ipsius caritatis quam fervoris ejus. Unde et peccatum infidelitatis, quod funditus separat hominem ab Ecclesiæ unitate, simpliciter loquendo, maxime hominem ineptum reddit ad susceptionem hujus sacramenti; quod est sacramentum ecclesiasticæ unitatis ut supra dictum est.[10] Unde et gravius peccat infidelis accipiens hoc sacramentum quam fidelis peccator; et magis contemnit Christum secundum quod est sub hoc sacramento, præsertim si non credat Christum vere sub hoc sacramento esse; quia quantum est in se diminuit sanctitatem hujus sacramenti, et virtutem Christi operantis in hoc sacramento, quod est contemnere ipsum sacramentum in seipso. Fidelis autem qui cum conscientia peccati sumit contemnit hoc sacramentum non in seipso, sed quantum ad usum, indigne accipiens. Unde et Apostolus assignans rationem hujus peccati, dicit, *Non dijudicans corpus Domini*,[11] idest *non discernens ipsum ab aliis cibis*;[12] quod maxime facit ille qui non credit Christum esse sub hoc sacramento.

---

[9]ad 1 above

[10]3a. 67, 2; 73, 2 & 4

and the same is the case with other circumstances.[d] And accordingly this sin can be the graver, for instance in those who, while conscious of sin, approach the sacrament from contempt. In others, however, it is less grave, for instance, who approach it, while conscious of sin, from fear of their sin being discovered.

So then it is clear that this sin of its kind is graver than many others, but nevertheless it is not the gravest of all.

Hence: 1. The sin of receiving this sacrament unworthily is compared to the sin of those who killed Christ on account of some likeness, for both are committed against his body, but not on account of the size of the crime. Theirs was a much graver sin; first, because it was against his proper natural body, whereas this is against his body under the sacramental species; second, because theirs sprang from the intention of hurting him, whereas this does not.

2. A fornicator receiving Christ's body is likened to Judas kissing Christ as to a resemblance of the sin, for both offer offence to Christ under the guise of friendship; but not as to the extent of the crime, as was observed above.[9] The comparison applies no less to other sinners than to fornicators; other mortal sins conflict with Christ's friendship, of which this sacrament is the sign, and all the more the graver they are. Yet in one respect fornication renders a person more unfit for receiving the sacrament, in that it enslaves the spirit to the flesh, and so damps the flame of affection that is called for.

However, the hindrance to charity itself outweighs that to its fervour. Accordingly the sin of unbelief which cuts off at root a person from the unity of the Church, makes him utterly unfit to receive this sacrament, which, as we have seen,[10] is the sacrament of the Church's unity. So the unbeliever who receives this sacrament sins more gravely than the sinful believer and shows great contempt towards Christ who is in this sacrament, and especially if he does not believe Christ to be really present, because, in so far as it lies in his power, he lessens the sacredness of the sacrament, and the power of Christ at work in it; this is to despise the sacrament in itself. The believer, while conscious of being in sin, by unworthily receiving it contemns the sacrament, not in itself but in its application. Hence St Paul in assigning the cause of this sin speaks of receiving *without discerning the body of the Lord*,[11] that is, *not distinguishing it from other food*.[12] This, indeed, is above all done by a person who does not believe that Christ is in this sacrament.

---

[11] 1 *Corinthians* 11, 29

[12] Interlinear gloss. Lombard. PL 191, 1647

[d] cf 1a2æ. 73, 6 & 7.

3. Ad tertium dicendum quod ille qui projiceret hoc sacramentum in lutum, multo gravius peccaret quam ille qui cum conscientia peccati mortalis ad hoc sacramentum accedit; primo quidem quia ille hoc faceret ex intentione injuriam faciendi huic sacramento, quod non intendit peccator indigne corpus Christi accipiens; secundo quia peccator est capax gratiæ: unde etiam magis est aptus ad suscipiendum hoc sacramentum quam quæcumque alia irrationalis creatura. Unde maxime inordinate uteretur hoc sacramento qui projiceret ipsum canibus ad manducandum, vel qui projiceret in lutum ad conculcandum.

articulus 6. utrum sacerdos debeat denegare corpus Christi peccatori petenti

AD SEXTUM sic proceditur:[1] 1. Videtur quod sacerdos debeat denegare corpus Christi peccatori petenti. Non enim est faciendum contra Christi præceptum propter vitandum scandalum, vel infamiam alicujus. Sed Dominus præcepit, *Nolite sanctum dare canibus*;[2] maxime autem datur sanctum canibus cum hoc sacramentum peccatoribus exhibetur. Ergo neque propter vitandum scandalum, neque propter vitandam infamiam alicujus, debet hoc sacramentum peccatori petenti dari.

2. Præterea, de duobus malis minus malum est eligendum. Sed minus malum esse videtur si peccator infametur, vel etiam si ei hostia non consecrata detur, quam si sumens corpus Christi mortaliter peccet. Videtur ergo hoc potius esse eligendum quod vel infametur peccator petens corpus Christi, vel etiam quod detur ei hostia non consecrata.

3. Præterea, corpus Christi interdum datur suspectis de crimine ad criminis manifestationem. Legitur enim in *Decr.*, *Sæpe contingit ut in monasteriis monachorum furta perpetrentur; idcirco statuimus ut quando ipsi fratres de talibus expurgare se debent, missa ab abbate celebretur, vel ab aliquo cui abbas præceperit, præsentibus fratribus; et sic, expleta missa, omnes communicent in hæc verba, Corpus Christi sit mihi hodie ad probationem.*[3] Et infra, *Si episcopo aut presbytero aliquod maleficium fuerit imputatum, pro singulis missam celebrare debet et communicare, et de singulis sibi imputatis innocentem se ostendere.*[4] Sed peccatores occultos non oportet manifestari, quia si frontem verecundiæ abjecerint, liberius peccabunt, ut Augustinus dicit.[5] Ergo peccatoribus occultis non est corpus Christi dandum, etiamsi petant.

---

[1]cf 3a. 81, 2. IV *Sent.* 9, 5, i; 11, 3, 2, i. *Quodl.* V, 6, 2
[2]*Matthew* 7, 6
[3]Gratian, *Decretum* II, 2, 5, 23. RF I, 464

3. He who cast this sacrament in the mud would sin much more gravely than one approaching it while conscious of mortal sin. First, because he intends to violate the sacrament, whereas in communicating the sinner has no such intent. Secondly, the sinner is open to grace, and hence more capable than any non-rational creature of receiving the sacrament. And so he would treat this sacrament most inordinately who threw it to the dogs to eat or flung it in the mud to be trodden on.

article 6. should a priest deny the body of Christ to a sinner who asks for it?

THE SIXTH POINT:[1a] 1. Yes, so it seems. For Christ's command is not to be acted against for the sake of avoiding scandal and loss of reputation.[b] But he commands, *Do not give dogs what is holy.*[2] This is especially exemplified in offering this sacrament to sinners. Therefore neither for the sake of avoiding scandal or of loss of reputation should this sacrament be given to a sinner who asks for it.

2. Besides, one should chose the lesser of two evils. Yet rather than sinning mortally by receiving Christ's body it seems to be a lesser evil to suffer loss of reputation or to be given an unconsecrated host. And this course is to be preferred.

3. Then also, Christ's body is sometimes given to those suspected of crime in order to put them to test. We read in the *Decretum*, *It often happens that thefts are perpetrated in monasteries of monks. Wherefore we enact that when the brethren have to exonerate themselves, the abbot or his deputy shall celebrate mass for the brethren and at the end all shall communicate under the words, May the Body of Christ prove me today.*[3] And further on, *If any evil deed is imputed to a bishop or priest, for each charge he must say mass and communicate and show his innocence on each charge.*[4] Now secret sinners must not be exposed, for as Augustine remarks,[5] once the blush of shame is dispelled they will indulge in sin the more. Therefore the body of Christ is not to be given to secret sinners, even if they ask for it.

---

[4]ibid 26. RF I, 465
[5]*Serm. ad Popul.* LXXXII, 4. PL 38, 509
[a]The remaining articles are mainly about the Eucharistic discipline in the 13th-century Latin Church.
[b]*Infamia*, a canonical concept: the loss of rights and privileges consequent on conviction for certain crimes.

SED CONTRA est quod, super illud *Psal., Manducaverunt, et adoraverunt omnes pingues terræ,*[6] dicit Augustinus, *Non prohibeat dispensator pingues terræ, idest peccatores, in mensa Domini manducare.*[7]

RESPONSIO: Dicendum quod circa peccatores distinguendum est: quidam enim sunt occulti, quidam vero manifesti, scilicet per evidentiam facti, sicut publici usurarii, aut publici raptores, vel etiam per aliquod judicium ecclesiasticum vel sæculare. Manifestis ergo peccatoribus non debet etiam petentibus sacra communio dari. Unde Cyprianus scribit ad quendam, *Pro dilectione tua consulendum me existimasti quid mihi videatur de histrione et mago illo qui apud vos constitutus adhuc in artis suæ dedecore perseverat, an talibus sacra communio cum cæteris Christianis debeat dari. Puto nec majestati divinæ, nec evangelicæ disciplinæ congruere, ut pudor et honor Ecclesiæ tam turpi et infami contagione fœdetur.*[8]

Si vero non sunt manifesti peccatores, sed occulti, non potest eis petentibus sacra communio denegari. Cum enim quilibet Christianus ex hoc ipso quod est baptizatus sit admissus ad dominicam mensam, non potest ei jus suum tolli, nisi pro aliqua causa manifesta. Unde super illud 1 *Cor., Si is qui frater nominatur inter vos,* etc.[9] dicit glossa Augustini, *Nos a communione quemquam prohibere non possumus, nisi aut sponte confessum, aut in aliquo judicio ecclesiastico vel seculari nominatum atque convictum.*[10] Potest tamen sacerdos, qui est conscius criminis, occulte monere peccatorem occultum, vel etiam in publico generaliter omnes, ne ad mensam Domini accedant, antequam de peccatis pœniteant et Ecclesiæ reconcilientur; nam post pœnitentiam et reconciliationem etiam publicis peccatoribus non est communio deneganda præcipue in articulo mortis. Unde in concilio Carthaginensi III legitur, *Scenicis atque histrionibus, cœterisque hujusmodi personis, vel apostatis conversis ad Deum reconciliatio non negetur.*[11]

1. Ad primum ergo dicendum quod sancta prohibentur dari canibus, idest peccatoribus manifestis; sed occulta non possunt publice puniri, sed sunt divino judicio reservanda.

2. Ad secundum dicendum quod licet pejus sit peccatori occulto peccare mortaliter, sumendo corpus Christi, quam infamari, tamen sacerdoti ministranti corpus Christi pejus est peccare mortaliter infamando injuste peccatorem occultum quam quod ille mortaliter peccet, quia nullus debet peccatum mortale committere ut alium liberet a peccato. Unde Augustinus

---

[6]*Psalms* 21, 30 [7]*Enarr. in Psalm.* on 48, 3. PL 86, 545

[8]*Epist.* LXI, ad Euchratium. PL 4, 373

[9]1 *Corinthians* 5, 11

[10]*Serm. ad Popul.* CCCLI, 4. PL 39, 1546. Lombard. PL 191, 1575

ON THE OTHER HAND, on the verse, *All the fat ones of the earth have eaten and adored,*[6] Augustine says, *Let not the dispenser hinder the fat ones of the earth,* that is, sinners, *from eating at the table of the Lord.*[7]

REPLY: Sinners are subjects for discrimination. Some are secret, some notorious, either because the fact is evident, as with public usurers or gangsters, or because of the judgement of a civil or ecclesiastical court. To such notorious sinners holy Communion should not be given even if they ask for it. Hence Cyprian[c] in a letter writes, *You were so kind as to consult me about actors and that magician who is installed among you and is addicted to the disgraceful practice of his art, as to whether holy Communion should be given to them along with others. I think that it beseems neither the divine majesty nor gospel discipline for the Church's decency and honour to be defiled by such shameful and infamous contagion.*[8]

Yet if these be hidden, not open, sinners, holy Communion should not be denied them if they request it, since every Christian, from the fact that he is baptized, is admitted to the Lord's table, cannot be robbed of his right except for some manifest reason. On the text, *If any one who bears the name of brother,*[9] a gloss from Augustine comments, *We cannot forbid Communion to anyone unless he has freely confessed or been summoned and convicted by some ecclesiastical or secular tribunal.*[10] Nevertheless a priest who is aware of the crime can privately warn the secret sinner, or publicly warn all in general terms, against approaching the Lord's table until they have repented and been reconciled to the Church. Thereafter Communion is not to be refused even to public sinners, especially at the hour of death. Accordingly we read in the Council of Carthage, *Reconciliation is not to be denied to stage-players or actors and the like and to apostates after their conversion to God.*[11d]

Hence: 1. We are forbidden to give holy things to dogs, that is to notorious sinners. Nevertheless hidden sins cannot be publicly punished, but should be left to God's judgement.

2. Though it is worse for a secret sinner to sin mortally in taking Christ's body than to suffer loss of his good name, nevertheless it is worse for the priest to sin mortally by unjustly defaming the secret sinner than by allowing him to sin mortally, because nobody ought to commit a mortal sin to prevent another from mortal sin. Accordingly Augustine

---

[11]Carthage III, can. 35, 398. Mansi III, 885. cf Gratian, *Decretum* III, 2, 96. RF I, 1352

[c]St Cyprian, Bishop of Carthage, d. 258.

[d]The teaching of this article is incorporated in the Code of Canon Law, can. 855. For a point of casuistry, cf *Quodl.* V, 6, 12.

dicit, *Periculosissime admittitur hæc compensatio, ut nos faciamus aliquid mali, ne alius gravius malum faciat.*[12] Peccator tamen occultus potius deberet eligere infamari, quam indigne ad mensam Domini accedere. Hostia tamen non consecrata nullo modo debet dari loco consecratæ; quia sacerdos hoc faciens, quantum in se est, facit idololatrare illos qui credunt esse hostiam consecratam, sive alios præsentes sive etiam ipsum sumentem, quia, ut Augustinus dicit in *Psalm.*, *nemo carnem Christi manducet, nisi prius adoret.*[13] Unde *Extra.* de homine dicitur, *Licet is qui pro sui criminis conscientia reputat se indignum, peccet graviter, si se ingerat irreverenter ad illud; gravius tamen videtur offendere qui fraudulenter illud præsumpserit simulare.*[14]

3. Ad tertium dicendum quod decreta illa sunt abrogata per contraria documenta Romanorum pontificum. Dicit enim Stephanus Papa, *Ferri candentis vel aquæ ferventis examinatione confessionem extorqueri a quolibet, sacri canones non concedunt; spontanea enim confessione vel testium approbatione publica delicta commissa sunt regimini nostro judicari; occulta vero et incognita illi sunt relinquenda qui solus novit corda filiorum hominum.*[15] Et idem habetur *Extra.*[16] In omnibus enim talibus esse videtur Dei tentatio; unde sine peccato fieri non possunt. Et gravius videretur, si in hoc sacramento, quod est institutum ad remedium salutis, aliquis incurreret judicium mortis. Unde nullo modo corpus Christi debet dari alicui suspecto de crimine, quasi ad examinationem.

articulus 7. utrum nocturna pollutio aliquem impediat a sumptione hujus sacramenti

AD SEPTIMUM sic proceditur:[1] 1. Videtur quod nocturna pollutio non impediat aliquem a sumptione corporis Christi. Nullus enim impeditur a sumptione corporis Christi nisi propter peccatum. Sed nocturna pollutio accidit sine peccato; dicit enim Augustinus, *Ipsa phantasia, quæ fit in cogitatione sermocinantis, cum sic expressa fuerit in visione somniantis, ut inter illam et veram conjunctionem corporum non discernatur, continuo movetur caro, et sequitur quod eum motum sequi solet; cum hoc tam sine peccato fiat quam sine peccato a vigilantibus dicitur, quod, ut diceretur, procul dubio cogitatum est.*[2] Ergo nocturna pollutio non impedit hominem ab hujus sacramenti sumptione.

---

[12] *Quæst. in Heptat.* I, 42. On *Genesis* 19, 8. PL 34, 559
[13] *Enarr. in Psalm.*, on 98, 5. PL 37, 1264
[14] *Decretals of Gregory IX*, III, 41, 7. RF II, 640
[15] Stephen V. *Fragm. Epist.* ad Leutbertum. Mansi, XVIII, 25. cf Gratian, *Decretum* II, 2, 5, 20. RF I, 463
[16] *Decretals of Gregory IX.* V, 34, 8. RF II, 871
[1] cf IV *Sent.* 9, 4, ii
[2] *Super Genes. ad litt.* XII, 15. PL 34, 466

writes, *It is a highly dangerous exchange for us to do evil lest others do a greater.*[12] All the same the sinner ought to prefer infamy rather than approach the Lord's table unworthily.

By no means should an unconsecrated host be given him instead of a consecrated host: a priest doing this, so far as he is concerned, makes others, whether the recipient or those present, commit idolatry by believing it is consecrated, since, as Augustine says, *Let no one eat Christ's flesh before he first worships it.*[13] Hence in the *Decretals,*[e] it is laid down, *Although he who reputes himself unworthy, through consciousness of his sin, sins gravely if he receives; nevertheless he who deceitfully has presumed to simulate it seems to sin more gravely.*[14]

3. Those decrees were abrogated by contrary enactments of the Roman Pontiffs. Pope Stephen,[f] says *The sacred canons do not allow of a confession being extorted from any person by trial with hot iron or boiling water. It is for our state authorities to judge of public crimes which are committed and made evident by spontaneous confession or the proof of witness: private and unknown crimes are to be left to him who alone knows the hearts of the sons of men.*[15] And the same is found in the *Decretals.*[16] Tempting God seems present in all such ordeals, and so their practice cannot be free from sin.[g] And it would seem the graver were anybody to receive the death-sentence through this sacrament, which was instituted to be a saving remedy. Consequently Christ's body should absolutely never be given to a suspect as part of his examination.

article 7. does nocturnal pollution hinder one from receiving the sacrament?

THE SEVENTH POINT:[1a] 1. It seems not, for no one is stopped from receiving the body of Christ except on account of sin. But nocturnal pollution happens without sin; Augustine says that *the same image that comes into the mind of a speaker may present itself to the mind of a dreamer, so that he is unable to distinguish image from reality and so is moved carnally, with the result that usually follows, and therefore there is as little sin in this as there is in speaking and therefore thinking of such things.*[2] Consequently nocturnal pollution does not stop a person from taking the sacrament.

---

[e]*The Decretals of Gregory IX.* A collection made by St Raymond of Peñafort at the command of Pope Gregory IX, who died 1241. The reference *Extra.* in the Latin text is to the *Extravagantes,* decretals which 'wandered outside' the *Decretum* of Gratian, but now usually reserved to decretals from the early 14th to the late 15th centuries.

[f]Stephen V, d. 891.

[g]The sin of tempting God, 2a2æ. 97, 1–3.

[a]Is nocturnal pollution a sin? 2a2æ. 154, 5.

2. Præterea, Gregorius dicit in epistola ad Augustinum episcopum Anglorum, *Si quis sua conjuge non cupidine voluptatis captus, sed tantum procreandorum liberorum gratia utitur, ille profecto sive de ingressu Ecclesiæ, sive de sumendo corporis dominici mysterio suo est judicio relinquendus; quia prohiberi a nobis non debet accipere qui in igne positus nescit ardere.*[3] Ex quo patet quod carnalis pollutio etiam vigilantis, si sit sine peccato, non prohibet hominem a sumptione corporis Christi. Multo igitur minus prohibet nocturna pollutio dormientis.

3. Præterea, nocturna pollutio videtur solam immunditiam corporalem habere. Sed aliæ immunditiæ corporales, quæ secundum legem impediebant ab ingressu sanctorum,[4] in nova lege non impediunt a sumptione hujus sacramenti: sicut de muliere pariente vel menstruata vel fluxum sanguinis patiente scribit B. Gregorius Augustino Anglorum episcopo.[5] Ergo videtur quod neque etiam nocturna pollutio impediat hominem a sumptione hujus sacramenti.

4. Præterea, peccatum veniale non impedit hominem a sumptione hujus sacramenti, nec etiam peccatum mortale post pœnitentiam. Sed dato quod nocturna pollutio provenerit ex aliquo peccato præcedenti, sive crapulæ sive turpium cogitationum, plerumque tale peccatum est veniale; et si aliquando sit mortale, potest contingere quod de mane pœniteat, et peccatum suum confiteatur. Ergo videtur quod non debeat impediri a sumptione hujus sacramenti.

5. Præterea, gravius peccatum est homicidii quam fornicationis. Sed si aliquis de nocte somniet se homicidium perpetrare aut furtum aut quodcumque aliud peccatum, non propter hoc impeditur a sumptione corporis Christi. Ergo videtur quod multo minus fornicatio somniata cum pollutione subsequente impediat a sumptione hujus sacramenti.

SED CONTRA est quod *Levit.* dicitur, *Vir de quo egredietur semen coitus immundus erit usque ad vesperum.*[6] Sed immundis non patet aditus ad sacramenta. Ergo videtur quod propter pollutionem nocturnam aliquis impediatur a sumptione hujus sacramenti, quod est maximum sacramentum.

RESPONSIO: Dicendum quod circa pollutionem nocturnam duo possunt considerari: unum quidem ratione cujus ex necessitate impedit hominem a sumptione hujus sacramenti; aliud autem ratione cujus non ex necessitate impedit hominem ab hujusmodi sacramenti perceptione, sed ex quadam congruentia.

---

[3] *Registrum* XI, 4, 64, 10. PL 77, 1197. cf Gratian, II, 33, 4, 7. RF I, 1249

2. Again, Gregory says in his letter to Augustine, Bishop of the English,[b] *If anyone knows his wife, not carried away by greed for pleasure, but only from desire to have children, it should be left to his conscience whether to enter the church and receive the mystery of the Lord's body: we ought not to forbid him since he has passed through the fire unscorched.*[3] From this it is clear that carnal pollution even when one is awake, if it be without sin, is no hindrance to receiving the body of Christ. Much less, then, is it so when it happens when one is asleep.

3. Also, nocturnal pollution seems to carry only bodily uncleanness. But other bodily uncleannesses, which according to the Old Law[4] forbade entrance into a holy place, do not according to the New Law prevent receiving this sacrament, as for instance a woman after childbirth, during her period, or suffering from an issue of blood: so writes blessed Gregory to Augustine, Bishop of the English.[5] It seems, then, that neither does nocturnal pollution hinder a man from the reception of this sacrament.

4. Besides, venial sin is no hindrance to receiving the sacrament, nor is mortal sin after repentance. Granted that nocturnal pollution arises from some foregoing sin, whether of intemperance or impure thoughts, often as not such sin is venial, and if mortal, one may repent and confess it. Consequently it seems he should not be stopped from receiving the sacrament.

5. Then as well, murder is worse than fornication. Yet if a man dreams he has committed murder, or theft, or any other sin, he is not on that account debarred from receiving the body of Christ. Therefore it seems that none should be debarred from receiving this sacrament because he has dreams of fornication with subsequent pollution.

ON THE OTHER HAND it is written, *If a man has an emission of seed he shall be unclean until the evening.*[6] For the unclean there is not access to the sacraments. Therefore it would seem that owing to a nocturnal pollution a man is debarred from taking this, the greatest of the sacraments.

REPLY: There can be two considerations about nocturnal pollution, one the reason which necessarily debars a man from receiving this sacrament, the other which debars him, not of necessity, but from a sense of propriety.

---

[4]*Leviticus* 12 & 15
[5]loc cit note 3. PL 77, 1195
[6]*Leviticus* 15, 16
[b]St Augustine of Canterbury, d. 604.

Ex necessitate quidem impedit hominem ab hujus sacramenti perceptione solum peccatum mortale. Et quamvis nocturna ipsa pollutio secundum se considerata peccatum mortale esse non possit, nihilominus tamen ratione suæ causæ, quandoque habet peccatum mortale annexum. Et ideo consideranda est causa pollutionis nocturnæ. Quandoque enim provenit a causa extrinseca spirituali, scilicet ex dæmonum illusione, qui, sicut in *Prima Parte* habitum est,[7] phantasmata commovere possunt, ex quorum apparitione pollutio interdum subsequitur. Quandoque vero provenit pollutio ex causa intrinseca spirituali, scilicet ex præcedentibus cogitationibus. Aliquando autem ex causa intrinseca corporali, vel ex superfluitate sive debilitate naturæ, sive etiam ex superfluitate cibi vel potus. Quælibet autem harum trium causarum potest et sine peccato, et cum peccato veniali vel mortali existere. Et si quidem sit sine peccato, vel cum peccato veniali, non ex necessitate impedit sumptionem hujus sacramenti, ita scilicet quod homo sumendo sit reus corporis et sanguinis Domini. Si vero sit cum peccato mortali, impedit ex necessitate.

Illusio enim dæmonum quandoque provenit ex præcedenti negligentia præparationis ad devotionem; quæ potest esse et mortale et veniale peccatum. Quandoque vero provenit ex sola nequitia dæmonum volentium impedire hominem a sumptione hujus sacramenti. Unde legitur in *Collationibus Patrum*,[8] quod cum quidam frater pateretur pollutionem semper in festis in quibus erat communicandum, seniores comperto quod nulla causa ab ipso præcesserat decreverunt quod propter hoc a communione non cessaret, et ita cessavit illusio dæmonum. Similiter etiam præcedentes cogitationes lascivæ quandoque possunt esse omnino sine peccato, puta cum aliquis causa lectionis vel disputationis cogitur de talibus cogitare; et si hoc fit sine concupiscentia et delectatione, non erunt cogitationes immundæ, sed honestæ; ex quibus tamen pollutio sequi potest, sicut patet ex auctoritate Augustini supra inducta.[9] Quandoque vero præcedentes cogitationes sunt ex concupiscentia et delectatione; et si adsit consensus, erit peccatum mortale; si autem desit, erit veniale. Similiter etiam et causa corporalis quandoque est sine peccato, puta cum est ex infirmitate naturæ, unde quidam etiam in vigilando absque peccato fluxum seminis patiuntur, vel etiam si sit ex superfluitate naturæ; sicut enim contingit sanguinem fluere absque peccato, ita et semen, quod est superfluitas sanguinis, secundum Philosophum.[10]

Quandoque vero est cum peccato, puta cum provenit ex superfluitate cibi vel potus; et hoc etiam potest esse peccatum veniale vel mortale; licet frequentius peccatum mortale accidat circa turpes cogitationes, propter

---

[7] 1a. 111, 3

[8] Cassian, XXII, 6. PL 49, 1255

Mortal sin alone stops a man from receiving this sacrament. And though nocturnal pollution considered in itself cannot be a mortal sin, nevertheless owing to its cause it sometimes is connected with mortal sin, which cause, therefore, is to be investigated. It sometimes comes from an external spiritual cause, namely the deception of demons, who, as we have seen in the *Prima Pars*,[7] can stir up images and from the apparition of these pollution sometimes follows. Sometimes it comes from an internal spiritual cause, such as preceding thoughts, sometimes from an internal bodily cause, as from excess or defect of nature, or from a surfeit of meat or drink. Now each of these causes may be without sin, or with sin, mortal or venial. If without sin or with venial sin, it does not necessarily prevent the receiving of this sacrament, such as would make a man guilty of the body and blood of the Lord. If, however, with mortal sin, it prevents it of necessity. Let us discuss this further.

Sometimes the demon's deceiving us may be because of preceding negligence about our preparatory devotion, and this can be either mortal or venial sin. At other times the illusion is solely from demons wishing to keep man from receiving the sacrament. And so we read in the *Conferences of the Fathers*,[8c] that when one of the brethren always suffered a pollution before a feast day when he was to receive Communion, the elders, having found out for certain there was no preceding fault on his part, ruled that he was not to abstain from Communion on that account, and thereupon the illusion of demons ceased. Likewise previous lascivious thoughts sometimes can be wholly without sin, as when because of a lecture or debate one is obliged to think of sex. If that be done without lust and delectation they will not be impure but decent, and yet pollution can come of them, on the clear authority of Augustine.[9] Sometimes, however, such thoughts come from lust and delectation, and should we consent, it will be mortal sin, otherwise it will be venial.[d] Likewise also the bodily cause can be without sin, as when pollution comes from natural infirmity, thus some suffer from it without sin even if they are awake; or as when it comes from natural abundance, for just as blood can issue without sin so also can semen, which, according to Aristotle,[10] is a superfluity of blood.

Sometimes however it is with sin, as when it is due to an excess of food or drink. This can be mortal or venial, though it is mortal more frequently with impure thoughts because consent is easier there than with taking

---

[9]loc cit note 2

[10]*De Generatione Animal*, I, 19. 726b9

[c]By John Cassian, d. *c.* 435.

[d]For the Augustinian teaching on *delectatio morosa* and *consensus*, see 1a2æ. 74, 6–8.

facilitatem consensus, quam circa sumptionem cibi et potus. Unde et Gregorius, scribens Augustino Anglorum episcopo,[11] dicit cessandum esse a communione, quando ex turpibus cogitationibus provenit, non autem quando provenit ex superfluitate cibi vel potus, præsertim si necessitas adsit. Sic igitur ex causa pollutionis considerari potest utrum nocturna pollutio impediat ex necessitate sumptionem hujus sacramenti.

Ex quadam vero congruentia impedit quantum ad duo. Quorum unum semper accidit, scilicet quædam fœditas corporalis, cum qua, propter reverentiam sacramenti, non decet ad altare accedere (unde et volentes tangere aliquid sacrum, manus lavant); nisi forte talis immunditia sit perpetua vel diuturna, sicut est lepra vel fluxus sanguinis vel aliquid hujusmodi. Aliud autem est evagatio mentis, quæ sequitur pollutionem nocturnam, præcipue quando cum turpi imaginatione contingit. Hoc tamen impedimentum, quod ex congruitate provenit, postponi debet propter aliquam necessitatem, puta ut Gregorius dicit, *cum fortasse aut festus dies exigit, aut exhibere ministerium, pro eo quod sacerdos alius deest, ipsa necessitas compellit.*[12]

1. Ad primum ergo dicendum quod ex necessitate quidem non impeditur homo a sumptione hujus sacramenti, nisi propter peccatum mortale; sed ex quadam convenientia potest homo impediri propter alias causas, sicut dictum est.[13]

2. Ad secundum dicendum quod coitus conjugalis, si sit sine peccato (puta si fiat causa prolis generandæ, vel causa reddendi debitum), non alia ratione impedit sumptionem hujus sacramenti, nisi sicut dictum est de pollutione nocturna quæ accidit sine peccato, scilicet propter immunditiam corporalem, et mentis distractionem; ratione cujus Hieronymus dicit, *Si panes propositionis ab his qui uxores tetigerant comedi non poterant, quanto magis ille panis qui de cœlo descendit, non potest ab his qui conjugalibus paulo ante hæsere complexibus, violari, atque contingi? Non quod nuptias condemnemus, sed quod eo tempore quo carnes agni manducaturi sumus vacare a carnalibus operibus non debeamus.*[14] Sed quia hoc secundum congruitatem, et non secundum necessitatem est intelligendum. Gregorius dicit quod *talis est suo judicio relinquendus.*[15] Si vero *non amor procreandæ sobolis, sed voluptas dominatur in opere commixtionis,* ut ibidem Gregorius subdit,[16] tunc prohiberi debet ne accedat ad hoc sacramentum.

3. Ad tertium dicendum quod, sicut Gregorius dicit in epistola supra dicta ad Augustinum Anglorum episcopum,[17] in veteri Testamento aliqui polluti dicebantur figuraliter, quod populus novæ legis spiritualiter intelligit. Unde hujusmodi corporales immunditiæ, si sint perpetuæ vel

---

[11]loc cit note 3. PL 77, 1198
[12]loc cit

food or drink. And so Gregory writes to Augustine, Bishop of the English,[11] that we should abstain from Communion when nocturnal pollution rises from impure thoughts but not from abundant food and drink, especially if necessity calls for Communion.

All the same a certain decency forbids Communion on two counts. One is always present, namely a certain bodily dross, with which, out of reverence for the sacrament, it is unbecoming to approach the altar, hence those who want to touch a sacred object wash their hands; an exception may be those whose uncleanness is chronic or of long standing, such as leprosy or issue of blood and the like. The other is the mental distraction which follows nocturnal pollution, especially when accompanied by impure imaginings. This obstacle, which arises from a sense of decency, can be set aside owing to necessity; Gregory says, *As when perhaps a feast day calls for Communion or when one must exercise his ministry because no other priest is available.*[12]

Hence: 1. Only mortal sin of necessity blocks reception of this sacrament: but for not receiving there may be other reasons, as explained above.[13]

2. Conjugal intercourse, if it be without sin, for instance if done for the sake of a baby or of rendering what is due, is no more reason for stopping the reception of this sacrament than nocturnal pollution without sin, unless because of uncleanness of body or distraction of mind, as we have explained. And so Jerome expresses himself in the following terms, *If the loaves of proposition*[e] *might not be eaten by those who have carnally known their wives, how much less may this bread which has come down from heaven be profaned and touched by those who shortly before have been clinging in conjugal embraces. It is not that we condemn marriage, but that at the time when we are going to eat the flesh of the Lamb, we should not have indulged in carnal deeds.*[14] But since this is to be understood of congruity, not necessity, Gregory says that a person *is to be left to his own judgement.*[15] He adds, *If voluptuousness prevails, not fruitful love, then going to the sacrament should be forbidden.*[16]

3. As Gregory says in his letter to Augustine, Bishop of the English,[17] that in the Old Law some were termed polluted figuratively, and this the people of the New Law understand spiritually. Hence these bodily uncleannesses, if they are chronic or of long standing, do not prevent the

---

[13]body of art.
[14]Pseudo-Jerome. *Epist.* XXVIII. PL 30, 231. cf Gratian, II, 33, 4, I. RF I 1247
[15]loc cit note 3. PL 77, 1195
[16]ibid
[17]loc cit note 11
[e]The hallowed bread given to David by Ahimelech, I *Samuel* 21, 6.

diuturnæ, non impediunt sumptionem hujus sacramenti salutaris, sicut impediebant accessum ad sacramenta figuralia; si vero cito transeant, sicut immunditia pollutionis nocturnæ, ex quadam congruentia impediunt sumptionem hujus sacramenti per illum diem quo hoc accidit. Unde et *Deut.* dicitur, *Si fuerit inter vos homo qui nocturno pollutus sit somnio, egredietur extra castra et non revertetur, priusquam ad vesperum lavetur aqua.*[18]

4. Ad quartum dicendum quod licet per contritionem et confessionem auferatur reatus culpæ, non tamen aufertur corporalis immunditia, et distractio mentis ex pollutione consecuta.

5. Ad quintum dicendum quod somnium homicidii non inducit corporalem immunditiam, nec etiam tantam distractionem mentis, sicut fornicatio somniata propter delectationis intensionem; si tamen somnium homicidii proveniat ex causa quæ est peccatum, præsertim mortale, impedit a sumptione hujus sacramenti ratione suæ causæ.

articulus 8. *utrum cibus vel potus præassumptus impediat sumptionem hujus sacramenti*

AD OCTAVUM sic proceditur:[1] 1. Videtur quod cibus vel potus præassumptus non impediat sumptionem hujus sacramenti. Hoc enim sacramentum est a Domino institutum in cœna. Sed Dominus, postquam cœnavit, hoc sacramentum discipulis suis tradidit, sicut patet *Luc.*,[2] et 1 *Cor.*[3] Ergo videtur quod etiam post alios cibos assumptos nos debeamus sumere hoc sacramentum.

2. Præterea, 1 *Cor.* dicitur, *Cum convenitis ad manducandum*, scilicet corpus Domini, *invicem expectate: si quis autem esurit, domi manducet.*[4] Et ita videtur quod postquam aliquis domi manducaverit possit in Ecclesia corpus Christi manducare.

3. Præterea, in concilio Carthaginensi III legitur, *Sacramenta altaris non nisi a jejunis hominibus celebrentur, excepto uno die anniversario quo cœna Domini celebratur.*[5] Ergo saltem illa die aliquis potest corpus Christi post alios cibos sumere.

4. Præterea, sumptio aquæ vel medicinæ, vel alterius cibi vel potus in minima quantitate vel reliquiarum cibi in ore manentium, neque jejunium Ecclesiæ solvit, neque sobrietatem tollit, quæ exigitur ad hoc quod aliquis reverenter sumat hoc sacramentum. Ergo per prædicta non impeditur aliquis a sumptione hujus sacramenti.

5. Præterea, quidam de nocte profunda comedunt aut bibunt, aut forte totam noctem insomnem ducentes, de mane percipiunt sacra mysteria

---

[18]*Deuteronomy* 23, 10

[1]cf 2a2æ. 147, 6 ad 2. IV *Sent.* 8, 1, 4, i & ii. In 1 *Cor.* 11, *lect.* 4

receiving of this saving sacrament, as they prevented approaching those figurative sacraments.[f] If they soon pass, like the uncleanness of nocturnal pollution, yet out of fittingness they hinder the reception for the day following. So it is written, *If there is among you any man who is not clean by means of what chances to him by night, then he shall go outside the camp, and shall not return before he washed himself in the evening.*[18]

4. Contrition and confession take away the guilt of fault, it is true, but not the bodily defilement, nor the resulting distraction of mind.

5. To dream of murder does not bring on bodily uncleanness nor such distraction of mind as to dream of fornication because of the intense pleasure that gives. Still, if the dream of murder springs from a sinful cause, especially if that be grievously wrong, then this hinders reception of this sacrament.

article 8. *does taking food or drink hinder reception of this sacrament?*

THE EIGHTH POINT:[1a] 1. It seems not. For this sacrament was instituted by our Lord at a supper. But when it was ended the Lord gave it to his disciples, as appears from *Luke*[2] and 1 *Corinthians*.[3] So it seems we ought to take it after receiving other food.

2. Again, it is written, *When you come together to eat, namely, the Lord's body, wait for one another; if any one is hungry, let him eat at home.*[4] Then it seems that after eating at home, a man may eat Christ's body in church.

3. Also, canon law repeats the ordinance of a Council of Carthage, *Let the sacrament of the altar be celebrated only by those who are fasting, with the exception of the anniversary day on which the Lord's Supper is celebrated.*[5] Therefore at least on that day one may receive the body of Christ after partaking of other food.

4. Also, to take water or medicine, or a slight quantity of food and drink, or to swallow the remains of food left in the mouth, neither breaks the Church's fast nor takes away the sobriety required for reverently receiving the sacrament, and consequently is no barrier to the reception of this sacrament.

5. Also, some eat and drink late at night, or possibly, after passing a sleepless night, receive the sacred mysteries in the morning when food is

[2]*Luke* 22, 20
[3]1 *Corinthians* 11, 25
[4]1 *Corinthians* 11, 33
[5]Carthage III, 29, 398. Mansi, III, 885. Gratian III, 1, 49. RF 1, 1307
[f]Sacraments of the Old Law; 1a2æ. 101–103. Vol. 29, ed. D. J. Bourke.
[a]This art. may be regarded largely as a period piece, since the rules of fasting communion have been relaxed in our days.

nondum plene digesti. Minus autem impediretur sobrietas hominis si in mane parum comederet, et postea circa nonam sumeret hoc sacramentum, cum etiam sit quandoque major distantia temporis. Ergo videtur quod talis cibi præassumptio non impediat hominen ab hoc sacramento.

6. Præterea, non minor reverentia debetur huic sacramento jam sumpto quam ante sumptionem. Sed sumpto sacramento, licet cibum aut potum sumere. Ergo et ante sumptionem.

SED CONTRA est quod Augustinus dicit, *Placuit Spiritui Sancto ut in honorem tanti sacramenti prius in os Christiani corpus dominicum intraret quam cæteri cibi.*[6]

RESPONSIO: Dicendum quod aliquid impedit sumptionem hujus sacramenti dupliciter. Uno modo secundum se, sicut peccatum mortale quod habet repugnantiam ad significatum hujus sacramenti, ut supra dictum est.[7] Alio modo propter prohibitionem Ecclesiæ, et sic impeditur aliquis a sumptione hujus sacramenti post cibum et potum assumptum, triplici ratione. Primo quidem, sicut Augustinus dicit, *in honorem hujus sacramenti,*[8] ut scilicet in os hominis intret nondum aliquo cibo vel potu infectum. Secundo propter significationem, ut scilicet detur intelligi quod Christus, qui est res hujus sacramenti, et caritas ejus, debet primo fundari in cordibus nostris, secundum illud *Matt.*, *Quærite primum regnum Dei.*[9] Tertio propter periculum vomitus et ebrietatis, quæ quandoque contingunt ex hoc quod homines inordinate cibis utuntur, sicut et Apostolus dicit, *Alius quidem esurit, alius autem ebrius est.*[10]

Ab hac tamen generali regula excipiuntur infirmi, qui statim communicandi sunt, etiam post cibum, si de eorum periculo dubitatur ne sine communione decedant, quia necessitas legem non habet. Unde dicitur, *Presbyter infirmum statim communicet, ne sine communione moriatur.*[11]

1. Ad primum ergo dicendum quod, sicut Augustinus dicit, *neque quia post cibos Dominus dedit, propterea pransi, aut cœnati fratres ad hoc sacramentum accipiendum convenire debent, aut mensis suis miscere, sicut faciebant, quos Apostolus arguit et emendat. Namque Salvator, quo vehementius commendaret mysterii illius altitudinem ultimum hoc voluit arctius infigere cordibus et memoriæ discipulorum; et ideo non præcepit quo deinceps tali ordine sumeretur, ut apostolis, per quos ecclesias dispositurus erat, servaret hunc modum.*[12]

2. Ad secundum dicendum quod illud verbum in glossa sic exponitur,

---

[6]*Epist.* LIV, 6, ad inquis. Januarii. PL 33, 203
[7]art. 4 above
[8]loc cit note 6

not fully digested. Now sobriety would be less affected if one took a little food first thing and then about the ninth hour took the sacrament: this would also ensure a longer interval. So then it seems that such taking of food beforehand does not keep a man away from this sacrament.

6. Also, no less reverence is due to the sacrament after receiving it than before. One may take food and drink after receiving it. Also, then, before.

ON THE OTHER HAND Augustine writes, *It has pleased the Holy Ghost that out of honour for such a great sacrament the Lord's body should enter the mouth of a Christian before other food.*[6]

REPLY: Something may bar the reception of this sacrament in two ways. One, in itself; such is mortal sin which is repugnant to the very meaning of this sacrament, as we have said.[7] Two, on account of the Church's discipline; such is taking no food and drink beforehand. There are three reasons for this. First, as Augustine notes,[8] *out of respect for the sacrament*, that it may enter a mouth not yet fouled by food and drink. Second, to bring out a meaning, that is, it gives us to understand that Christ, who is the reality in this sacrament, and his charity, should be the first to be established in our heart, according to the words, *Seek first the kingdom of God.*[9] Third is the risk of vomiting and drunkenness, which sometimes arise from over-indulgence, to which St Paul refers, *One is hungry and another is drunk.*[10]

Nevertheless the sick are an exception to this general rule, for they are to be given Communion at once, even after food, should their danger be in any doubt, lest they die without it, because necessity knows no law. Here it is laid down in canon law, *Let the priest at once take Communion to the sick person, lest he die without Communion.*[11]

Hence 1. In the same book Augustine writes, *Because our Lord gave the sacrament after food is no reason why the brethren should come together after dinner or supper, or to receive it with their meals, as did those whom the Apostle reproves and corrects. For our Saviour in order to recommend more strongly the height of the mystery wished to fix it in the hearts and memories of the disciples, and therefore did not command it be received in that order, leaving this to the Apostles, to whom he was about to entrust the government of the Church.*[12]

2. A gloss paraphrases the text as follows, *If any man be hungry and being*

---

[9]*Matthew* 6, 33
[10] 1 *Corinthians* 11, 21
[11]Gratian, *Decretum* III, 2, 93. RF I, 1351
[12]loc cit note 6

Si quis esurit, et impatiens non vult expectare alios, manducet domi cibos suos, idest pane terreno pascatur, nec post Eucharistiam sumat.[13]

3. Ad tertium dicendum quod capitulum illud loquitur secundum consuetudinem aliquando apud aliquos observatam, ut in repræsentationem dominicæ cœnæ illo die a non jejunis corpus Christi sumeretur. Sed nunc hoc abrogatum est; nam, sicut Augustinus dicit, *per universum orbem mos iste servatur,*[14] ut scilicet corpus Christi a jejunis sumatur.

4. Ad quartum dicendum quod, sicut in *Secunda Parte* habitum est,[15] duplex est jejunium. Primum est jejunium naturæ, quod importat privationem cujuscumque præassumpti per modum cibi vel potus; et tale jejunium requiritur ad hoc sacramentum propter prædicta.[16] Et ideo neque post assumptionem aquæ vel alterius cibi aut potus, vel etiam medicinæ, in quantumcumque parva quantitate, licet hoc sacramentum accipere. Nec refert utrum aliquid hujusmodi nutriat vel non nutriat, aut per se aut cum aliis, dummodo sumatur per modum cibi vel potus. Reliquiæ tamen cibi remanentes in ore, si casualiter transglutiantur, non impediunt sumptionem hujus sacramenti, quia non trajiciuntur per modum cibi, sed per modum salivæ; et eadem ratio est de reliquiis aquæ vel vini, quibus os abluitur, dummodo non trajiciantur in magna quantitate, sed permixtæ salivæ, quod vitari non potest. Aliud autem est jejunium Ecclesiæ, quod instituitur ad carnis macerationem; et tale jejunium per prædicta non impeditur, quia prædicta non multum nutriunt, sed magis ad alterandum sumuntur.

5. Ad quintum dicendum quod cum dicitur quod hoc sacramentum prius quam alii cibi debet in os Christiani mitti, non est intelligendum absolute respectu totius temporis, alioquin qui semel comedisset vel bibisset, nunquam posset postea hoc sacramentum accipere; sed est intelligendum quantum ad eundem diem; et licet principium diei secundum diversos diversimode sumatur (nam quidam a meridie, quidam ab occasu, quidam a media nocte, quidam ab ortu solis diem incipiunt), Ecclesia tamen secundum Romanos diem a media nocte incipit.[17] Et ideo si post mediam noctem aliquis sumpserit aliquid per modum cibi vel potus, non potest eadem die hoc sumere sacramentum; potest vero, si ante mediam noctem. Nec refert utrum post cibum vel potum assumptum dormierit, aut etiam digestus sit, quantum ad rationem præcepti; refert autem quantum ad perturbationem mentis, quam patiuntur homines propter insomnietatem vel indigestionem; ex quibus si mens multum perturbetur, homo redditur ineptus ad sumptionem hujus sacramenti.

6. Ad sextum dicendum quod maxima devotio requiritur in ipsa sumptione hujus sacramenti, quia tunc percipitur sacramenti effectus, quæ

---

[13]Interlinear. On 11, 34. Lombard, PL 191, 1649

impatient does not wish to wait for the rest, let him eat his food at home, that is feed on earthly bread, without receiving the Eucharist afterwards.[13]

3. This decree is worded in accordance with a former custom observed by some of receiving the body of Christ non-fasting in order to represent the Lord's supper. This is now abrogated. For, as Augustine says,[14] *through the whole world it is customary* to receive Christ's body fasting.

4. As stated in the *Secunda Pars*,[15] there are two kinds of fast. First, there is physical fast which implies not taking anything whatsoever by way of food and drink. Such a fast is required for this sacrament for the reasons given above.[16] It is never lawful to receive this sacrament after taking water, or other food or drink, or even medicine, however slight the quantity may be. Nor does it matter whether it nourishes or not, whether it is taken by itself or together with other things, provided it be taken in the manner of food or drink. But the remains of food left in the mouth, if they happen to be swallowed, do not hinder receiving, because they pass in the mode of saliva, not food. The same holds good of the remains of wine or water with which the mouth is rinsed, provided they are not swallowed in great amount, but mixed with saliva, which is unavoidable. Secondly, there is the fast of the Church, which is instituted for the mortification of the flesh, and this fast is not broken by the things mentioned in the objection, for they do not give much nourishment, but are taken rather as digestives.

5. When it is said that this sacrament ought to enter into a Christian's mouth before any other food, this is to be understood, not absolutely of the whole of time, otherwise those who had eaten and drunk could never afterwards receive the sacrament, but of the same day. When a day begins is variously reckoned; some start from noon, others from sunset, some at midnight, others at dawn. The Roman Church begins it at midnight.[17] Consequently after midnight if a person takes something by way of food or drink he may not receive the sacrament on that day; food or drink before midnight offers no impediment. Nor does it matter, as far as the precept is concerned, whether he has slept after taking it or has digested it. It matters, however, as to the mental disturbance one suffers as a result of insomnia or indigestion, for if it be serious it unfits a man for receiving this sacrament.

6. The taking of this sacrament requires the greatest devotion for its effect to be obtained. This devotion is hindered more by what comes before

[14]loc cit note 6
[15]2a2æ. 147, 6 ad 2
[16]body of art.
[17]*Decretals of Gregory IX*, I, 29, 24. RF II, 170

quidem devotio magis impeditur per præcedentia quam per sequentia. Et ideo magis est institutum quod homines jejunent ante sumptionem hujus sacramenti quam post. Debet tamen esse aliqua mora inter sumptionem hujus sacramenti et reliquos cibos. Unde et in missa oratio gratiarum actionis post communionem dicitur, et communicantes etiam suas privatas orationes dicunt.

Secundum tamen antiquos canones statutum fuit a Papa Clemente I, *Si mane dominica portio editur, usque ad sextam jejunent ministri qui eam sumpserunt, et si tertia vel quarta hora acceperint, jejunent usque ad vesperum.*[18] Antiquitus enim rarius missarum solemnia celebrabantur, et cum majori præparatione. Nunc autem quia oportet frequentius sacra mysteria celebrare, non posset de facili observari, et ideo per contrariam consuetudinem est abrogatum.

articulus 9. utrum non habentes usum rationis debeant suscipere hoc sacramentum

AD NONUM sic proceditur:[1] 1. Videtur quod non habentes usum rationis non debeant hoc sacramentum suscipere. Requiritur enim quod aliquis ad hoc sacramentum cum devotione et præcedente sui examinatione accedat, secundum illud 1 *Cor.*, *Probet seipsum homo, et sic de pane illo edat, et de calice bibat.*[2] Sed hoc non potest esse in his qui carent usu rationis. Ergo non debet eis hoc sacramentum dari.

2. Præterea, inter illos qui carent usu rationis, sunt etiam arreptitii, qui *energumeni* dicuntur. Sed tales etiam ab inspectione hujus sacramenti arcentur, secundum Dionysium.[3] Ergo carentibus usu rationis hoc sacramentum dari non debet.

3. Præterea, inter alios carentes usu rationis maxime pueri videntur esse innocentes. Sed pueris hoc sacramentum non exhibetur. Ergo multo minus aliis carentibus usu rationis.

SED CONTRA est quod legitur in concilio Arausicano I et habetur in *Decreto*, *Amentibus quæcumque pietatis sunt, conferenda sunt;*[4] et ita est eis conferendum hoc sacramentum, quod est sacramentum pietatis.

RESPONSIO: Dicendum quod aliqui dicuntur non habere usum rationis dupliciter. Uno modo quia habent debilem usum rationis, sicut dicitur non videns, qui male videt; et quia tales possunt aliquam devotionem

---

[18]Pseudo-Clement I. Mansi I, 125. Gratian, *Decretum* III, 2, 23. RF I, 1321
[1]cf IV *Sent.* 9, 5, iii & iv; 23, 2, 2, iii & iv. *In Joan.* 6, *lect.* 7
[2]1 *Corinthians* 11, 28

than by what comes after. Accordingly a preceding rather than a subsequent fast was ordained. Nevertheless, there ought to be some interval between receiving this sacrament and other food. Consequently the prayer of thanksgiving in the Postcommunion of the Mass is said, and the communicants also say their own private prayers.

However, according to the ancient canons it was laid down by Pope Clement,[b] *If the Lord's portion be eaten in the morning, the ministers who have taken it shall fast until the sixth hour, if they take it at the third or fourth hour, they shall fast until evening.*[18] For in olden times the priest celebrated more rarely and with more preparation. But now this practice may no longer be observed so easily, for the sacred mysteries have to be celebrated oftener, and so it has been abrogated by contrary custom.

article 9. ought those not having the use of reason receive the sacrament?

THE NINTH POINT:[1] 1. It seems not. For devotion and previous self-examination are required to approach this sacrament. Thus St Paul says, *Let a man examine himself, and so eat the bread and drink of the cup.*[2] But those who lack the use of reason cannot do this. Therefore they should not be given this sacrament.

2. Besides, among those who lack the use of reason are the possessed, who are called energumens. But such are kept even from beholding the sacrament, according to Dionysius.[3] And so those who lack the use of reason ought not to be given it.

3. Then also, among those who lack the use of reason are the most innocent of all. But this sacrament is not offered to children. Much less, then, to others lacking the use of reason.

ON THE OTHER HAND we read in a council of Orange, and it is repeated in the *Decretum*, *All things that pertain to piety are to be given to the insane.*[4] And as this sacrament is the sacrament of piety, it is to be granted to them.

REPLY: Some are said to lack reason in two ways. First, when they are feeble-minded, as a man is said not to see when he has poor eye-sight. And because such are able to conceive some devotion to the sacrament, it

[3] *De Eccles. Hier.* 3. PG 3, 433

[4] Orange I (441), can. 13. Mansi VI, 438. Gratian, *Decretum* II, 26, 6, 7. RF I, 1038

[b] St Clement I, *fl. c.* 96. The ascription is without foundation.

hujus sacramenti concipere, non est eis hoc sacramentum denegandum. Alio modo dicuntur aliqui non habere totaliter usum rationis. Aut igitur nunquam habuerunt usum rationis, sed sic a nativitate permanserunt; et sic talibus non est hoc sacramentum exhibendum, quia in eis nullo modo præcessit hujus sacramenti devotio. Aut non semper caruerunt usu rationis; et tunc, si prius quando erant compotes suæ mentis, apparuit in eis devotio hujus sacramenti, debet eis in articulo mortis hoc sacramentum exhiberi; nisi forte timeatur periculum vomitus vel expuitionis. Unde in concilio Carthaginensi IV legitur, et habetur in *Decreto*, *Is qui in infirmitate pœnitentiam petit, si casu dum ad eum sacerdos invitatus venit, oppressus infirmitate obmutuerit, vel in phrenesim conversus fuerit, dent testimonium qui eum audierunt, et accipiat pœnitentiam; et si continuo creditur moriturus, reconcilietur per manus impositionem, et infundatur ori ejus Eucharistia.*[5]

1. Ad primum ergo dicendum quod carentes usu rationis possunt devotionem ad sacramentum habere, quantum ad aliquos quidem præsentem, quantum ad alios autem præteritam.

2. Ad secundum dicendum quod Dionysius loquitur ibi de energumenis nondum baptizatis, in quibus scilicet nondum est vis dæmonis extincta, quæ viget in eis per originale peccatum. Sed de baptizatis qui corporaliter ab immundis spiritibus vexantur est eadem ratio et de aliis amentibus. Unde Cassianus dicit, *Eis qui ab immundis vexantur spiritibus, communionem sacrosanctam a senioribus nostris nunquam meminimus interdictam.*[6]

3. Ad tertium dicendum quod eadem ratio est de pueris recenter natis, et de amentibus qui nunquam habuerunt usum rationis. Unde talibus non sunt sacra mysteria danda. Quamvis quidam Græci contrarium faciant, propter hoc quod Dionysius, dicit baptizatis esse sacram communionem dandam, non intelligentes quod Dionysius ibi loquitur de baptismo adultorum.[7] Nec tamen per hoc aliquod detrimentum vitæ patiuntur, propter hoc quod Dominus dicit. *Nisi manducaveritis carnem Filii hominis, et biberitis ejus sanguinem, non habebitis vitam in vobis*;[8] quia, sicut Augustinus scribit Bonifacio, *tunc unusquisque fidelium corporis et sanguinis Domini particeps fit*, scilicet spiritualiter, *quando in baptismate membrum corporis Christi efficitur.*[9] Sed quando jam pueri incipiunt aliqualem usum rationis habere ut possint devotionem concipere hujus sacramenti, tunc potest eis hoc sacramentum conferri.

---

[5]Carthage IV (398) cap. 76. Mansi III, 957. Gratian, *Decretum* II, 26, 6, 8. RF I, 1038

[6]*Collationes* VII, 30. PL 49, 710

is not to be denied them. Second, some seem to be quite bereft of the use of reason. Either they never had it and remained so from birth; and such are not to be offered it for there has not been any preceding devotion at all towards the sacrament. Or else they were not always so, and when they were in their right mind manifested devotion towards the sacrament; such ought to be granted the sacrament at the hour of their death, unless danger of vomiting or spitting it out is feared. Accordingly we read in the Council of Carthage IV, and in canon law, *If a man asks for the sacrament of penance, and when the priest sent for comes to him, he be so weak as to be unable to speak, or he become delirious, let them who heard him ask bear witness and let him receive the sacrament of penance: then if it be thought that he is going to die shortly, let him be reconciled by the imposition of hands, and let the Eucharist be placed in his mouth.*[7]

Hence: 1. Those lacking the use of reason can have devotion towards the sacrament, present devotion in some cases, and past in others.

2. Dionysius is speaking there of energumens who are not yet baptized, in whom the devil's power is not yet extinct, but thrives through original sin. As to the baptized who are vexed in body by unclean spirits, the same reason holds for them as for others who are demented. Accordingly Cassian says, *We do not remember holy Communion having been denied by our elders to those who were vexed with unclean spirits.*[8]

3. The same reason holds good for young babies and for the insane who have never had the use of reason; consequently the sacred mysteries are not to be given them, though the practice of certain Greeks is contrary, because Dionysius says[7] that holy Communion is to be given to them that are baptized: they do not appreciate that he is referring to the baptism of adults.[a] Babies and the insane, however, do not suffer from lethal harm thereby, despite our Lord's saying, *Unless you eat the flesh of the Son of man and drink his blood, you have no life in you,*[8] because, as Augustine writes, *When one is made a member of Christ's body in baptism, it is then that each one of the faithful becomes a partaker*, that is, spiritually, *of the body and blood of the Lord.*[9b] But when children once begin to have some use of reason so as to be able to conceive some devotion for the sacrament, then it may be granted them.

---

[7]*De Eccl. Hier.* 2. PG 3, 396

[8]*John* 6, 54

[9]*Epist.* XCVIII, ad Bonifacium. PL 33, 364. cf 3a. 73, 3 ad 1

[a]And because of the need for the Bread of Life affirmed in *John* 6.

[b]The *res* of the Eucharist is received in Baptism according to the *votum* of the Church; 3a. 73, 3. Vol. 38, ed. W. Barden. cf note *f* to art. 1 above.

articulus 10. *utrum liceat quotidie hoc sacramentum suscipere*

AD DECIMUM sic proceditur:[1] 1. Videtur quod non liceat quotidie hoc sacramentum suscipere. Sicut enim baptismus repræsentat dominicam passionem, ita et hoc sacramentum. Sed non licet pluries baptizari, sed semel tantum, quia *Christus semel* tantum *pro peccatis nostris mortuus* est, ut dicitur 1 *Pet.*[2] Ergo videtur quod non liceat hoc sacramentum quotidie suscipere.

2. Præterea, veritas debet respondere figuræ. Sed agnus paschalis, qui fuit figura præcipua hujus sacramenti, ut supra dictum est,[3] non manducabatur nisi semel in anno; semel etiam in anno Ecclesia celebrat Christi passionem, cujus hoc sacramentum est memoriale. Ergo videtur quod non liceat quotidie sumere hoc sacramentum, sed solum semel in anno.

3. Præterea, huic sacramento in quo totus Christus continetur maxima reverentia debetur. Ad reverentiam autem pertinet quod aliquis ab hoc sacramento abstineat; unde et laudatur centurio qui dixit, *Domine, non sum dignus ut intres sub tectum meum*;[4] et Petrus qui dixit, *Exi a me, Domine quia homo peccator ego sum.*[5] Ergo non est laudabile quod homo quotidie hoc sacramentum suscipiat.

4. Præterea, si esset laudabile frequenter hoc sacramentum accipere, quanto frequentius sumeretur tanto esset laudabilius. Sed major esset frequentia si homo pluries in die sumeret hoc sacramentum. Ergo esset laudabile quod homo pluries in die communicaret, quod tamen non habet Ecclesiæ consuetudo. Non ergo videtur esse laudabile quod aliquis quotidie hoc sacramentum accipiat.

5. Præterea, Ecclesia intendit suis statutis fidelium utilitati providere. Sed ex statuto Ecclesiæ fideles tenentur solum semel communicare in anno; unde dicitur *Extra.*, *Omnis utriusque sexus fidelis suscipiat reverenter, ad minus in Pascha, Eucharistiæ sacramentum; nisi forte de proprii sacerdotis consilio ob aliquam rationabilem causam ad tempus ab ejus perceptione duxerit abstinendum.*[6] Non ergo est laudabile quod quotidie hoc sacramentum sumatur.

SED CONTRA est quod Augustinus dicit, *Iste panis quotidianus est, accipe quotidie, ut quotidie tibi prosit.*[7]

RESPONSIO: Dicendum quod circa usum hujus sacramenti duo possunt considerari. Unum quidem ex parte ipsius sacramenti, cujus virtus est hominibus salutaris, et ideo utile est quotidie ipsum sumere, ut homo

---

[1]cf IV *Sent.* 12, 3, 1. *In* 1 *Cor.* 11, *lect.* 7

article 10. is it lawful to receive this sacrament daily?

THE TENTH POINT:[1] 1. It would seem not. As Baptism represents our Lord's Passion, so does this sacrament. Now one may be baptized only once, not several times, because *Christ died for sins once for all.*[2] Therefore it seems unlawful to receive this sacrament every day.

2. Moreover, the reality and the figure ought to correspond. But the paschal lamb, which was the figure of this sacrament, as we have seen,[3] was eaten only once a year, and the Church, too, celebrates Christ's Passion, of which this sacrament is the memorial, once in the year. It seems, then, that it is lawful to receive it only annually, not daily.

3. Further, the greatest reverence is due to this sacrament, for it holds Christ. But it is a token of reverence to refrain from receiving this sacrament: accordingly the centurion is praised for confessing, *Lord, I am not worthy to have you come under my roof*;[4] and Peter for crying, *Depart from me, for I am a sinful man, O Lord.*[5] So then it is not praiseworthy to receive this sacrament daily.

4. Besides, were it praiseworthy to receive this sacrament often, then the oftener it were received the more praiseworthy it would be. And so several times a day. Yet this is not the Church's custom. Therefore to receive it daily does not seem praiseworthy.

5. Again, the Church's intention in legislating is to provide for the welfare of the faithful. But the law requires Communion once a year; *Let every person of either sex devoutly receive the sacrament of the Eucharist at least at Easter, unless by the advice of his parish priest and for some reasonable cause, he is led to defer it for a time.*[6] Therefore it is not praiseworthy to receive this sacrament daily.

ON THE OTHER HAND Augustine says, *This is our daily bread: take it daily that it may profit you daily.*[7]

REPLY: Two considerations about the reception of this sacrament. The first regards the sacrament itself, the virtue of which is salutary to man: consequently it is profitable to receive daily so as to gather its fruits

---

[2] *1 Peter* 3, 18
[3] 3a. 73, 6
[4] *Matthew* 8, 8
[5] *Luke* 5, 8
[6] *Decretals of Gregory IX*, V, 38, 12. RF II, 887
[7] *Sermo suppos.* LXXXIV. PL 39, 1908

quotidie ejus fructum percipiat. Unde Ambrosius dicit, *Si quotiescumque effunditur sanguis Christi, in remissionem peccatorum effunditur, debeo semper accipere, qui semper pecco, debeo semper habere medicinam.*[8] Alio modo potest considerari ex parte sumentis, in quo requiritur ut cum magna devotione et reverentia ad hoc sacramentum accedat. Et ideo si aliquis se quotidie ad hoc paratum inveniat, laudabile est quod quotidie sumat. Unde Augustinus cum dixisset, *Accipe quotidie, ut quotidie tibi prosit*, subjungit, *Sic vive, ut quotidie merearis accipere.*[9] Sed quia multoties in pluribus hominum multa impedimenta hujus devotionis occurrunt, propter corporis indispositionem vel animæ, non est utile omnibus hominibus quotidie ad hoc sacramentum accedere; sed quotiescumque se ad illud homo invenerit præparatum. Unde in lib. de *Eccles. Dogm.* dicitur, *Quotidie Eucharistiæ communionem accipere nec laudo, nec vitupero.*[10]

1. Ad primum ergo dicendum quod per sacramentum baptismi configuratur homo morti Christi, in se suscipiens ejus characterem. Et ideo sicut Christus semel mortuus est, ita solum semel debet homo baptizari. Sed per hoc sacramentum non recipit homo Christi characterem, sed ipsum Christum, cujus virtus manet in æternum. Unde *Heb.* dicitur, *Una oblatione consummavit in sempiternum sanctificatos.*[11] Et ideo quia quotidie homo indiget salutifera Christi virtute, quotidie potest laudabiliter hoc sacramentum suscipere. Et quia præcipue baptismus est spiritualis regeneratio, ideo sicut homo semel carnaliter nascitur, ita debet semel spiritualiter renasci per baptismum, ut Augustinus dicit super illud *Joan.*, *Quomodo potest homo nasci, cum sit senex?*[12] Sed hoc sacramentum est cibus spiritualis; unde sicut cibus corporalis quotidie sumitur, ita et hoc sacramentum quotidie sumere laudabile est. Unde Dominus docet petere, *Panem nostrum quotidianum da nobis hodie*;[13] in cujus expositione Augustinus dicit, *Si quotidie accipis* (scilicet hoc sacramentum), *quotidie Christus resurgit; hodie enim est quando Christus resurgit.*[14]

2. Ad secundum dicendum quod agnus paschalis præcipue fuit figura hujus sacramenti quantum ad passionem Christi, quæ repræsentatur per hoc sacramentum; et ideo semel tantum in anno sumebatur, quia Christus semel mortuus est. Et propter hoc etiam Ecclesia celebrat semel in anno memoriam passionis Christi. Sed in hoc sacramento traditur nobis quotidie sumitur; et ideo quantum ad hoc significatur per manna, quod memoriale passionis Christi per modum cibi, qui quotidie dabatur populo in deserto.

3. Ad tertium dicendum quod reverentia hujus sacramenti habet timorem amori conjunctum: unde timor reverentiæ ad Deum dicitur timor filialis, ut in *Secunda Parte* dictum est.[15] Ex amore enim provocatur

---

[8] *De Sacram.* IV 6. PL 16, 464. Gratian, III, 2, 14. RF I, 1319
[9] loc cit note 7. PL 39, 1909

daily. Hence Ambrose says, *If whenever Christ's blood is shed, it is shed for the forgiveness of sins, I, who sin often, should receive it often; I need a frequent remedy.*[8] The second regards the recipient, who is required to approach this sacrament with great reverence and devotion. Consequently if someone finds he has these dispositions every day, he does well to receive daily. However, Augustine, after saying, *Receive daily, that it may profit you daily,* adds, *So live as to deserve to receive it daily.*[9] Since many are often held from such devotion, however, on account of their many bodily and spiritual drawbacks, it is not expedient for all to approach this sacrament daily, but as often as they find themselves properly prepared. So we are told, *Neither praise nor blame daily reception of the Eucharist.*[10]

Hence: 1. A person is conformed in the sacrament of baptism to Christ's death by receiving his character, and accordingly as Christ died but once, so a person is but once to be baptized. But he does not receive Christ's character in this sacrament, he receives Christ himself, whose virtue lasts for ever: *By a single offering he has perfected for all times those who are sanctified.*[11] Consequently, since a person needs Christ's health-giving virtue every day, he may commendably receive the sacrament every day. Moreover, since baptism above all is a spiritual rebirth, so as a man is born in nature but once, so is he born in the spirit but once, as Augustine says when commenting on *John, How can a man be born when he is old?*[12] This sacrament, however, is spiritual food, and so, as bodily food is taken every day, so is it well to receive it every day. Hence our Lord teaches us to pray, *Give us this day our daily bread.*[13] In explaining this Augustine says, *If you receive it daily,* that is, this sacrament, *every day is for you to-day, and Christ rises every day in you, for to-day it is when Christ rises.*[14]

2. The paschal lamb was the chief figure of this sacrament with respect to Christ's Passion there represented, and accordingly was received once a year, since Christ died but once. On this account the Church celebrates once a year the memorial of Christ's Passion. But in this sacrament is delivered to us the memorial by way of food which is taken daily. In this way it is signified by the manna which was bestowed every day on the people in the desert.

3. Reverence for this sacrament is compounded of fear and love. Reverential fear of God is called filial fear, as we noted in the *Secunda Pars.*[15] The desire of receiving is called forth by love, the modesty about

---

[10] Gennadius, *De Ecclesiasticis Dogmatibus* 53. PL 58, 994

[11] *Hebrews* 10, 14

[12] *Super Joan.* XI. On 3, 4. PL 35, 1478

[13] *Luke* 11, 3

[14] loc cit note 7. PL 39, 1909

[15] 1a2æ. 67, 4 ad 2. 2a2æ. 19, 19, 11 & 12

desiderium sumendi, ex timore autem consurgit humilitas reverendi. Et ideo utrumque pertinet ad reverentiam hujus sacramenti, et quod quotidie sumatur et quod aliquando abstineatur. Unde Augustinus dicit, *Si dixerit quispiam, non quotidie accipiendam Eucharistiam, alius contra, faciat unusquisque quod secundum fidem suam pie credit esse faciendum; neque enim litigaverunt inter se Zacchæus et ille centurio, cum alter eorum gaudens suscepit Dominum, alter dixit, Non sum dignus ut intres sub tectum meum; ambo Salvatorem honorificantes, quamvis non uno modo.*[16] Amor tamen et spes, ad quæ semper Scriptura nos provocat, præferuntur timori. Unde et cum Petrus dixisset, *Exi a me, Domine, quia homo peccator sum,* respondit Jesus, *Noli timere.*[17]

4. Ad quartum dicendum quod quia Dominus dicit, *Panem nostrum quotidianum da nobis hodie,*[18] non est pluries in die communicandum, ut saltem per hoc quod aliquis semel in die communicat repræsentetur unitas passionis Christi.

5. Ad quintum dicendum quod secundum diversum statum Ecclesiæ diversa circa hoc statuta emanaverunt. Nam in primitiva Ecclesia quando magis vigebat devotio fidei christianæ statutum fuit ut quotidie fideles communicarent: unde Anacletus Papa, et habetur *de Consecrat.*, dicit, *Peracta consecratione, omnes communicent qui noluerint ecclesiasticis carere liminibus; sic enim et apostoli statuerunt, et sancta Romana tenet Ecclesia.*[19] Postmodum vero, diminuto fidei fervore, Fabianus Papa, et habetur *de Consecrat.*, indulsit *ut si non frequentius, saltem ter in anno omnes communicent scilicet in Pascha, Pentecoste, et Natali Domini.*[20] Soter etiam Papa, in cœna Domini dicit esse communicandum, ut habetur in *de Consecrat.*[21] Postmodum propter iniquitatis abundantiam refrigescente caritate multorum,[22] statuit Innocentius III in concil. Lateran. IV, ut saltem semel in anno, scilicet in Pascha, fideles communicent.[23] Consulitur tamen in lib. *de Eccles. Dogm.* omnibus diebus dominicis esse communicandum.[24]

articulus 11. *utrum liceat omnino a communione cessare*

AD UNDECIMUM sic proceditur:[1] 1. Videtur quod liceat cessare omnino a communione. Laudatur enim centurio de hoc quod dicit, *Domine, non sum dignus ut intres sub tectum meum,*[2] cui comparatur ille qui reputat a communione sibi esse abstinendum, ut dictum est.[3] Cum ergo nunquam legatur Christum in ejus domum venisse, videtur quod liceat alicui toto tempore vitæ suæ a communione abstinere.

---

[16]*Epist.* LIV, 3, ad Januarium. PL 33, 201. *Luke* 19, 6. *Matthew* 8, 8

[17]*Luke* 5, 8 & 10

[18]*Luke* 11, 3

[19]*Epist.* I, 2. Mansi I, 602. Gratian, III, 2, 10. RF I, 1317

[20]Council of Tours III. 50 (813). Mansi XIV, 91. Gratian, III, 2, 16. RF I, 1319

receiving rises from fear: both are part of reverence towards the sacrament, alike as to receiving it every day and holding back sometimes. Accordingly Augustine writes, *If someone says the Eucharist should not be received daily, and another the contrary, let each one genuinely do as his devotion thinks right. For Zaccheus and the centurion are not in conflict, where one received the Lord with joy, and the other said, I am not worthy that you should enter under my roof, since both honoured our Saviour, though not in the same way.*[16] However, love and hope, to which the Scriptures constantly urge us, are preferable to fear, and so when Peter said, *Depart from me for I am a sinful man, O Lord,* Jesus replied, *Fear not.*[17]

4. Because our Lord said, *Give us this day our daily bread,*[18] we are not therefore to communicate several times every day: once a day at least sets forth the oneness of Christ's Passion.

5. Various statutes have been passed according to the various ages of the Church. In the primitive Church when the devotion of Christians flourished, it was enacted that the faithful should communicate daily. Pope Anacletus[a] says, *When the consecration is over, let all communicate who do not wish to cut Church bounds, so the Apostles have ordained, and the Holy Roman Church holds.*[19] Later on when the fervour of faith diminished, Pope Fabian allowed that *if not more often, all should communicate at least three times a year, at Easter, Pentecost and Christmas.*[20] Pope Soter declared that Communion should be received on Holy Thursday, as is set forth in canon law.[21b] Later on, *when wickedness was multiplied and love grew cold,*[22] Pope Innocent III commanded that the faithful should communicate at least once a year, namely at Easter.[23] However the faithful are counselled to communicate on all Sundays.[24]

article 11. *is it lawful to abstain altogether from Communion?*

THE ELEVENTH POINT:[1] 1. So it seems. The centurion is praised who said, *Lord, I am not worthy for you to come under my roof.*[2] He is compared, as has been noted,[3] to one who thinks he should refrain from Communion. Since then we do not read of Christ entering his house, it seems to be lawful to abstain from Communion all one's life.

---

[21]Council of Chalon-sur-Saône II, 47 (813). Mansi XIV, 103. Gratian, III, 2, 17. RF I, 1320
[22]*Matthew* 24, 12
[23]Lateran IV, 21. Mansi XXII, 1010. *Decretals of Gregory IX*, V, 38, 12. RF II, 887
[24]loc cit note 10
[1]cf IV *Sent.* 12, 3, 2, i. *In Joan.* 6, *lect.* 7
[2]*Matthew* 8, 8
[3]art. 10 ad 3 above
[a]Anacletus, or Cletus, first-century pope. Ascription not established.
[b]Pope Fabian, d. 250. Pope Soter, a doubtfully historical figure.

2. Præterea, cuilibet licet abstinere ab his quæ non sunt de necessitate salutis. Sed hoc sacramentum non est de necessitate salutis ut supra dictum est.[4] Ergo licet a sumptione hujus sacramenti omnino cessare.

3. Præterea, peccatores non tenentur communicare: unde Fabianus Papa, cum dixisset, *Ter in anno omnes communicent*, adjunxit, *Nisi forte quis majoribus criminibus impediatur.*[5] Si ergo illi qui non sunt in peccato tenentur communicare, videtur quod melioris conditionis sint peccatores quam justi, quod est inconveniens. Ergo videtur quod etiam justis liceat a communione cessare.

SED CONTRA est quod Dominus dicit, *Nisi manducaveritis carnem Filii hominis, et biberitis ejus sanguinem, non habebitis vitam in vobis.*[6]

RESPONSIO: Dicendum quod, sicut supra dictum est,[7] duplex est modus percipiendi hoc sacramentum, scilicet spiritualis et sacramentalis. Manifestum est autem quod omnes tenentur saltem spiritualiter manducare, quia hoc est Christo incorporari, ut supra dictum est.[8] Spiritualis autem manducatio includit votum seu desiderium percipiendi hoc sacramentum, ut supra dictum est.[9] Et ideo sine voto percipiendi hoc sacramentum non potest homini esse salus. Frustra autem esset votum nisi impleretur quando opportunitas adesset. Et ideo manifestum est quod homo tenetur hoc sacramentum sumere, non solum ex statuto Ecclesiæ, sed ex mandato Domini dicentis, *Hoc facite in meam commemorationem.*[10] Ex statuto autem Ecclesiæ sunt determinata tempora exequendi Christi præceptum.

1. Ad primum ergo dicendum quod, sicut Gregorius dicit, *illa est vera humilitas, cum ad respuendum quod utiliter præcipitur pertinax non est.*[11] Et ideo non potest esse laudabilis humilitas, si contra præceptum Christi et Ecclesiæ aliquis omnino a communione abstineat. Neque enim centurioni præceptum fuit ut Christum in sua domo reciperet.

2. Ad secundum dicendum quod hoc sacramentum dicitur non esse necessitatis, sicut baptismus, quantum ad pueros, quibus potest esse salus sine hoc sacramento, non autem sine sacramento baptismi; quantum vero ad adultos, utrumque est necessitatis.

3. Ad tertium dicendum quod peccatores magnum detrimentum patiuntur ex hoc quod repelluntur a perceptione hujus sacramenti, unde per hoc non sunt melioris conditionis: et licet in peccatis permanentes non excusentur propter hoc a transgressione præcepti, pœnitentes tamen qui, ut Innocentius dicit,[12] *secundum concilium sacerdotis abstinent excusantur.*

---

[4]3a. 73, 3 [5]loc cit note 20 art. 10 above [6]*John* 6, 54

2. Besides, it is lawful for anyone to refrain from things not needful for salvation. But this sacrament is not, as we agreed,[4] of necessity for salvation. Therefore it is lawful to abstain from Communion altogether.

3. Again, sinners are not bound to communicate, hence when Pope Fabian says, *Let all communicate three times a year*, he adds, *except, at least one who is burdened by serious crime.*[5] If then those who are not in sin are obliged to go to Communion, it seems that sinners are better off, which is rather odd. Then it seems that good people also may lawfully refrain from Communion.

ON THE OTHER HAND our Lord says, *Unless you eat the flesh of the Son of man and drink his blood, you have no life in you.*[6]

REPLY: As we have stated,[7] the manner of receiving this sacrament is twofold, spiritual and sacramental. Now it is clear that all are bound to eat it at least spiritually for them to be incorporated in Christ, as we have said.[8] Spiritual eating, we have noted,[9] includes the purpose or desire of receiving the sacrament. And so a man cannot be saved without the desire of receiving this sacrament. Now a desire would be pointless unless it could be fulfilled when the opportunity presents itself. So it is clear that a person is bound to receive this sacrament, not only by virtue of the Church's ordinance, but also of our Lord's command, *Do this in memory of me.*[10] Yet the Church's law prescribes the times for fulfilling his command.

Hence: 1. As Gregory says, *True humility is that which is not obstinate in accepting what is prescribed for one's good.*[11] That humility is not praiseworthy when one abstains from Communion altogether against the command of Christ and the Church. In fact the centurion was not commanded to receive Christ into his house.

2. This sacrament is not said to be of the same necessity as Baptism with respect to children; they can be saved without it, but not without Baptism.[a] Both, however, are necessary to adults.

3. Sinners suffer great loss in being held back from receiving this sacrament, so on that account they are not better off. And although while continuing in sin they are not excused thereby from transgressing the precept, nevertheless those who are penitent are excused, as Innocent III says, *who hold back on the advice of their priest.*[12]

---

[7]art. 1 above
[8]3a. 73, 3 ad 1. art. 8 ad 3 above
[9]arts. 1 ad 3 & 2 above
[10]*Luke* 22, 19
[11]*Regula Pastoralis* 1, 6. PL 77, 19
[12]loc cit note 23 art. 10 above
[a]Necessity of baptism, 3a. 68, 1 & 2. cf 2a2æ. 2, 3–8, Vol. 31, ed. T. C. O'Brien.

articulus 12. *utrum liceat sumere corpus Christi sine sanguine*

AD DUODECIMUM sic proceditur:[1] 1. Videtur quod non liceat sumere corpus Christi sine sanguine. Dicit enim Gelasius Papa, et habetur *de Consecrat.*, *Comperimus quod quidam, sumpta tantummodo corporis sacri portione, a calice sacrati cruoris abstinent; qui procul dubio, quoniam nescio qua superstitione docentur adstringi, aut integra sacramenta percipiant, aut ab integris arceantur.*[2] Non ergo licet sumere corpus Christi sine ejus sanguine.

2. Præterea, ad perfectionem hujus sacramenti concurrit et manducatio corporis et potatio sanguinis, ut supra habitum est.[3] Si ergo sumatur corpus sine sanguine, erit sacramentum imperfectum, quod ad sacrilegium pertinere videtur; unde ibidem Gelasius subdit, *Quia divisio unius ejusdemque mysterii sine grandi sacrilegio provenire non potest.*[4]

3. Præterea, hoc sacramentum celebratur in memoriam dominicæ passionis, ut supra dictum est,[5] et sumitur pro animæ salute. Sed passio Christi magis exprimitur in sanguine quam in corpore; sanguis etiam pro salute animæ offertur, ut supra habitum est.[6] Potius ergo esset abstinendum a sumptione corporis quam a sumptione sanguinis. Ergo accedentes ad hoc sacramentum non debent sumere corpus Christi sine ejus sanguine.

SED CONTRA est multarum ecclesiarum usus, in quibus populo communicanti datur corpus Christi sumendum, non autem sanguis.

RESPONSIO: Dicendum quod circa usum hujus sacramenti duo possunt considerari: unum ex parte ipsius sacramenti, aliud ex parte sumentium. Ex parte quidem ipsius sacramenti convenit quod utrumque sumatur, scilicet et corpus et sanguis, quia in utroque consistit perfectio sacramenti, et ideo quia ad sacerdotem pertinet hoc sacramentum consecrare et perficere, nullo modo debet corpus Christi sumere sine sanguine.

Ex parte autem sumentium requiritur summa reverentia et cautela, ne aliquid accidat quod vergat ad injuriam tanti mysterii. Quod præcipue posset accidere in sanguinis sumptione, qui quidem si incaute sumeretur de facili posset effundi. Et quia crevit multitudo populi christiani, in qua

---

[1]cf IV *Sent.* 12, 3, 2, ii. *In Joan.* 6, *lect* 7

[2]Gelasius I. *Epist.* XXXVII. Thiel 451. Gratian, III, 2, 12. RF I, 1318

[3]3a. 73, 2; 74, 1; 76, 2

[4]loc cit note 2

[5]3a. 66, 9 ad 5; 73, 4 & 5; 74, 1

[6]3a. 74, 1; 76, 2 ad 1

[a]Communion under both kinds was the practice in the early Church, though exceptions were soon allowed: the consecrated bread might be taken home or given to travellers or prisoners, the consecrated wine given to babies after baptism or to the dying as viaticum. The practice of Communion under one kind was established in the West by the 12th century. The reasons for it are purely practical; though

article 12. is it lawful to receive the body without the blood of Christ?

THE TWELFTH POINT:[1a] 1. It seems not. For Pope Gelasius[b] says, and he is repeated in canon law, *We have learnt that some after taking just a portion of the sacred body, abstain from the chalice of the sacred blood, doubtless from some superstition, I know not what, but let them either receive the integral sacrament or be kept back.*[2] Therefore it is not lawful to receive the body of Christ without his blood.

2. Further, it has been stated[3] that the eating of the body and the drinking of the blood come together for the completion of this sacrament. If the body be taken without the blood the sacrament will be incomplete. This smacks of sacrilege. And so Pope Gelasius adds, *Dividing one and the same mystery cannot be without great sacrilege.*[4]

3. Moreover, the sacrament is celebrated in memory of Christ's Passion, as has been stated,[5] and it is received for the health of the soul. But Christ's Passion is expressed by blood rather than by body; the blood also is offered for the health of the soul, as stated above.[6] Better, then, to refrain from receiving the body, not the blood. Therefore those coming to Communion ought not to take Christ's body without his blood.

ON THE OTHER HAND it is the custom of many churches for people to be given Communion with the body, not with the blood of Christ.[c]

REPLY: Note two points with regard to the use of this sacrament, one on the part of the sacrament, the other on that of the receiver. On the part of the sacrament, it is appropriate that both body and blood should be taken, for in both together lies its completeness. And so, because it is the priest's office to consecrate and complete the sacrament, never ought he receive Christ's body without the blood.

On the part of the receiver, however, the greatest reverence and care are called for lest anything happen that would dishonour such a mystery. This could happen in receiving the blood, which if incautiously taken

---

admittedly less expressive liturgically and sacramentally, it is underpinned by the doctrine of the presence of the whole Christ under either species by natural concomitance; 3a. 37, 1–3, Vol. 58, ed. W. Barden. Attacked by the Hussites, it was confirmed at the time of the Councils of Constance and Basel. While invoking the principles maintained at Trent defending the practice, Vatican II (*On the Mystery of the Eucharist*, II, 55) cautiously reintroduced Communion under two kinds.

[b]Pope Gelasius, d. 496.

[c]Note that the appeal is to the usage of many churches, not of the Universal Church.

continentur senes, et juvenes, et parvuli, quorum quidam non sunt tantæ discretionis ut cautelam debitam circa usum hujus sacramenti adhibeant, ideo provide in quibusdam ecclesiis observatur ut populo sanguis sumendus non detur, sed solum a sacerdote sumatur.

1. Ad primum ergo dicendum quod Gelasius loquitur quantum ad sacerdotes, qui sicut totum consecrant sacramentum, ita etiam toti communicare debent. Ut enim legitur in concilio Toletano, *quale erit sacrificium, cui nec ipse sacrificans particeps esse dignoscitur?*[7]

2. Ad secundum dicendum quod perfectio hujus sacramenti non est in usu fidelium, sed in consecratione materiæ. Et ideo nihil derogat perfectioni hujus sacramenti, si populus sumat corpus sine sanguine, dummodo sacerdos consecrans sumat utrumque.

3. Ad tertium dicendum quod repræsentatio dominicæ passionis agitur in ipsa consecratione hujus sacramenti, in qua non debet corpus sine sanguine consecrari: potest autem a populo corpus sine sanguine sumi; nec exinde sequitur aliquod detrimentum, quia sacerdos in persona omnium sanguinem offert et sumit; et sub utraque specie totus Christus continetur, ut supra habitum est.[8]

---

[7]Toledo XII, cap. 5. (681). Mansi XI, 1033. Gratian, III, 2, 11. RF I, 1318

might easily be spilt. Because of growth in numbers of Christian people, including old and young and children, some of whom have not discretion enough to use due care in taking the sacrament, it is the prudent custom in some churches for the blood not to be offered for reception by the people, but received by the priest alone.

Hence: 1. Gelasius is speaking of priests; since they consecrate the sacrament entire, so ought they to receive it. As we read in the Council of Toledo, *What kind of sacrifice is that where not even the offerer is known to have a share?*[7]

2. The completion of this sacrament lies in the consecration of the matter, not in the receiving of it by the faithful. Hence then nothing takes away from its completeness if the people receive the body without the blood provided that the consecrating priest receives both.

3. Our Lord's Passion is set forth in the consecration itself of this sacrament, in which the body ought not to be consecrated without the blood. But the body can be received by the people without the blood, and this without any loss to the sacrament. The priest in the person of all offers the blood and consumes it, and under either species the whole Christ is present, as we have explained.[8]

---

[8] 3a. 76, 2

Quæstio 81. de modo quo Christus usus est hoc sacramento

DEINDE CONSIDERANDUM EST de usu hujus sacramenti, quo Christus usus est in prima sui institutione. Et circa hoc quæruntur quantuor:

1. utrum Christus sumpserit suum corpus et sanguinem;
2. utrum Judæ dederit;
3. quale corpus sumpserit aut dederit, utrum scilicet passibile vel impassibile;
4. quomodo se habuisset Christus sub hoc sacramento, si fuisset in triduo mortis reservatum aut consecratum.

articulus 1. *utrum Christus sumpserit suum corpus et sanguinem*

AD PRIMUM sic proceditur:[1] 1. Videtur quod Christus non sumpserit corpus suum et sanguinem. Non enim de factis Christi et dictis asseri debet quod auctoritate sacræ Scripturæ non traditur. Sed in Evangeliis non habetur quod Christus corpus suum manducaverit aut sanguinem suum biberit. Non ergo est hoc asserendum.

2. Præterea, nihil potest esse in seipso, nisi forte ratione partium, prout scilicet una pars ejus est in alia, ut habetur *Physic.*[2] Sed illud quod manducatur et bibitur est in manducante et bibente. Cum igitur totus Christus sit sub utraque specie sacramenti, videtur impossibile fuisse quod ipse sumpserit hoc sacramentum.

3. Præterea, duplex est sumptio hujus sacramenti, scilicet spiritualis et sacramentalis. Sed spiritualis non competebat Christo, quia nihil a sacramento accipit; et per consequens nec sacramentalis, quæ sine spirituali est imperfecta, ut supra habitum est.[3] Ergo Christus nullo modo hoc sacramentum sumpsit.

SED CONTRA est quod Hieronymus dicit ad Heldibiam, *Dominus Jesus Christus ipse conviva et convivum, ipse comedens et qui comeditur.*[4]

RESPONSIO: Dicendum quod quidam[5] dixerunt quod Christus in cœna corpus et sanguinem suum discipulis suis tradidit, non tamen ipse sumpsit.

---

[1]cf 3a. 84. 7 ad 4. IV *Sent.* 11, 3, 1

[2]Aristotle, *Physics* IV, 4. 211a30

[3]3a. 80, 1

[4]*Epist.* CXX. PL 28, 986. Gratian, III, 2, 87. RF I, 1350

[5]e.g. Peter of Poitiers. *Sent.* V, 13. PL 211, 1254

Question 81. the first Eucharist

NOW TO BE DISCUSSED is Christ's giving of this sacrament at its institution.[a] Here there are four points of inquiry:

1. whether he received his own body and blood;
2. whether he gave the sacrament to Judas;
3. whether the body he received and gave was passible or impassible;
4. how would have been the condition of Christ's body under this sacrament had it been consecrated and reserved during the three days he lay dead.

article 1. did Christ receive his own body and blood?

THE FIRST POINT:[1] 1. No, it seems. For nothing should be asserted of the sayings and doings of Christ which is not warranted by the authority of sacred Scripture. But the Gospels do not record that Christ ate his own body or drank his own blood.[b] Therefore it is not to be asserted that he did.

2. Besides, according to the *Physics*,[2] nothing can be within itself except maybe by reason of its parts, for instance inasmuch as one part is in another. What is eaten and drunk is in the eater and drinker. Since the whole Christ is under each sacramental species, it seems impossible for him to have received this sacrament.

3. Also, the taking of the sacrament is twofold, namely spiritual and sacramental. But spiritual reception was not for Christ, who gains nothing from this sacrament. Consequently neither is sacramental reception, which, as we have seen,[3] is imperfect without spiritual reception. Hence Christ in no wise received this sacrament.

ON THE OTHER HAND there is Jerome, *The Lord Jesus Christ is himself the guest and the banquet, the partaker and the food.*[4]

REPLY: It has been held[5c] that at the Last Supper Christ gave his body and blood to his disciples, but did not himself receive. Yet it is not in keeping

---

[a]More literally, the sacramental use Christ adopted in founding the Eucharist, that is, towards the end of the Last Supper. cf *Matthew* 26, 1–29. *Mark* 14, 1–25. *Luke* 22, 1–23. *John* 13, 1–38. 1 *Corinthians* 11, 17–35.

[b]The NT recounts how Christ ate the pasch with his disciples, but does not leave the impression that he received the elements which he had consecrated. The matter is not raised in St Thomas's Scriptural exposition, *In Matt.* 13 and *In* 1 *Cor.* 11.

[c]Peter of Poitiers, d. 1205.

Sed hoc non videtur convenienter dici, quia Christus ea quæ ab aliis observanda instituit ipse primitus observavit. Unde et ipse prius baptizari voluit quam aliis baptismum imponeret, secundum illud *Act.*, *Cœpit Jesus facere et docere.*[6] Unde et primo ipse corpus suum et sanguinem sumpsit, et postea discipulis sumendum tradidit. Et hoc est quod *Ruth*, super illud, *Cumque comedisset et bibisset*, etc.,[7] dicit Glossa quod *Christus comedit et bibit in cœna, cum corporis et sanguinis sui sacramentum discipulis tradidit. Unde quia pueri communicaverunt carni et sanguini, et ipse participavit eisdem.*[8]

1. Ad primum ergo dicendum quod in Evangeliis legitur quod Christus *accepit panem et calicem*;[9] non est autem intelligendum quod acceperit solum in manibus, ut quidam dicunt;[10] sed eo modo accepit quo aliis accipiendum tradidit; unde cum discipulis dixerit, *Accipite et comedite;* et iterum, *Accipite et bibite*, intelligendum est quod ipse accipiens comederit et biberit. Unde et quidam metrice dixerunt:

Rex sedet in cœna
Turba cinctus duodena;
Se tenet in manibus,
Se cibat ipse cibus.[11]

2. Ad secundum dicendum quod, sicut supra dictum est,[12] Christus secundum quod est sub hoc sacramento, comparatur ad locum non secundum proprias dimensiones, sed secundum dimensionem specierum sacramentalium, ita quod in quocumque loco ubi sunt illæ species, est ipse Christus; et quia species illæ potuerunt esse in manibus et in ore Christi, ipse totus Christus potuit esse in suis manibus et in suo ore. Non autem hoc potuisset esse, secundum quod comparatur ad locum per proprias dimensiones.

3. Ad tertium dicendum quod, sicut supra dictum est,[13] effectus hujus sacramenti est non solum augmentum habitualis gratiæ, sed etiam quædam actualis delectatio spiritualis dulcedinis. Quamvis autem Christo gratia non fuerit augmentata ex susceptione hujus sacramenti, habuit tamen quamdam spiritualem delectationem in nova institutione hujus sacramenti. Unde ipse dicebat, *Desiderio desideravi hoc Pascha manducare vobiscum*;[14] quod Eusebius exponit de novo mysterio novi Testamenti, quod tradebat discipulis.[15] Et ideo spiritualiter manducavit, et similiter sacramentaliter, inquantum corpus suum sub sacramento sumpsit, quod sacramentum sui

---

[6]*Acts* 1, 1
[7]*Ruth* 3, 7
[8]*Ordinaria*. An echo of *Hebrews* 2, 14
[9]*Matthew* 26, 26
[10]e.g. Peter of Poitiers, loc cit note 5

to say this.[d] For what Christ instituted for others to observe he began by observing himself. Thus he willed first to be baptized before imposing baptism on others,[e] and so also it is written, *Jesus began to do and to teach.*[6] That is why he first took his body and blood, and afterward gave it to the disciples to receive. Accordingly on *Ruth*, *When he had eaten and drunk,*[7] the Gloss observes, *Christ ate and drank at the Last Supper when he gave the sacrament of his body and blood to the disciples. And so, because the children are partakers of his body and blood, he also was a partaker.*[8]

Hence: 1. We read in the Gospels that Christ *took the bread and the cup.*[9] Do not think that this means that he took them only in his hands, as some say,[10] but that he took them in the manner they were given for others to receive. Accordingly, when he said to the disciples, *Take and eat*, and again, *Take and drink*, it is to be understood that the Lord himself took and ate and drank. Hence the verse:

The King sat at supper
Girdled by the twelve
In his hands he held himself
And gave himself that food.[11]

2. As we have said,[12] Christ, inasmuch as he is present under this sacrament, is related to it according to the dimensions of the sacramental elements, not his own dimensions, so that where the elements are there is Christ. And because those elements can be in his hands and in his mouth, so also can the whole Christ. This would not be possible were he there related to place according to his own proper dimensions.

3. As we have said,[13] the effect of this sacrament is not only the growth of habitual grace,[f] but also a certain actual enjoyment of spiritual sweetness. Though Christ's grace was not increased from receiving this sacrament,[g] he had a certain spiritual joy in its new institution. He said, *With desire I have desired to eat this pasch with you,*[14] which Eusebius[h] explains of the new mystery of the New Testament which he delivered to his disciples.[15] And so he ate spiritually and likewise sacramentally; he received his own body in this sacrament, the sacrament of his body planned and

---

[11]Given by Albert, *Sent.* IV, 12, 15, 6. Also Hugh of St Cher, on *Luke* 22, 16
[12] 3a. 76, 5 [13]3a. 79, 1 ad 2 [14]*Luke* 22, 15
[15]Eusebius of Cæsarea, *De Solemn. Paschali.* PG 24, 704. *Catena Aurea*
[d]Note the cautious introduction to a recommendatory argument, *argumentum ex convenientia.*
[e]Why Christ was baptized, 3a. 39, 1.
[f]Habitual grace, the abiding quality of being in love with God; 1a2æ. 110, 2–4.
[g]cf 3a. 7, 1 & 12.
[h]Eusebius, d. *c.* 340.

corporis intellexit et disposuit; aliter tamen quam cæteri sacramentaliter et spiritualiter sumant; qui augmentum gratiæ suscipiunt, et sacramentalibus signis indigent ad veritatis perceptionem.

articulus 2. utrum Christus dederit Judæ corpus suum

AD SECUNDUM sic proceditur:[1] 1. Videtur quod Christus Judæ non dederit corpus suum, Ut enim legitur *Matt.*, postquam dedit Dominus corpus suum et sanguinem discipulis, dixit eis, *Non bibam amodo de hoc genimine vitis usque in diem illum cum illud bibam vobiscum novum in regno Patris mei.*[2] Ex quo videtur quod illi quibus corpus suum et sanguinem dederat, cum eo essent iterum bibituri. Sed Judas postea cum ipso non bibit. Ergo non accepit cum aliis discipulis corpus Christi in sanguinem.

2. Præterea, Dominus implevit quod præcepit secundum illud *Act.*, *Cœpit Jesus facere et docere.*[3] Sed ipse præcepit, *Nolite sanctum dare canibus.*[4] Cum ergo ipse cognosceret Judam esse peccatorem, videtur quod ei corpus suum et sanguinem non dederit.

3. Præterea, Christus specialiter legitur Judæ panem intinctum porrexisse, *Joan.*[5] Si ergo corpus suum ei dedit, videtur quod sub buccella ei dederit: præcipue cum legatur ibidem quod *post buccellam introivit in eum Satanas*; ubi Augustinus dicit, *Hinc nos docemur quam sit cavendum male accipere bonum. Si enim corripitur qui non dijudicat, idest non discernit corpus Domini a cæteris cibis, quomodo non damnabitur qui ad ejus mensam fingens se amicum, accedit inimicus?*[6] Sed cum buccella intincta non accepit corpus Christi: ut enim Augustinus dicit super illud *Joan.*, *Cum intinxisset panem, dedit Judæ Simonis Iscariotæ, non, ut putant quidam negligenter legentes, tunc Judas corpus Christi accepit.*[7] Ergo videtur quod Judas corpus Christi non acceperit.

SED CONTRA est quod Chrysostomus dicit, *Judas particeps existens mysteriorum conversus non est; unde fit scelus ejus utrinque immanius, tum quia tali proposito imbutus adit mysteria, tum quia adiens melior factus non fuit nec metu, nec beneficio, nec honore.*[8]

RESPONSIO: Dicendum quod Hilarius posuit, quod Christus Judæ corpus suum et sanguinem non dedit.[9] Et hoc quidem conveniens fuisset, considerata malitia Judæ. Sed quia Christus nobis debuit esse exemplum

---

[1]cf IV *Sent.* 11, 3, 2, i & ii. *In Matt.* 26. *In Joan.* 18, *lect.* 3 & 4

[2]*Matthew* 26, 29

[3]*Acts* 1, 1

[4]*Matthew* 7, 6

[5]*John* 13, 26

[6]*Super Joan.* LXII. PL 35, 1801

[7]loc cit On 13, 27

carried into effect by himself. Yet otherwise than the rest of us who receive it spiritually and sacramentally, for under the sacramental species we receive the increase of grace we need for laying hold of the reality.

article 2. did Christ give his body to Judas?

THE SECOND POINT:[1] 1. Apparently not. For as we read in *Matthew* that after the Lord gave his body and blood to his disciples he said to them, *I will not drink from henceforth of the vine until that day when I shall drink it with you new in the kingdom of my Father.*[2] From which it seems that those to whom he had given his body and blood were to drink of it again with him. But Judas was not among them. Therefore he did not receive the body and blood of Christ with the other disciples.

2. Besides, our Lord fulfilled what he commanded, according to *Acts, Jesus began to do and to teach.*[3] But he commands, *Do not give what is holy to the dogs.*[4] Since he knew Judas to be a sinner, it would seem that he did not give him his body and blood.

3. Again, we read explicitly that Christ gave Judas *bread dipped.*[5] If therefore he gave his body, it would seem that he gave it as a morsel, as we read, *and after that Satan entered into him*, on which Augustine comments, *Here we are now warned as to accepting good badly. If they are corrected who do not distinguish, that is who do not discern the Lord's body from other food, how shall those not be condemned who come to the table as an enemy when they pretend to be a friend?*[6] But Judas did not receive Christ's body with the dipped morsel; as Augustine says, *When he dipped the bread, he gave to Judas Simon Iscariot, not, as some careless readers think, that Judas then received the body of Christ.*[7] Consequently it would seem that Judas did not receive Christ's body.

ON THE OTHER HAND Chrysostom says, *Judas, a sharer in the mysteries, was not converted. And so on both counts guilty of an outrage, he came to the mysteries with his design in mind, and did not come to a better heart, neither from awe, nor from gratitude, nor by honour.*[8a]

REPLY: Hilary[b] affirms that Christ did not give his body and blood to Judas.[9] This would be all very well if we looked only at the wickedness of Judas. Yet because Christ should be to us a model of justice, it did not

[8] *In Matt.* LXXXII. PG 58, 737

[9] *Super Matt.* 30. PL 9, 1065

[a] The common view is that Judas did not receive Communion; a difference arises from the accounts of the Evangelists. The conclusion this article arrives at, guardedly and *ex convenientia*, can be supported by *Luke*, but not by *Matthew, Mark*, and *John*. See Scriptural commentaries.

[b] St Hilary of Poitiers, d. 367.

justitiæ, non conveniebat ejus magisterio ut Judam occultum peccatorem sine accusatore et evidenti probatione ab aliorum communione separaret; ne per hoc daretur exemplum prælatis Ecclesiæ similia faciendi, et ipse Judas exasperatus inde sumeret occasionem peccandi. Et ideo dicendum est quod Judas cum aliis discipulis corpus Domini et sanguinem suscepit, ut dicit Dionysius[10] et Augustinus.[11]

1. Ad primum ergo dicendum quod illa est ratio Hilarii,[12] ad ostendendum quod Judas corpus Christi non sumpsit; non tamen cogit, quia Christus loquitur discipulis, a quorum collegio Judas se separavit. Non autem Christus eum exclusit; et ideo Christus, quantum est in se, etiam cum Juda vinum in regno Dei bibit; sed hoc convivium ipse Judas repudiavit.

2. Ad secundum dicendum quod Christo nota erat Judæ iniquitas, sicut Deo; non autem erat ei nota per modum quo hominibus innotescit. Et ideo Christus Judam non repulit a communione ut daret exemplum, tales peccatores occultos non esse ab aliis sacerdotibus expellendos.

3. Ad tertium dicendum quod sine dubio Judas sub pane intincto corpus Christi non sumpsit, sed simplicem panem. *Significatur autem fortassis*, ut Augustinus ibidem dicit, *per panis intinctionem fictio Judæ; ut enim inficiantur nonnulla intinguntur. Si autem bonum aliquid hic significat tinctio* (scilicet dulcedinem bonitatis divinæ, quia panis ex intinctione sapidior redditur), *eidem bono ingratum non immerito est secuta damnatio.*[13] Et propter hanc ingratitudinem id quod est bonum factum est ei malum, sicut accidit circa sumentes corpus Christi indigne; et, sicut Augustinus ibidem dicit, *intelligendum est quod Dominus jam antea distribuerat omnibus discipulis suis sacramentum corporis et sanguinis sui, ubi et ipse Judas erat, sicut Lucas narrat; ac deinde ad hoc ventum est, ubi secundum narrationem Joannis, Dominus per buccellam tinctam atque porrectam suum exprimit proditorem.*[14]

articulus 3. *utrum Christus sumpserit, et discipulis dederit corpus suum impassibile.*

AD TERTIUM sic proceditur:[1] 1. Videtur quod Christus sumpserit et discipulis dederit corpus suum impassibile, quia super illud *Matt.*, *Transfinuratus est ante eos*,[2] dicit quædam Glossa,[3] *Illud corpus quod habuit per naturam dedit discipulis in cœna, non mortale et passibile.* Et *Levit.* super

---

[10] *De Eccles. Hier.* 3. PG 3, 428. cf 453
[11] *Super Joan.* LXII. On 13, 26. PL 35, 1802
[12] loc cit note 8
[13] loc cit note 11
[14] ibid
[1] cf IV *Sent.* 11, 9, 3; 12, 1, 3, i

befit his authority that Judas, a hidden sinner, should be separated from Communion without evident charge and proof, lest Church rulers should thereby be given a precedent for doing the same; also lest Judas, turning ugly, should make of it an occasion of sin. Therefore, it is to be held that together with the other disciples Judas received the Lord's body and blood; so say Dionysius[10] and Augustine.[11]

Hence: 1. This is the argument used by Hilary to show that Judas did not receive Christ's body.[12] Nevertheless it is not convincing. For Christ was speaking to the disciples, from whose company Judas was parting. It was not Christ that excluded him. And so Christ for his part drinks in the Kingdom of heaven with Judas, but Judas it was who refused the feast.

2. The wickedness of Judas was evident to Christ as God, yet it was not evident in the manner that men could come to know of it. Accordingly Christ did not expel Judas from Communion, that he might give an example that priests are not to repel such secret sinners.

3. There is no doubt that by the bread dipped Judas did not receive Christ's body, but ordinary bread. *Perhaps*, says Augustine, *it signified the pretence of Judas, as things are dipped before they are dyed. And if anything good is here signified*, for instance the sweetness of divine goodness, for dipped bread is more relished; *from that good ungratefully received not unfairly follows condemnation*, on account of that ingratitude *what is good is made into evil*,[13] as is the case with those who receive Christ's body unworthily. And as Augustine says in the same place. *It is to be understood that the Lord had already distributed to all his disciples the sacrament of his body and blood when Judas was there, as Luke narrates. And then we come to this, where according to John's report, the Lord by dipping bread and giving it indicated his betrayer.*[14]

article 3. did Christ take and give to the disciples his impassible body?

THE THIRD POINT:[1a] 1. So it would seem. For on the text, *He was transfigured before them*,[2] the Gloss comments, *That body which he had by birth he gave to the disciples at the Last Supper, not mortal or passible.*[3] And on *Levit.*, *If thy offering be not of blood*,[4] the Gloss comments, *The Cross,*

---

[2] *Matthew* 17, 2

[3] *Ordinaria*

[a] Passible; capable of suffering, liable to mortality. The theological principle behind the discussion is that the entire Christ is in the sacrament, 3a. 76, 2. Also that the sacramental reality is Christ as he exists in fact. The present inquiry, unlike that in the following art., is not hypothetical: the sacrament of Christ's body was consecrated before his death. But note the distinction in the Reply: a passible body, but present in an impassible sacramental mode.

illud, *Si oblatio tua fuerit de sartagine*,[4] dicit Glossa, *Crux super omnia fortis carnem Christi, quæ ante passionem non videbatur esui apta, post aptam fecit.*[5] Sed Christus dedit corpus suum ut aptum ad manducandum. Ergo dedit tale quale habuit post passionem, scilicet impassibile et immortale.

2. Præterea, omne corpus passibile per contactum et manducationem patitur. Si ergo corpus Christi erat passibile, per contactum et comestionem discipulorum passum fuisset.

3. Præterea, verba sacramentalia non sunt modo majoris virtutis quando proferuntur a sacerdote in persona Christi, quam tunc quando fuerunt prolata ab ipso Christo. Sed nunc virtute verborum sacramentalium in altari consecratur corpus Christi impassibile et immortale. Ergo multo magis tunc.

SED CONTRA est quod, sicut Innocentius III dicit, *tale corpus tunc dedit discipulis, quale habuit.*[6] Habuit autem tunc corpus passibile et mortale. Ergo corpus passibile et mortale discipulis dedit.

RESPONSIO: Dicendum quod Hugo de Sancto Victore posuit[7] quod Christus ante passionem diversis temporibus quatuor dotes corporis glorificati assumpserit, scilicet subtilitatem in nativitate, quando exivit de clauso utero Virginis; agilitatem, quando ambulavit siccis pedibus super mare; claritatem in transfiguratione; impassibilitatem in cœna, quando corpus suum discipulis tradidit manducandum. Et secundum hoc dedit discipulis suis corpus suum impassibile et immortale.

Sed quidquid sit de aliis, de quibus supra dictum est,[8] quid sentiri debeat, circa impassibilitatem tamen impossibile est esse quod dicitur. Manifestum est enim quod idem verum corpus Christi erat quod a discipulis tunc in propria specie videbatur, et in specie sacramenti sumebatur. Non autem erat impassibile secundum quod in propria specie videbatur; quinimmo erat passioni paratum. Unde nec ipsum corpus Christi quod in specie sacramenti dabatur impassibile erat.

Impassibili tamen modo erat sub specie sacramenti quod in se erat passibile, sicut invisibiliter quod in se erat visibile. Sicut enim visio requirit contactum corporis quod videtur ad circumstans medium visionis, ita passio requirit contactum corporis quod patitur, ad ea quæ agunt. Corpus autem Christi, secundum quod est sub sacramento, ut supra dictum est,[9] non comparatur ad ea quæ circumstant, mediantibus propriis

---

[4]*Leviticus* 2, 5 [5]*Ordinaria*. Hesychius, *In Levit.* I. PG 93, 808
[6]*De Sacro Altaris Mysterio* IV, 12. PL 217, 864
[7]cf Innocent III. loc cit note 6. Also *Serm.* XIV. PL 217, 382
[8]3a. 28, 2 ad 3; 45, 2; 54, I ad I. cf *Suppl.* 45, 2

mighty above all, bore the flesh of Christ, which before the Passion did not seem adapted for nourishment afterwards made it so.[5] But Christ gave his body apt to be eaten. Therefore he gave it such as it was after the Passion, namely impassible and immortal.

2. Besides, touching and eating involves a change in any passible body. If, then, Christ's body were passible, it would have undergone change by being touched and eaten by the disciples.

3. In addition, the sacramental words are not of greater virtue now when they are pronounced by a priest in the person of Christ than they were when they were uttered by Christ. But now in virtue of the sacramental words at the altar the body of Christ is consecrated impassible and immortal.

ON THE OTHER HAND is Pope Innocent III, *The body he then gave to the disciples was the body such as he then had.*[6]

REPLY: Hugh of St Victor[7b] held that Christ at diverse times assumed the four endowments of the human body in heaven,[c] namely fineness, when he came from the closed womb of the Virgin; lissomeness, when he walked dry-shod on the sea; resplendence, in the Transfiguration; impassibility when at the Last Supper he gave his body to the disciples as food. According to this position, he gave the disciples his body impassible and immortal.

Yet, whatever may be the case about the others, and we have discussed[8] the matter and decided what we should hold, nevertheless the above position cannot be sustained. Clearly it was the same body of Christ that the disciples knew in its proper appearance and that which they received in its sacramental appearance. It was not impassible when seen in its proper human guise, rather indeed it was all ready to undergo the Passion, nor, consequently, was it impassible when it was given under the sacramental species.

Nevertheless though passible in itself, yet under the sacramental species it was in an impassible mode; just as that was there invisibly which of itself was visible. For as seeing requires a contact of the body which is seen with the corresponding medium of vision, so undergoing changes requires contact of the body which is changed with factors acting on it. But Christ's body, as it is in the sacrament is, as we have said,[9] related to its

---

[9]3a. 76, 4, 5 & 6. art. 1 and 2 above

[b]Hugh of St Victor, d. 1141.

[c]The four endowments, *dotes*, parts of the dowry of the body in heaven. cf *Supplementum* 82–85. 95, 1–3.

dimensionibus, quibus corpora se tangunt, sed mediantibus dimensionibus specierum panis et vini; et ideo species illæ sunt quæ patiuntur et videntur, non autem ipsum corpus Christi.

1. Ad primum ergo dicendum quod Christus dicitur in cœna non dedisse corpus suum mortale et passibile, quia non dedit mortali et passibili modo. Crux autem fecit carnem Christi aptam manducationi inquantum hoc sacramentum repræsentat passionem Christi.

2. Ad secundum dicendum quod ratio illa procederet, si corpus Christi, sicut erat passibile, ita passibili modo fuisset sub hoc sacramento.

3. Ad tertium dicentum quod sicut supra dictum est,[10] accidentia corporis Christi sunt in sacramento ex reali concomitantia, non autem ex vi sacramenti, ex qua est ibi substantia corporis Christi. Et ideo virtus verborum sacramentalium ad hoc se extendit ut sit sub sacramento corpus Christi, scilicet quibuscumque accidentibus realiter in eo existentibus.

articulus 4. *utrum si hoc sacramentum tempore mortis Christi fuisset servatum vel consecratum ibi moreretur*

AD QUARTUM sic proceditur:[1] 1. Videtur quod si hoc sacramentum tempore mortis Christi fuisset servatum in pixide, vel ab aliquo Apostolorum consecratum, non ibi moreretur. Mors enim Christi accidit per ejus passionem. Sed Christus impassibili modo etiam tunc erat in hoc sacramento. Ergo non poterat mori in hoc sacramento.

2. Præterea, in morte Christi separatus fuit sanguis ejus a corpore. Sed in hoc sacramento simul est corpus Christi et sanguis. Ergo Christus in hoc sacramento non moreretur.

3. Præterea, mors accidit per separationem animæ a corpore. Sed in hoc sacramento continetur tam corpus quam anima Christi. Ergo in hoc sacramento non poterat Christus mori.

SED CONTRA est quod idem Christus qui erat in cruce fuisset in sacramento. Sed in cruce moriebatur. Ergo et in sacramento conservato moreretur.

RESPONSIO: Dicendum quod corpus Christi idem in substantia est in hoc sacramento et in propria specie, sed non eodem modo: nam in propria specie contingit circumstantia corpora per proprias dimensiones; non

---

[10] 3a. 76, 4

[1] cf IV *Sent.* 10, 2, i; 11, 3, 4, i & 2. *CG* IV, 64. *In* I *Cor.* 11, *lect.* 6. *In Joan.* 6, *lect.* 7. *Quodl.* V, 6, 1

[a] The inquiry may seem dictated by a sense more of logic than of history, more of doctrinal implication than of likely fact. Yet it brings out of principles of art. 3

surroundings by means, not of his proper dimensions whereby bodies touch, but of those of the species of bread and wine. It is those which undergo change and are seen, not Christ's own body.

Hence: 1. Christ is said not to have given his mortal and passible body, because he did not give it as a mortal and passible man. And the Cross made Christ's body apt to be eaten inasmuch as this sacrament represents his Passion.

2. The reasoning here would follow if Christ's body, passible as it then was, would have to be present in the sacrament in a passible manner.

3. As we have said above,[10] the properties of Christ's body in this sacrament are present by real concomitance, but not in virtue of the sacrament whereby the substance of Christ's body is there. And so the virtue of the sacramental words extends to this, that Christ's body is present under the sacrament, whatever be the accidents existing in it.

article 4. if it had been consecrated or reserved at the time Christ died would he have died in the sacrament?

THE FOURTH POINT:[1] 1. Had it been consecrated or reserved in a pyx by an Apostle at the time of Christ's death, it would seem that Christ would have not died in the sacrament. His death came about through his Passion. But Christ was in the sacrament in an impassible manner. Therefore he could not have died in this sacrament.

2. Besides, in the death of Christ his body was separated from his blood. Now Christ's body and blood are both in the sacrament. Therefore in it he would not have died.

3. Also, death comes about by the separation of soul from body. Now this sacrament contains Christ's soul as well as his body. Therefore Christ could not have died in this sacrament.

ON THE OTHER HAND the same Christ who was on the cross is present in the sacrament. And on a cross he died. Therefore in the sacrament, had it then been reserved, he would have died.

REPLY: Christ's body in this sacrament and in proper species under his own appearance is the same in substance, but not in manner, for under his own species he touches surrounding bodies through his own proper dimensions, whereas this is not so by his presence in the sacrament, as we have noted

above, see note *a*. It supposes the teaching of 3a. 50, 2–4, that Christ's dead body was not just a corpse but united to the person of the Word, as was his soul in the harrowing of hell, 3a. 52, 3.

autem prout est in hoc sacramento, ut supra dictum est.[2] Et ideo quidquid pertinet ad Christum secundum quod in se est potest attribui ei et in propria specie et in sacramento existenti, sicut vivere, mori, dolere, animatum vel inanimatum esse, et cætera hujusmodi. Quæcumque vero conveniunt ei per comparationem ad corpora extrinseca possunt ei attribui in propria specie existenti, non autem prout est in sacramento, sicut irrideri, conspui, crucifigi, flagellari, et cætera hujusmodi. Unde et quidam metrice dixerunt:

Pixide servato poteris sociare dolorem
Innatum; sed non illatus convenit illi.[3]

1. Ad primum ergo dicendum quod, sicut dictum est,[4] passio convenit corpori passo per comparationem ad agens extrinsecum. Et ideo Christus, secundum quod est sub hoc sacramento, pati non potest, potest tamen mori.

2. Ad secundum dicundum quod, sicut supra dictum est,[5] sub specie panis est corpus Christi ex vi consecrationis, sanguis autem sub specie vini. Sed nunc quidem, quando realiter sanguis Christi non est separatus ab ejus corpore, ex reali concomitantia et sanguis Christi est sub specie panis simul cum corpore, et corpus sub specie vini simul cum sanguine. Sed si tempore passionis Christi, quando realiter sanguis fuit separatus a corpore Christi, fuisset hoc sacramentum consecratum, sub specie panis fuisset solum corpus, et sub specie vini fuisset solus sanguis.

3. Ad tertium dicendum quod, sicut supra dictum est,[6] anima Christi est in hoc sacramento ex reali concomitantia, quia non est sine corpore, non autem ex vi consecrationis. Et ideo si tunc fuisset hoc sacramentum consecratum vel servatum,* quando anima erat a corpore realiter separata, non fuisset anima Christi sub hoc sacramento, non propter defectum virtutis verborum, sed propter aliam dispositionem rei.

---

*Piana: *peractum*

[2]art. 3 above

[3]Given by Albert, in *Sent.* IV, 12, 14

above.[2] And consequently whatever is attributed to Christ as he is in himself may be attributed to him both under his own proper appearances and as present in the sacrament, for instance to live, to die, to suffer, to be alive or not alive, and the like. But whatsoever is his in relationship to external bodies can be attributed to him as existing under his own proper species, but not as present under this sacrament, thus to be mocked, spat upon, scourged, and crucified. Hence the verse:

When reserved in the pyx he can grieve
from within, yet cannot be hurt from without.[3]

Hence: 1. As we have said above,[4] suffering is of a body that undergoes it in respect of some outside body. So therefore Christ in this sacrament cannot suffer. Nevertheless he can die.

2. As we have said already,[5] the body of Christ is under the species of bread, his blood under the species of wine: this is in virtue of the consecration. But now his blood is not really separated from his body; consequently his blood is present together with the body under the species of the bread, and his body with the blood under the species of the wine: this is in virtue of their concomitance in reality. At the time when Christ suffered, however, when his blood was really separated or flowed out of his body, if this sacrament had been then consecrated, the body only would have been present under the species of bread, and the blood only under the species of wine.

3. As we have explained,[6] it is by real concomitance that Christ's soul, which is not apart from his body, is present in this sacrament: it is not in virtue of the sacramental consecration. And so if this sacrament had been consecrated or reserved when his soul was really separated from his body, his soul would not have been present in this sacrament, not from any defect of the sacramental words, but because the reality was then disposed otherwise.

---

[4]body of art.
[5]3a. 76, 2
[6]3a. 76, 1 ad 1

Quæstio 82. de ministro hujus sacramenti

DEINDE CONSIDERANDUM EST de ministro hujus sacramenti; et circa hoc quæruntur decem:

1. utrum consecrare hoc sacramentum sit proprium sacerdotis;
2. utrum plures sacerdotes simul possint eandem hostiam consecrare;
3. utrum dispensatio hujus sacramenti pertineat ad solum sacerdotem;
4. utrum liceat sacerdoti consecranti a communione abstinere;
5. utrum sacerdos peccator possit conficere hoc sacramentum;
6. utrum missa mali sacerdotis minus valeat quam boni;
7. utrum hæretici, schismatici vel excommunicati possint conficere hoc sacramentum;
8. utrum degradati;
9. utrum peccent a talibus communionem recipientes;
10. utrum liceat sacerdoti omnino a celebratione abstinere.*

articulus 1. utrum consecratio hujus sacramenti sit propria sacerdotis

AD PRIMUM sic proceditur:[1] 1. Videtur quod consecratio hujus sacramenti non sit propria sacerdotis. Dictum est enim supra[2] quod hoc sacramentum consecratur virtute verborum, quæ sunt forma hujus sacramenti. Sed illa verba non mutantur, sive dicantur a sacerdote sive a quocumque alio. Ergo videtur quod non solus sacerdos, sed etiam quilibet alius possit hoc sacramentum consecrare.

2. Præterea, sacerdos hoc sacramentum conficit in persona Christi. Sed laicus sanctus est unitus Christo per caritatem. Ergo videtur quod etiam laicus possit hoc sacramentum conficere; unde et Chrysostomus dicit quod *omnis sanctus est sacerdos.*[3]

3. Præterea, sicut baptismus ordinatur ad hominum salutem, ita et hoc sacramentum, sicut ex supra dictis patet.[4] Sed etiam laicus potest baptizare, ut supra dictum est.[5] Non ergo est proprium sacerdotis conficere hoc sacramentum.

---

*The Leonine Edition prints art. 10 as art. 5, and arts 6–9 are re-numbered accordingly, arts 7–10

Question 82. the minister of this sacrament

WE NOW COME TO DISCUSS the minister of the sacrament, and here there are ten points of inquiry:

1. whether to consecrate this sacrament is proper only to a priest;
2. whether several priests can consecrate the same host;
3. whether giving this sacrament is only for priests;
4. when it is lawful for the consecrating priest not to take Communion;
5. whether a priest in sin can consecrate;
6. whether the mass of a bad priest is of less value than that of a good priest;
7. whether heretics, schismatics and excommunicates can consecrate;
8. whether those who have suffered degradation;
9. whether it is sinful to receive Communion from such;
10. whether it is lawful for a priest to refrain altogether from celebrating mass.*

article 1. *is the consecration of the sacrament proper only to priests?*

THE FIRST POINT:[1] 1. Apparently not. For it has been said[2] that this sacrament is consecrated in virtue of the words which are its form. Now these words do not alter whether they are pronounced by a priest or anyone else. So then it seems that anyone, not just a priest, can consecrate this sacrament.

2. Further, a priest effects this sacrament in the person of Christ. Yet a lay person in grace is united to Christ through charity. Consequently it seems that such a lay person can effect this sacrament. Accordingly Chrysostom holds, *Every holy person is a priest.*[3]

3. Also, this sacrament is ordained for man's salvation as Baptism is; this has already appeared.[4] But a lay person can baptize, so we have agreed.[5] To effect this sacrament, therefore, is not proper only to a priest.

---

[1]cf 3a. 67, 2. IV *Sent.* 13, 1, i & ii
[2]3a. 78, 4
[3]Pseudo-Chrysostom. *In Matt.* XLIII. On 23, 2. PG 56, 876
[4]3a. 74, 1; 79, 2
[5]3a. 67, 3

4. Præterea, hoc sacramentium perficitur in consecratione materiæ. Sed alias materias consecrare, scilicet chrisma et oleum sanctum et oleum benedictum, pertinet ad solum episcopum; quarum tamen consecratio non est tantæ dignitatis, sicut consecratio Eucharistiæ, in qua est totus Christus. Ergo non est proprium sacerdotis, sed solius Episcopi hoc sacramentum conficere.

SED CONTRA est quod Isidorus dicit in quadam epistola et habetur in *Decreto*, *Ad presbyterum pertinet sacramentum corporis et sanguinis Domini in altari Dei conficere.*[6]

RESPONSIO: Dicendum quod, sicut supra dictum est,[7] hoc sacramentum est tantæ dignitatis quod non conficitur nisi in persona Christi. Quicumque autem aliquid agit in persona alterius oportet hoc fieri per potestatem ab illo concessam. Sicut autem baptizato conceditur a Christo potestas sumendi hoc sacramentum, ita sacerdoti cum ordinatur confertur potestas hoc sacramentum consecrandi in persona Christi. Per hoc enim ponitur in gradu eorum quibus dictum est a Domino, *Hoc facite in meam commemorationem.*[8] Et ideo dicendum est quod proprium est sacerdotum conficere hoc sacramentum.

1. Ad primum ergo dicendum quod virtus sacramentalis in pluribus consistit, et non in uno tantum, sicut virtus baptismi consistit in ipsis verbis et in aqua. Unde et virtus consecrativa non solum constitit in ipsis verbis, sed etiam in potestate sacerdoti tradita in sua consecratione et ordinatione, cum ei dicitur ab episcopo, *Accipe potestatem offerendi in Ecclesia sacrificium tam pro vivis quam pro mortuis.*[9] Nam et virtus instrumentalis in pluribus instrumentis consistit, per quæ agit principale agens.

2. Ad secundum dicendum quod laicus justus unitus est Christo unione spirituali per fidem et caritatem, non autem per sacramentalem potestatem; et ideo habet spirituale sacerdotium ad offerendum spirituales hostias de quibus dicitur in *Psal.*, *Sacrificium Deo spiritus contribulatus*;[10] et *Rom.*, *Exhibeatis corpora vestra hostiam viventem.*[11] Unde et 1 *Pet.* dicitur, *Sacerdotium sanctum offerre spirituales hostias.*[12]

3. Ad tertium dicendum quod perceptio hujus sacramenti non est tantæ necessitatis sicut perceptio baptismi, ut ex supra dictis patet.[13] Et ideo licet in necessitatis articulo laicus possit baptizare, non tamen potest hoc sacramentum conficere.

---

[6] *Epist.* 1, ad Leudefredum. PL 83, 895. Gratian, 1, 25, 1. RF 1, 90
[7] 3a. 78, 1 & 4 [8] *Luke* 22, 19 [9] Roman Ordinal
[10] *Psalms* 50, 19 [11] *Romans* 12, 1 [12] 1 *Peter* 2, 5
[13] 3a. 65, 3 & 4; 73, 3; 80, 11 ad 2

4. Besides, this sacrament is accomplished in the consecration of the matter. But the consecration of materials for other sacraments, such as the chrism, the holy oil, and blessed oil, is only for a bishop.[a] Yet their consecration is not of such grandeur as that of the Eucharist where the whole Christ is present. Therefore it is not for a priest, but for a bishop alone, to consecrate this sacrament.

ON THE OTHER HAND Isidore[b] writes, and he is quoted in canon law, *It belongs to a priest to consecrate this sacrament of the Lord's body and blood upon God's altar.*[6]

REPLY: We have observed[7] that such is the dignity of this sacrament that it is effected only as in the person of Christ.[c] Now whoever performs an act in another's stead must do so through the power of that other. As a baptized person is granted by Christ the power of receiving this sacrament, so on a priest at his ordination is conferred the power of consecrating in the person of Christ. For it is by this that he ranked among those to whom the Lord said, *Do this in memory of me.*[8] So it is for priests alone to consecrate this sacrament.

Hence: 1. Sacramental virtue depends on several components, not merely one: thus the virtue of Baptism is from the words and the water.[d] Accordingly the consecrating virtue is not only in the words of consecration, but also in the power delivered to the priest when he is dedicated and ordained, when the bishop says to him, *Receive the power of offering sacrifice in the Church for the living as well as the dead.*[9e] For the instrumental power lies in the several instruments through which the principal agent works.

2. Devout layfolk are one with Christ by spiritual union through faith and charity, but not by sacramental power. They have a spiritual priesthood for offering spiritual sacrifice of which it is said, *The sacrifice acceptable to God is a broken spirit,*[10] and, *Present your bodies as a living sacrifice.*[11] And so, *To be a holy priesthood, to offer up spiritual sacrifice.*[12]

3. As is evident from what has been said,[13] the receiving of this sacrament is not of such necessity as the receiving of Baptism. So though in case of need a lay person can baptize, he cannot consecrate this sacrament.

---

[a]Chrism, a mixture of oil and balsam, used in the three sacraments that confer a character, also in other dedications. Other oils are the oil of the sick and the oil of the catechumens.

[b]St Isidore of Seville, d. 636.

[c]In the person of Christ. The minister is more closely identified with Christ here than when he acts as the instrument of the other sacraments, as is shown by the words of consecration, *This is my body . . . my blood. Conficere sacramentum,* to consecrate the sacrament, according to technical usage.

[d]cf 3a. 60, 5–7.

[e]Now not regarded as an essential part of the rite of priestly ordination.

4. Ad quartum dicendum quod episcopus accipit potestatem ut agat in persona Christi super corpus ejus mysticum, idest super Ecclesiam: quam quidem potestatem non accipit sacerdos in sua consecratione, licet possit eam habere ex episcopi commissione. Et ideo ea quæ non pertinent ad dispositionem corporis mystici non reservantur episcopo, sicut consecratio hujus sacramenti. Ad episcopum vero pertinet tradere non solum populo, sed etiam sacerdotibus ea ex quibus possunt propriis officiis uti. Et quia benedictio chrismatis, et olei sancti, et olei infirmorum, et aliorum quæ consecrantur, puta altaris, Ecclesiæ, vestium et vasorum, præstat quandam idoneitatem ad sacramenta perficienda, quæ pertinent ad officium sacerdotum, ideo tales consecrationes episcopo reservantur, tanquam principi totius ecclesiastici ordinis.

articulus 2. utrum plures sacerdotes possint unam et eandem hostiam consecrare

AD SECUNDUM sic proceditur:[1] 1. Videtur quod plures sacerdotes non possint unam et eandem hostiam consecrare; dictum est enim supra[2] quod plures non possunt simul unum baptizare. Sed non minor vis est sacerdotis consecrantis quam hominis baptizantis. Ergo etiam non possunt simul plures unam hostiam consecrare.

2. Præterea, quod potest fieri per unum superflue fit per multos. In sacramentis autem nihil debet esse superfluum. Cum ergo unus sufficiat ad consecrandum, videtur quod plures non possint unam hostiam consecrare.

3. Præterea, sicut dicit Augustinus hoc sacramentum est *sacramentum unitatis.*[3] Sed contrarium unitati esse videtur multitudo. Ergo non videtur conveniens esse huic sacramento quod plures sacerdotes eandem hostiam consecrent.

SED CONTRA est quod secundum consuetudinem quarundam ecclesiarum sacerdotes, cum de novo ordinantur, concelebrant episcopo ordinanti.

RESPONSIO: Dicendum quod, sicut dictum est,[4] sacerdos, cum ordinatur, constituitur in gradu eorum qui a Domino acceperunt potestatem consecrandi in cœna. Et ideo secundum consuetudinem quarundam ecclesiarum, sicut apostoli Christo cœnanti concœnaverunt, ita novi ordinati episcopo ordinanti concelebrant. Nec propter hoc iteratur consecratio super eandem hostiam, quia, sicut Innocentius III dicit, *omnium intentio debet ferri ad idem instans consecrationis.*[5]

---

[1]cf IV *Sent.* 13, 1, 2, ii
[2]3a. 67, 6
[3]*Super Joan.* XXVI. On 6, 41. PL 35, 1613
[4]art. 1 above
[5]*De Sacro Altaris Myst.* IV, 25. PL 217, 873

4. A bishop receives power to act in the person of Christ on his mystical body, which is the Church, which power a priest does not receive in his ordination, though he may have it by commission from the bishop.[f] Consequently such matters which do not belong to the organization of the mystical body, such as the consecration of this sacrament, are not reserved to the bishop. It belongs to the bishop to deliver, not only to the people, but also to priests such things as serve them in the fulfilment of their office. And because the blessing of chrism, the holy oil, and the oil of the sick, and other consecrated things, such as altars, vestments, sacred vessels, fits them for use in applying the sacraments, which is the function of priests, this is reserved to a bishop as to a prince in the whole ecclesiastical system.

article 2. can several priests consecrate one and the same host?

THE SECOND POINT:[1a] 1. It would seem not. We have agreed that several cannot baptize one person.[2] Now the priest's power in consecrating is not less than that of a person in baptizing. Therefore several cannot consecrate one host at the same time.

2. Besides, it is superfluous to do by many what can be done by one. And in the sacraments there should be nothing superfluous. Since one is enough for consecrating, it seems that several cannot consecrate one single host.

3. Also, Augustine speaks of the Eucharist as the *sacrament of unity.*[3] Plurality, however, seems opposed to unity. Therefore it seems inconsistent with this sacrament to have several priests consecrating the same offering.

ON THE OTHER HAND is the custom of some Churches for priests at their ordination to concelebrate with the bishop ordaining.

REPLY: As we have said,[4] a priest when ordained is ranked with those who received consecrating power from our Lord at the Last Supper. And so, according to the custom of some of the Churches, as the Apostles ate together with Christ at the Last Supper, so the newly ordained concelebrate with the ordaining bishop. Nor is the consecration on that account repeated over the same bread because, as Innocent III says,[5] *the intention of all should bear together at the same instant of the consecration.*

---

[f]cf 2a2æ. 185. Vol. 47, ed. J. Aumann.

[a]Concelebration, restored as a normal practice by Vatican II (*Constitution for the Liturgy* 57, 58). Not so firmly rooted in the West as to grow into a custom, it was unknown in the Middle Ages, apart from the mass of ordination. Durandus of Saint-Pourçain thought it dangerous, and to be put down rather than kept. Even Cajetan felt obliged to address himself to a difficulty regarding the split-second timing of the words of consecration.

1. Ad primum ergo dicendum quod Christus non legitur simul baptizasse cum apostolis quando injunxit eis officium baptizandi, et ideo non est similis ratio.

2. Ad secundum dicendum quod si quilibet sacerdotum operaretur in virtute propria, superfluerent alii celebrantes, uno sufficienter celebrante. Sed quia sacerdos non consecrat nisi in persona Christi, multi autem *sunt unum in Christo*,[6] ideo non refert utrum per unum aut per multos hoc sacramentum consecretur, nisi quod oportet ritum Ecclesiæ servari.

3. Ad tertium dicendum quod Eucharistia est sacramentum unitatis ecclesiasticæ, quæ attenditur secundum hoc quod multi sunt unum in Christo.

articulus 3. *utrum dispensatio hujus sacramenti pertineat solum ad sacerdotem*

AD TERTIUM sic proceditur:[1] 1. Videtur quod non pertineat solum ad sacerdotem dispensatio hujus sacramenti. Sanguis enim Christi non minus pertinet ad hoc sacramentum quam corpus. Sed sanguis Christi dispensatur per diaconos; unde et beatus Laurentius dixit beato Sixto, *Experire utrum idoneum ministrum elegeris, cui commisisti dominici sanguinis dispensationem.*[2] Ergo et pari ratione dispensatio corporis Christi non pertinet ad solos sacerdotes.

2. Præterea, sacerdotes constituuntur ministri sacramentorum. Sed hoc sacramentum perficitur in consecratione materiæ, non in usu, ad quem pertinet dispensatio. Ergo videtur quod non pertineat ad sacerdotem corpus Domini dispensare.

3. Præterea, Dionysius dicit[3] quod hoc sacramentum habet perfectivam virtutem, sicut et chrisma. Sed signare chrismate baptizatos non pertinet ad sacerdotem, sed ad episcopum. Ergo etiam dispensare hoc sacramentum pertinet ad episcopum, non ad sacerdotem.

SED CONTRA est quod dicitur *de Consecr.*, *Pervenit ad notitiam nostram quod quidam presbyteri laico aut feminæ corpus Domini tradunt ad deferendum infirmis. Igitur interdicit synodus ne talis præsumptio ulterius fiat, sed presbyter per semetipsum infirmos communicet.*[4]

RESPONSIO: Dicendum quod, ad sacerdotem pertinet dispensatio corporis Christi, propter tria. Primo quidem quia, sicut dictum est,[5] ipse consecrat in persona Christi. Ipse autem Christus sicut consecravit corpus suum in cœna, ita et aliis sumendum dedit. Unde sicut ad sacerdotem pertinet

---

[6] *Galatians* 3, 28

[1] cf IV *Sent.* 13, 1, 3, i & ii

[2] Matins, 2nd responsory. Dominican Breviary, 10th Aug.

Hence: 1. We do not read of Christ baptizing simultaneously with the Apostles when he committed to them the office of baptizing. And so there is no parallel.

2. Were each priest to act in his own power, then other celebrants would be superfluous and one would be enough. Yet because he does not consecrate save in the person of Christ, and many *are one in Christ*[6], it is irrelevant whether this sacrament be consecrated by one or by many, so long as the usage of the Church is observed.

3. The Eucharist is the sacrament of ecclesiastical unity, which requires that many be one in Christ.

article 3. is the dispensing of this sacrament only for a priest?

THE THIRD POINT:[1a] Apparently not. For Christ's blood is part of the sacrament no less than his body. But the blood of Christ is dispensed by deacons; St Lawrence said to St Sixtus,[b] *Try whether you have chosen a fit minister, to whom you entrusted the dispensing of the Lord's blood.*[2] With equal reason, the dispensing of the Lord's body is not for priests alone.

2. Again, priests are the appointed ministers of the sacraments. Now this sacrament is completed in the consecration of the matter, not in the application to which the dispensing belongs. So it seems then that the dispensing is not for a priest.

3. Besides, Dionysius compares[3] this sacrament to chrism for its bringing to perfection. But it is for bishops, not priests, to sign with the chrism. Likewise, therefore, this sacrament is for bishops to give, not priests.

ON THE OTHER HAND it is written in canon law, *It has come to our knowledge that some priests deliver the Lord's body to a layman or woman to carry it to the sick. Therefore the Synod forbids such presumption. Let the priest himself give Communion to the sick.*[4]

REPLY: The dispensing of Christ's body is a priest's office for three reasons. First, because, as was said above,[5] he consecrates in the person of Christ, who consecrated his body at the Last Supper and also gave it to others to receive. Accordingly as the consecrating is for a priest so also is the

---

[3]*De Eccles. Hier.* 3. PG 3, 425
[4]Gratian, *Decretum* III, 2, 29. RF I, 1323
[5]art. I above
[a]Recent legislation has extended to laypeople the office of giving Communion. The art. is to be read as a period piece, an *apologia ex convenientia* for contemporary, and perhaps provincial, practice. Note the reserve about deacons giving the host.
[b]St Lawrence, Deacon and Martyr. St Sixtus II, Pope and Martyr. Both d. 258.

consecratio corporis Christi, ita ad eum pertinet dispensatio. Secundo quia sacerdos constituitur medius inter Deum et populum; unde sicut ad eum pertinet dona populi Deo offerre, ita ad eum pertinet dona sanctificata divinitus populo tradere. Tertio quia in reverentiam hujus sacramenti, a nulla re contingitur nisi consecrata; unde et corporale et calix consecrantur, et similiter manus sacerdotis, ad tangendum hoc sacramentum; unde nulli alii tangere licet, nisi in necessitatem, puta si caderet in terram, vel in aliquo alio necessitatis casu.

1. Ad primum ergo dicendum quod diaconus quasi propinquus ordini sacerdotali aliquid participat de ejus officio, ut scilicet dispenset sanguinem, non autem corpus, nisi in necessitate, jubente episcopo vel presbytero. Primo quidem quia sanguis Christi continetur in vase, unde non oportet quod tangatur a dispensante, sicut tangitur corpus Christi. Secundo quia sanguis designat redemptionem a Christo in populum derivatam; unde et sanguini admiscetur aqua, quæ significat populum. Et quia diaconi sunt inter sacerdotem et populum magis convenit diaconis dispensatio sanguinis quam dispensatio corporis.

2. Ad secundum dicendum quod ejusdem est hoc sacramentum dispensare et consecrare, ratione jam dicta.[6]

3. Ad tertium dicendum quod sicut diaconus in aliquo participat *illuminativam virtutem*[7] sacerdotis inquantum dispensat sanguinem, ita sacerdos participat perfectivam dispensationem episcopi, inquantum dispensat hoc sacramentum, quo perficitur homo secundum se per conjunctionem ad Christum. Aliæ autem perfectiones, quibus homo perficitur per comparationem ad alios, episcopo reservantur.

articulus 4. utrum sacerdos consecrans teneatur sumere hoc sacramentum

AD QUARTUM sic proceditur:[1] 1. Videtur quod sacerdos consecrans non teneatur sumere hoc sacramentum. In aliis enim consecrationibus ille qui consecrat materiam, non utitur ea, sicut episcopus consecrans chrisma non linitur eodem. Sed hoc sacramentum consistit in consecratione materiæ. Ergo sacerdos perficiens hoc sacramentum non necesse habet uti eodem, sed potest licite a sumptione ejus abstinere.

2. Præterea, in aliis sacramentis minister non præbet sacramentum sibi ipsi; nullus enim baptizare potest seipsum, ut supra dictum est.[2] Sed sicut baptismus ordinate dispensatur, ita et hoc sacramentum. Ergo sacerdos perficiens hoc sacramentum non debet ipsum sumere a seipso.

3. Præterea, contingit quandoque quod miraculose corpus Christi in altari apparet sub specie carnis, et sanguis sub specie sanguinis; quæ non

---

[6]body of art.

dispensing. Second, a priest is the appointed intermediary between God and the people. Accordingly as it belongs to him to offer the gifts of the people to God, so also to deliver the hallowed gifts to the people.
Third, because out of reverence, nothing touches this sacrament but what is blessed, thus the corporal and chalice, and likewise the priest's hands. Nobody else may lawfully touch it, except from necessity, for instance were it to fall to the ground, or some such case.

Hence: 1. A deacon, as being close to the priestly order, has a certain share in its duties, so that he may dispense the blood, but not the body, unless in case of necessity at the bidding of a bishop or priest. First, because Christ's blood is contained in a vessel, so that, unlike the body, it need not be touched. Second, because the blood signifies redemption flowing from Christ to the people, accordingly water, symbolizing the people, is mixed with the blood. And because deacons are between priests and people, their dispensing of the blood, rather than of the body, is more fitting.

2. For the reason given above,[6] it is for the same person to consecrate and dispense this sacrament.

3. As in some measure a deacon shares in a priest's *enlightening power*[7] in dispensing the blood, so a priest shares in the crowning administration of a bishop in dispensing this sacrament, which fulfils a man in himself by union with Christ. Other blessings, however, relative to others in the Church, are reserved to a bishop.

article 4. *is the consecrating priest bound to receive this sacrament?*

THE FOURTH POINT:[1] 1. Apparently not. Because in the other sacraments he who consecrates the matter does not have it applied to himself, for instance, a bishop consecrating the chrism. This sacrament consists in the consecration of the matter. Therefore a priest effecting this sacrament need not receive it but may lawfully refrain.

2. Further, in the other sacraments the minister does not give the sacrament to himself; for instance, nobody can baptize himself; on this we have agreed.[2] And as Baptism is given in due order, so also is this sacrament. Therefore the priest effecting it ought not to receive it at his own hands.

3. Besides, a miracle sometimes happens and Christ's body on the altar appears under the appearance of flesh and his blood under that of blood,

---

[7]Dionysius, *De Eccles. Hier.* 3. PG 3, 465
[1]cf IV *Sent.* 10, 4, iii ad 2; 12, 3, 2, ii
[2]3a. 66, 5 ad 4

sunt apta cibo et potui; unde, sicut supra dictum est,[3] propter hoc alia specie traduntur, ne sint horrori sumentibus. Ergo sacerdos consecrans non semper tenetur sumere hoc sacramentum.

SED CONTRA est quod in concilio Toletano XII legitur, et habetur *de Consecrat.*, *Modis omnibus tenendum est ut quotiescumque sacrificans corpus et sanguinem Domini nostri Jesu Christi in altari immolat, toties perceptionis corporis et sanguinis Christi participem se præbeat.*[4]

RESPONSIO: Dicendum quod, sicut supra dictum est,[5] Eucharistia non solum est sacramentum, sed etiam sacrificium. Quicumque autem sacrificium offert, debet sacrificii fieri particeps, quia exterius sacrificium, quod offertur, signum est interioris sacrificii, quo quis seipsum offert Deo, ut Augustinus dicit.[6] Unde per hoc quod participat sacrificio ostendit ad se sacrificium interius pertinere. Similiter etiam per hoc quod sacrificium populo dispensat, ostendit se esse dispensatorem divinorum populo, quorum ipse primo debet esse particeps, sicut Dionysius dicit.[7] Et ideo ipse ante sumere debet quam populo dispenset. Unde et in prædicto canone legitur, *Quale est sacrificium, cui nec ipse sacrificans particeps esse dignoscitur?*[8] Per hoc autem fit particeps quod de sacrificio sumit, secundum illud Apostoli I *Cor.*, *Nonne qui edunt hostias, participes sunt altaris?*[9] Et ideo necesse est quod sacerdos quotiescumque consecrat sumat integre hoc sacramentum.

1. Ad primum ergo dicendum quod consecratio chrismatis vel cujuscumque alterius materiæ non est sacrificium, sicut consecratio Eucharistiæ; et ideo non est similis ratio.

2. Ad secundum dicendum quod sacramentum baptismi perficitur in ipso usu materiæ, et ideo nullus potest baptizare seipsum, quia in sacramento non potest esse idem agens et patiens. Unde nec in hoc sacramento sacerdos consecrat seipsum, sed panem et vinum, in qua consecratione perficitur sacramentum. Usus autem sacramenti est consequenter se habens ad hoc sacramentum, et ideo non est simile.

3. Ad tertium dicendum quod si miraculose corpus Christi in altari sub specie carnis appareat, aut sanguis sub specie sanguinis, non est sumendum. Dicit enim Origenes super *Levit.*, et habetur *de Consecrat.*, *De hac quidem hostia, quæ in Christi commemoratione mirabiliter fit edere licet; de illa vero quam Christus in ara crucis obtulit, secundum se nulli edere licet.*[10] Nec propter hoc sacerdos transgressor efficitur, quia ea quæ miraculose fiunt legibus non subduntur. Consulendum tamen esset sacerdoti quod iterato corpus et sanguinem Domini consecraret et sumeret.

---

[3] 3a. 75, 5
[4] Toledo XII, 5 (681). Mansi XI, 1033. Gratian, *Decretum* III, 2, 11. RF I, 1318

which are not suitable for food and drink, on that account, as we have seen,[3] they are given under another species to prevent revulsion in the communicant. Not always, then, is the consecrating priest bound to receive this sacrament.

ON THE OTHER HAND the acts of a Council of Toledo, repeated by canon law, state, *This must be observed thoroughly, as often as the priest offers the body and blood of our Lord Jesus Christ upon the altar he must himself behave as a partaker of the body and blood.*[4]

REPLY: We have stated[5] that the Eucharist is a sacrifice as well as a sacrament. Now whoever offers a sacrifice must also be a partaker in the sacrifice. For the outward sacrifice the priest offers is a sign of the inward sacrifice whereby he offers himself to God, as Augustine writes.[6] And so by partaking in the sacrifice he shows that inwardly it is also his. Likewise by dispensing the sacrifice to the people he shows himself to be a dispenser of divine things, of which he himself ought to be first to participate, as Dionysius says.[7] And so he ought himself to receive, before giving it to the people. Accordingly we read, *What kind of sacrifice is that in which the sacrificer is not known to have a part?*[8] Now it is by the receiving of it that he participates in it, according to St Paul, *Are not those who eat the sacrifices partners in the altar?*[9] This is why the priest, as often as he consecrates, must needs receive this sacrament in its integrity.

Hence: 1. The consecration of chrism, or any such matter, is not a sacrifice as the Eucharist is. Consequently, there is no parallel.

2. The sacrament of Baptism is accomplished in the application of its matter. So nobody can baptize himself because the same person cannot be both active and passive in a sacrament. Accordingly neither in this sacrament does the priest consecrate himself; he consecrates the bread and wine, and in this consecration the sacrament is made completely ready to be received. The reception is a consequence of the sacrament being constituted. Consequently there is no parallel.

3. If by a miracle Christ's body appeared under the guise of flesh, or his blood under that of blood, it is not to be received. Canon law quotes Origen, *It is lawful to eat of this sacrifice which is wonderfully offered in memory of Christ, but not for anybody to eat of that one which Christ offered on the altar of the cross.*[10] Nor does the priest transgress on that account, for miraculous happenings are not subject to laws. He would be well advised, nevertheless, to consecrate again and receive the Lord's body and blood.

---

[5] 3a. 79, 5 & 7
[6] *De Civit. Dei* x, 5 & 6. PL 41, 282 & 283
[7] *De Eccles. Hier.* 3. PG 3, 445
[8] Gratian loc cit note 4
[9] 1 *Corinthians* 10, 18
[10] *In Levit.* VII, on 10, 6. PG 12, 477. Gratian, III, 2, 76. RF 1, 1345

*articulus 5. utrum malus sacerdos Eucharistiam consecrare possit**

AD QUINTUM sic proceditur:[1] 1. Videtur quod malus sacerdos Eucharistiam consecrare non possit. Dicit enim Hieronymus, *Sacerdotes, qui Eucharistiæ serviunt, et sanguinem Domini populis dividunt, impie agunt in legem Christi, putantes Eucharistiam peccantis facere verba, non vitam, et necessariam esse tantum solemnem orationem, et non sacerdotis merita: de quibus dicitur, Sacerdos in quacumque fuerit macula, non accedat offerre oblationes Domino.*[2] Sed sacerdos peccator, cum sit maculosus, nec vitam habet nec merita huic convenientia sacramento. Ergo sacerdos peccator non potest consecrare Eucharistiam.

2. Præterea, Damascenus dicit quod *panis et vinum per adventum Sancti Spiritus supernaturaliter transit in corpus et sanguinem Domini.*[3] Sed Gelasius Papa dicit, sicut habetur in *Decreto*, *Quomodo ad divini mysterii consecrationem cœlestis Spiritus invocatus adveniet, si sacerdos, qui eum adesse deprecatur, criminosis plenus actionibus comprobetur?*[4] Ergo per malum sacerdotem non potest Eucharistia consecrari.

3. Præterea, hoc sacramentum sacerdotis benedictione consecratur. Sed benedictio sacerdotis peccatoris non est efficax ad consecrationem hujus sacramenti, cum scriptum sit, *Maledicam benedictionibus vestris;*[5] et Dionysius dicit, *Perfecte cecidit a sacerdotali ordine qui non est illuminatus; et audax quidem nimium mihi videtur talis, sacerdotalibus manum apponens, et audet immundas infamias (non enim dicam orationes) super divina symbola christiformiter enuntiare.*[6]

SED CONTRA est quod Augustinus dicit, *Intra Ecclesiam catholicam, in mysterio corporis et sanguinis Domini, nihil a bono majus, nihil a malo minus perficitur sacerdote, quia non in merito consecrantis, sed in verbo perficitur Creatoris, et virtute Spiritus Sancti.*[7]

RESPONSIO: Dicendum quod, sicut supra dictum est,[8] sacerdos consecrat hoc sacramentum non virtute propria, sed sicut minister Christi, in cujus persona consecrat hoc sacramentum. Non autem ex hoc ipso desinit aliquis minister esse Christi quod est malus; habet enim Dominus bonos et malos ministros seu servos. Unde Dominus dicit, *Quis putas est fidelis*

---

*Leonine: article 6

[1]cf 3a. 64, 5

[2]*Super Sophoniam* 3, 4. PL 35, 1440. *Leviticus* 21, 12 (Septuagint)

[3]*De Fide Orth.* IV, 13. PG 94, 1145

[4]Gelasius. *Epist. fragm.* VII. Ad Elphidium. Thiel 486 Gratian, II, I, I, 92. RF I, 391

[5]*Malachi* 2, 2

*article 5. can a bad priest consecrate the Eucharist?**

THE FIFTH POINT[1] It would seem not. For Jerome, commenting on *Zephaniah*, writes, *The priests who celebrate the Eucharist and distribute the Lord's blood to the people, act impiously against Christ's law, in counting that the Eucharist is wrought by words rather than by a good life, and that only the solemn prayer is requisite, and not the priest's merits, of whom it is said 'the priest who has a blemish shall not come near to offer the Lord's offerings.'*[2] A sinful priest is blemished, and his life and merits are unworthy of the sacrament. And so he cannot consecrate the Eucharist.

2. Moreover, Damascene writes that *the bread and wine by the coming of the Holy Spirit are changed supernaturally into the body and blood of the Lord.*[3] Pope Gelasius, however, writes, and he is incorporated in canon law, *How shall the Holy Spirit when invoked come to the consecration of the divine mysteries, if the priest imploring him be proved full of guilty deeds?*[4] Therefore the Eucharist is not to be consecrated by a sinful priest.

3. Besides, this sacrament is consecrated by the priest's blessing. But a sinful priest's blessing is not effective for consecrating this sacrament, since it is written, *I will curse your blessings.*[5] And Dionysius writes to the monk Demophilus,[a] *He who is not enlightened has fallen away altogether from the priestly order, and I wonder how such a man may dare to employ his hands in priestly action, and conformably with Christ utter over the divine symbols his unclean infamies, I will not call them prayers.*[6]

ON THE OTHER HAND Augustine[b] writes, *Within the Catholic Church, in the mystery of the Lord's body and blood, nothing greater is done by a good priest, nothing less is done by a bad priest, because it is not by the merits of the consecrator that the sacrament is wrought, but by the Creator's word and the power of the Holy Spirit.*[7]

REPLY: As we have said,[8] the priest consecrates this sacrament, not by his own power, but as Christ's minister in whose person he acts. However, from the fact of being wicked he does not cease to be Christ's minister, for the Lord has good and bad ministers as servants. Accordingly, he asks,

[6]*Epist.* VIII. Ad Demophilum monachum. PG 3, 1093

[7]Paschasius Radbertus. *De Corp. et Sang. Dom.* 12. PL 120, 1310. Gratian, II, I, I, 77. RF I, 385

[8]arts I, 2 ad 2, 3 above

[a]Ministerial instrumentality, 3a, 64, 5; 78, 4.

[b]Paschasius Radbertus, d. *c.* 860. In the earliest doctrinal monograph on the Eucharist.

servus, et prudens? etc., et postea subdit, *Si autem dixerit malus iste servus in corde suo*, etc.[9] Et Apostolus dicit, *Sic nos existimet homo, ut ministros Christi;* et tamen postea subdit, *Nihil mihi conscius sum; sed non in hoc justificatus sum.*[10] Erat ergo certus se esse ministrum Christi; tamen non erat certus se esse justum. Potest ergo aliquis esse minister Christi etiamsi justus non sit. Et hoc ad excellentiam Christi pertinet, cui, sicut vero Deo, serviunt non solum bona sed etiam mala, quæ per ipsius providentiam in ejus gloriam ordinantur. Unde manifestum est quod sacerdotes, etiamsi non sint justi, sed peccatores, possunt Eucharistiam consecrare.

1. Ad primum ergo dicendum quod Hieronymus per illa verba improbat errorem sacerdotum qui credebant se digne posse Eucharistiam consecrare, ex hoc solo quod sunt sacerdotes etiamsi sint peccatores; quod improbat Hieronymus per hoc quod maculosi ad altare accedere prohibentur; non tamen removetur quin, si accesserint, sit verum sacrificium quod offerunt.

2. Ad secundum dicendum quod ante illa verba Gelasius Papa præmittit, *Sacrosancta religio, quæ catholicam continet disciplinam, tantam sibi reverentiam vindicat, ut ad eam quilibet, nisi pura conscientia, non audeat pervenire.*[11] Ex quo manifeste apparet ejus intentionem esse quod peccator sacerdos non debeat ad hoc sacramentum accedere. Unde per hoc quod subdit, *quomodo cœlestis Spiritus advocatus adveniet?* intelligi oportet quod non advenit ex merito sacerdotis, sed ex virtute Christi, cujus verba profert sacerdos.

3. Ad tertium dicendum quod sicut eadem actio, inquantum fit ex prava intentione ministri, potest esse mala; bona autem, inquantum fit ex bona intentione Domini; ita benedictio sacerdotis peccatoris, inquantum ab ipso indigne fit, est maledictione digna, et quasi infamia, sive blasphemia, et non oratio reputatur; inquantum autem profertur ex persona Christi, est sancta et efficax ad sanctificandum. Unde signanter dicitur, *Maledicam benedictionibus vestris.*

articulus 6. *utrum missa mali sacerdotis minus valeat quam missa sacerdotis boni**

AD SEXTUM sic proceditur:[1] 1. Videtur quod missa sacerdotis mali non minus valeat quam missa sacerdotis boni. Dicit enim Gregorius, *Heu in quam magnum laqueum incidunt qui divina et occulta mysteria plus ab aliis sanctificata posse fieri credunt; cum unus idemque Spiritus Sanctus ea mysteria occultet, atque invisibiliter operando sanctificet.*[2] Sed hæc occulta mysteria celebrantur in missa. Ergo missa mali sacerdotis non minus valet quam missa boni.

*Leonine: article 7

Who then is the faithful and wise servant? and then goes on to speak of *that wicked servant who mutters to himself* etc.[9] And St Paul says, *This is how one should regard oneself, as minister of Christ,* and admits, *I am not aware of anything against myself, but I am not thereby acquitted.*[10] Accordingly he was certain that he was Christ's minister, but not that he was in God's grace. Consequently a man may be Christ's minister even though he be not righteous. And this is part of Christ's greatness, whom, as the true God, things serve both good and bad, since all by his providence are to his glory. And so it is clear that priests even if not righteous but sinful can consecrate the Eucharist.

Hence: 1. In those words Jerome is condemning the error of priests who believed they could consecrate the Eucharist worthily from the mere fact of being priests, even though they were sinners. He objects to this because persons blemished are forbidden to approach the altar. This does not prevent them from offering a true sacrifice if they do.

2. Before the words quoted Pope Gelasius writes, *That holy religion which holds the Catholic discipline claims such reverence that nobody unless he has a clean conscience should dare to come to it.*[11] Clearly his meaning is that a priest who is a sinner ought not to approach this sacrament. Hence when he goes on, *How shall the heavenly Spirit we plead for come?* this must be understood that he comes, not through the merits of the priest, but from the power of Christ whose words the priest utters.

3. As the same action can be both evil from the wicked intention of a servant, and good from the right intention of the master, so the blessing of a sinful priest inasmuch as he acts unworthily is deserving of a curse, and is reputed an infamy and blasphemy, not a prayer, yet inasmuch as it is pronounced in the person of Christ it is holy and effective for salvation. That is why it is written, *I will curse your blessings.*

*article 6. is the mass of a bad priest worth less than the mass of a good priest**

THE SIXTH POINT:[1] 1. It seems not. For Gregory writes, *Alas into what a great snare they fall who believe that the divine and hidden mysteries can be hallowed more by some than by others, since it is one and the same Holy Spirit who hiddenly and invisibly hallows them.*[2] Now these hidden mysteries are celebrated in the Mass. Therefore the mass of a bad priest is not worth less than the mass of a good priest.

---

[9] *Matthew* 24, 45
[10] 1 *Corinthians* 4, 1
[11] loc cit note 4
[1] cf IV *Sent.* 13, 1, 1, v
[2] Gratian, *Decretum* II, 1, 1, 84. RF 1, 387. cf Isidore, *Etymol.* VI, 19. PL 82, 255

2. Præterea, sicut baptismus traditur a ministro in virtute Christi qui baptizat, ita et hoc sacramentum in persona Christi consecratur. Sed non melior baptismus datur a meliori ministro, ut supra dictum est.[3] Ergo etiam neque melior missa est, quæ celebratur a meliori sacerdote.

3. Præterea, sicut merita sacerdotum differunt per bonum et melius ita etiam differunt per bonum et malum. Si ergo missa melioris sacerdotis est melior, sequitur quod missa mali sacerdotis sit mala, quod est inconveniens, quia *malitia ministrorum non potest redundare in Christi mysteria*, sicut Augustinus dicit.[4] Ergo neque missa melioris sacerdotis est melior.

SED CONTRA est quod habetur in *Decreto*, *Quanto sacerdotes fuerint digniores, tanto facilius in necessitatibus, pro quibus clamant, exaudiuntur.*[5]

RESPONSIO: Dicendum quod in missa duo est considerare, scilicet ipsum sacramentum, quod est principale, et orationes quæ in missa fiunt pro vivis et mortuis. Quantum ergo ad sacramentum, non minus valet missa sacerdotis mali quam boni, quia utrobique idem conficitur sacramentum. Oratio etiam quæ fit in missa potest considerari dupliciter. Uno modo inquantum habet efficaciam ex devotione sacerdotis orantis, et sic non est dubium quod missa melioris sacerdotis magis est fructuosa. Alio modo inquantum oratio in missa profertur a sacerdote in persona totius Ecclesiæ, cujus sacerdos est minister; quod quidem ministerium etiam in peccatoribus manet, sicut supra dictum est de ministerio Christi.[6] Unde etiam quantum ad hoc est fructuosa non solum oratio sacerdotis peccatoris in missa, sed etiam omnes ejus orationes quas facit in ecclesiasticis officiis in quibus gerit personam Ecclesiæ; licet orationes ejus privatæ non sint fructuosæ, secundum illud *Prov.*, *Qui declinat aures suas, ne audiat legem, oratio ejus erit execrabilis.*[7]

1. Ad primum ergo dicendum quod Gregorius loquitur ibi quantum ad sanctitatem divini sacramenti.

2. Ad secundum dicendum quod in sacramento baptismi non fiunt solemnes orationes pro omnibus fidelibus, sicut in missa. Et ideo quantum ad hoc non est simile; est autem simile quantum ad effectum sacramenti.

3. Ad tertium dicendum quod per virtutem Spiritus Sancti, qui per unitatem caritatis communicat invicem bona membrorum Christi, fit quod bonum privatum, quod est in missa sacerdotis boni, est fructuosum aliis; malum autem privatum unius hominis non potest alteri nocere, nisi per aliquem consensum, ut Augustinus dicit.[8]

---

[3] 3a. 64, 1 ad 2; 5

[4] *De Bapt. contra Donat.* 12. PL 43, 120. *Contra Epist. Parmen.* II, 12. PL 43, 69. *Contra Litt. Petiliani* II, 47. PL 43, 298

2. Further, as Baptism is conferred by the minister in the virtue of Christ who baptizes, so likewise this sacrament is consecrated in the person of Christ. We have agreed[3] that Baptism is no better when given by a worthier minister. Neither then is mass the better when celebrated by a worthier priest.

3. Again, as the merits of priests differ in the degree of good and better, so too in being good or bad. Were the mass of a better priest to be better, it follows that the mass of a bad priest would be bad. This is inaccurate, for *the wickedness of the ministers cannot redound to Christ's mysteries*, as Augustine writes.[4] Therefore neither is the mass of a better priest the better.

ON THE OTHER HAND it is stated in the *Decretum*, *The worthier the priest the more readily is he heard in the needs for which he prays.*[5]

REPLY: There are two points to consider in the mass, namely the sacrament itself, which is chief, and the prayers offered therein for the living and the dead. As for the first, the mass of a bad priest is no less worth than the mass of a good priest, for by both the same sacrament is wrought. As for the prayers, they can be considered in two respects. First, in so far as they have efficacy from the devotion of the priest who prays, and here there is no doubt that the mass of a better priest is more fruitful. Second, in so far as they are said in the person of the whole Church, of which the priest is the minister. This ministry remains even in the case of sinful men, as was noticed above when speaking of Christ's ministry.[6] Accordingly, with regard to this, the prayers even of a sinful priest are fruitful, not only those of the mass, but also those he says in the ecclesiastical office in which he acts in the person of the Church. Notwithstanding his private prayers are not fruitful, according to *Proverbs*, *He that turns his ears from hearing the Law, his prayer is an abomination.*[7]

Hence: 1. The quotation refers to the holiness of the divine sacrament.

2. In the sacrament of Baptism solemn prayers are not made for all the faithful as in the mass. And so there is no parallel in this respect, though there is resemblance with regard to the sacramental effect.

3. By the power of the Holy Spirit who, through the union of charity, grants to each the blessings of being members of Christ, his personal goodness makes a priest's mass fruitful for others. But his personal evil cannot harm another, unless the other in some way consents, as Augustine remarks.[8]

---

[5]Gratian, II, I, I, 91. RF I, 391 [6]art. 5 above [7]*Proverbs* 28, 9
[8]*Contra Epist. Parmen.* II, 17 & 21. PL 43, 78 & 80

*articulus 7. utrum hæretici, schismatici et excommunicati possint consecrare**

AD SEPTIMUM sic proceditur:[1] 1. Videtur quod hæretici, schismatici et excommunicati Eucharistiam consecrare non possint. Dicit enim Augustinus quod *extra Ecclesiam catholicam non est locus veri sacrificii*;[2] et Leo Papa dicit (habetur in Decret.), *Aliter*, scilicet quam in Ecclesia, quæ corpus Christi est, *nec rata sunt sacerdotia nec vera sacrificia.*[3] Sed hæretici, schismatici et excommunicati sunt ab Ecclesia separati. Ergo non possunt verum sacrificium conficere.

2. Præterea, sicut ibidem legitur, Innocentius I Papa dicit, *Arianos cæterasque ejusmodi pestes, quia laicos eorum sub imagine pœnitentiæ suscipimus, non videtur clericos eorum cum sacerdotii, aut cujuspiam ministerii suscipi debere dignitate, quibus solum baptisma ratum esse permittimus.*[4] Sed non potest aliquis consecrare Eucharistiam, nisi sit cum sacerdotii dignitate. Ergo hæretici et cæteri hujusmodi non possunt Eucharistiam consecrare.

3. Præterea, ille qui est extra Ecclesiam non videtur aliquid posse agere in persona totius Ecclesiæ. Sed sacerdos consecrans Eucharistiam hoc agit in persona totius Ecclesiæ, quod patet ex hoc quod omnes orationes proponit in persona Ecclesiæ. Ergo videtur quod illi qui sunt extra Ecclesiam, scilicet hæretici, schismatici et excommunicati, non possint consecrare Eucharistiam.

SED CONTRA est quod Augustinus dicit, *Sicut Baptismus in eis*, scilicet hæreticis, schismaticis et excommunicatis, *ita ordinatio mansit integra.*[5] Sed ex vi ordinationis sacerdos potest consecrare Eucharistiam. Ergo hæretici, schismatici et excommunicati, cum in eis maneat ordinatio integra, videtur quod possint consecrare Eucharistiam.

RESPONSIO: Dicendum quod quidam[6] dixerunt quod hæretici, schismatici et excommunicati, quia sunt extra Ecclesiam, non possunt conficere hoc sacramentum. Sed in hoc decipiuntur, quia, sicut Augustinus dicit, *aliud est aliquid omnino non habere, aliud autem non recte habere*; et similiter etiam *est aliud non dare, et aliud non recte dare.*[7] Illi igitur qui intra Ecclesiam constituti receperunt potestatem consecrandi Eucharistiam in ordinatione sacerdotii, recte quidem habent potestatem, sed non recte ea

---

*Leonine: article 8

[1]cf 3a. 64, 9 ad 2. IV *Sent.* 13, 1, 1, iii; 19, 1, 2, iii ad 1. *Quodl.* XII, 11, 1

[2]Prosper of Aquitaine, *Sent.* 15. PL 41, 430

[3]*Epist.* LXXX. 2 Ad Anatolium. PL 20, 614. Gratian II, 1, 1, 68. RF 1, 382

article 7. heretics, schismatics, and excommunicates, can they consecrate?[*a]

THE SEVENTH POINT:[1] 1. It seems not. For Augustine[b] writes that *outside the Catholic Church there is no place for the true sacrifice.*[2] And Pope Leo writes, and he is repeated by canon law, *Elsewhere*, that is than in the Church, which is Christ's body, *there is no valid priesthood nor true sacrifice.*[3] Heretics, schismatics, and excommunicates are separated from the Church. Therefore they are unable to consecrate the true sacrifice.

2. Again, the *Decretum* quotes Pope Innocent I,[c] *As for Arians, and other pests, if we receive their laity if they seem to repent, it does not follow that their clerics are received with the dignity of the priesthood or of any other office, only their baptism is allowed.*[4] But none can consecrate the Eucharist unless he have the dignity of the priesthood. Therefore heretics and the like cannot consecrate the Eucharist.

3. Besides, one outside the Church cannot do anything in the person of the Church. Now when a priest consecrates the Eucharist he does so in the person of the whole Church, as is evident from his putting up all prayers in the person of the Church. So then it seems that those who are outside the Church, such as heretics, schismatics, and excommunicates, cannot consecrate the Eucharist.

ON THE OTHER HAND there is Augustine, *Just as Baptism remains in them*, namely heretics, schismatics, and excommunicates, *so do their Holy Orders remain entire.*[5] Now in virtue of his ordination a priest can consecrate the Eucharist. Since their Orders remain intact it appears that heretics, schismatics, and excommunicates, can consecrate the Eucharist.

REPLY: Some[6] held that heretics, schismatics, and excommunicates, because they are outside the Church, cannot effect the sacrament. In this, however, they are mistaken. For, as Augustine remarks, *it is one thing not to have something altogether, another not to have it rightly; and likewise it is one thing not to bestow, and another not to bestow rightly.*[7] Accordingly such as are within the Church receive the power of consecrating the

---

[4]Gratian, ibid 73. RF I, 384. Innocent I, *Epist.* XXIV, 3. PL. 20, 549
[5]*Contra Epist. Parmen.* II, 13. PL 43, 70
[6]cf Pelagius I. Mansi IX, 732. Gerhoh of Reichersberg, PL 194, 1204 & 1363. Pseudo-Hugh of St Victor, PL 176, 146. Peter of Poitiers, PL 211, 1256
[7]loc cit note 5
[a]Arts 7–9 develop the teaching of St Augustine against the Donatists.
[b]Prosper of Aquitaine, d. *c.* 463. [c]St Innocent I, d. 417.

utuntur, si postmodum per hæresim, aut schisma, vel excommunicationem ab Ecclesia separantur. Qui autem sic separati ordinantur, nec recte habent potestatem nec recte utuntur. Quod tamen utrique potestatem habeant, patet per hoc quod, sicut Augustinus ibidem dicit,[8] cum redeunt ad unitatem Ecclesiæ, non reordinantur, sed recipiuntur in suis ordinibus. Et quia consecratio Eucharistiæ est actus consequens ordinis potestatem, illi qui sunt ab Ecclesia separati per hæresim, aut schisma, vel excommunicationem, possunt quidem consecrare Eucharistiam, quæ ab eis consecrata verum corpus et sanguinem Christi continet; non tamen hoc recte faciunt, sed peccant facientes; et ideo fructum sacrificii non percipiunt, quod est sacrificium spirituale.

1. Ad primum ergo dicendum quod auctoritates illæ et similes intelligendæ sunt quantum ad hoc quod non recte extra Ecclesiam sacrificium offertur. Unde extra Ecclesiam non potest esse spirituale sacrificium, quod est verum veritate fructus, licet sit verum veritate sacramenti; sicut etiam supra dictum est[9] quod peccator sumit corpus Christi sacramentaliter, sed non spiritualiter.

2. Ad secundum dicendum quod solus baptismus permittitur esse ratus hæreticis et schismaticis, quia possunt licite baptizare in articulo necessitatis; in nullo autem casu licite possunt Eucharistiam consecrare, vel alia sacramenta conferre.

3. Ad tertium dicendum quod sacerdos in missa in orationibus quidem loquitur in persona Ecclesiæ, in cujus unitate consistit; sed in consecratione sacramenti loquitur in persona Christi, cujus vicem in hoc gerit per ordinis potestatem. Et ideo si sacerdos ab unitate Ecclesiæ præcisus missam celebret, quia potestatem ordinis non amittit, consecrat verum corpus et sanguinem Christi, sed quia est ab Ecclesiæ unitate separatus, orationes ejus efficaciam non habent.

articulus 8. *utrum sacerdos degradatus possit hoc sacramentum conficere**

AD OCTAVUM sic proceditur:[1] 1. Videtur quod sacerdos degradatus non possit hoc sacramentum conficere. Nullus enim conficit hoc sacramentum nisi per potestatem consecrandi, quam habet. Sed *degradatus non habet potestatem consecrandi, licet habeat potestatem baptizandi*, ut dicit canon in appendice Gratiani.[2] Ergo videtur quod presbyter degradatus non possit Eucharistiam consecrare.

---

*Leonine: article 9

[8]loc cit note 5

[9]3a. 80, 3

Eucharist at their priestly ordination rightly have the power, but they use it not rightly if afterward they are separated from the Church by heresy, schism, or excommunication. Such as are ordained while so separated neither have the power rightly nor do they use it rightly. But that they have the power indeed is clear from the fact, noted by Augustine,[8] that when they return to the Church they are not re-ordained, but are received in their Orders. And because the consecration of the Eucharist is an act based on the power of Holy Orders, those who are separated from the Church by heresy, schism, or excommunication, are able to consecrate the Eucharist, which when consecrated contains Christ's true body and blood; yet they act not rightly and sin by so doing. Consequently they do not gather the fruit of the sacrifice, which is a spiritual sacrifice.

Hence: 1. Such and similar authoritative texts are to be taken to refer to the sacrifice not rightly being offered outside the Church. It cannot be the true spiritual sacrifice, that is truly fruitful, though it is authentically sacramental. As we have said,[9] a sinner receives Christ's body sacramentally, but not spiritually.

2. Only Baptism is allowed to be certain when conferred by heretics and schismatics, for these may lawfully baptize in case of necessity. But in no case can they lawfully consecrate the Eucharist or confer other sacraments.

3. In reciting the prayers of the mass the priest speaks in the person of the Church. In consecrating the sacrament, however, he speaks in the person of Christ, whose role he plays by the power of Holy Orders. If, therefore, a priest cut off from the unity of the Church celebrates mass, since he has not lost the power of Holy Orders, he consecrates the true body and blood, but because he is apart from the unity of the Church, his prayers have no effectiveness.[d]

*article 8. can a canonically degraded priest consecrate this sacrament?**

THE EIGHTH POINT:[1a] 1. Apparently not. For no one can consecrate except he have the power. Yet it is pointed out in canon law that a priest *who has been degraded does not have the power of consecrating, though he has the power of baptizing.*[2] So then it seems that he cannot consecrate the Eucharist.

---

[1]cf IV *Sent.* 13, 1, 1, iv. *Quodl.* XII, 11, 1

[2]*Decretum* II, 1, 1, 97 append. RF 1, 395

[d]i.e. as prayers of the Church.

[a]Degradation: canonical penalty of deposition from office, reduction to ranks.

2. Præterea, ille qui aliquid dat potest etiam auferre. Sed episcopus dat presbytero potestatem consecrandi, ordinando ipsum. Ergo etiam potest ei auferre degradando eum.

3. Præterea, sacerdos per degradationem aut amittit potestatem consecrandi aut solam executionem. Sed non solam executionem, quia sic non plus admitteret degradatus quam excommunicatus, qui etiam executione caret. Ergo videtur quod amittat potestatem consecrandi; et ita videtur quod non possit conficere hoc sacramentum.

SED CONTRA est quod Augustinus probat quod apostatæ a fide *non carent baptismate*, per hoc *quod per pœnitentiam redeuntibus non restituitur, et ideo amitti non posse judicatur.*[3] Sed similiter degradatus, si reconcilietur, non est iterum ordinandus. Ergo non amisit potestatem consecrandi, et ita sacerdos degradatus potest conficere hoc sacramentum.

RESPONSIO: Dicendum quod potestas consecrandi Eucharistiam pertinet ad characterem sacerdotalis ordinis. Character autem quilibet, quia cum quadam consecratione datur, indelebilis est, ut supra dictum est,[4] sicut et quarumcumque rerum consecrationes perpetuæ sunt, nec amitti nec reiterari possunt. Unde manifestum est quod potestas consecrandi non amittitur per degradationem. Dicit enim Augustinus, *Utrumque*, scilicet baptismus et ordo, *sacramentum est, et quadam consecratione utrumque homini datur; illud, cum baptizatur; istud, cum ordinatur; ideoque non licet a Catholicis utrumque iterari.*[5] Et sic patet quod sacerdos degradatus potest conficere hoc sacramentum.

1. Ad primum ergo dicendum quod canon ille non loquitur assertive, sed inquisitive, sicut ex circumstantia litteræ haberi potest.

2. Ad secundum dicendum quod episcopus non dat potestatem sacerdotalis ordinis propria virtute, sed instrumentaliter, sicut minister Dei, cujus effectus per hominem tolli non potest, secundum illud *Matt.*, *Quod Deus conjunxit, homo non separet.*[6] Et ideo episcopus non potest hanc potestatem auferre, sicut nec ille qui baptizat, potest auferre characterem baptismalem.

3. Ad tertium dicendum quod excommunicatio est medicinalis. Et ideo excommunicatis non aufertur executio sacerdotalis potestatis quasi in perpetuum, sed ad correctionem usque ad tempus; degradatis autem aufertur executio, quasi in perpetuum condemnatis.

---

[3]*Contra Epist. Parmen.* II, 13. PL 43, 72
[4]3a. 63, 5
[5]loc cit note 3

2. Besides, he who gives can take away. But the bishop in ordaining gives the power to consecrate. Therefore he can take it away by degrading the priest.

3. Again, by degradation a priest loses either the power of consecration or the exercise of it. Not just the latter, for so he would lose no more than an excommunicate does, who also is deprived of exercising his Orders. Therefore it would seem that he loses the power of consecrating, and consequently cannot effect the sacrament.

ON THE OTHER HAND Augustine shows that apostates from the faith *are not deprived of their Baptism* from the fact *that it is not granted again when they return repentant, and therefore it is judged that it cannot be lost.*[3] Likewise a priest who has been canonically degraded when reconciled has not to be re-ordained. Therefore he has not lost the power of consecrating, and so can effect this sacrament.

REPLY: The power to consecrate comes from the sacramental character of priestly Orders. Now every sacramental character, since it is given with a certain dedication, is indelible, as we have noted above,[4] just as the dedication of any other thing is perpetual, and cannot either be lost or repeated. Clearly then the power to consecrate is not lost by degradation. Augustine writes of Baptism and Orders, *Both are sacraments, both are given to men with a certain dedication, the first when they are baptized, the second when they are ordained. Consequently it is not lawful for Catholics to repeat either of them.*[5] So it is evident that a canonically degraded priest can effect this sacrament.

Hence: 1. That particular canon is not laying down the law, but opening an inquiry, as may be gathered from the context.

2. The bishop does give priestly power by a causality, not his own as principal, but instrumental as God's minister, the effect of which man cannot take away; *What God has joined together, let no man put asunder.*[6b] Consequently the bishop cannot take this power away, just as neither can he who baptizes take away the baptismal character.

3. Excommunication is medicinal. Accordingly the exercise of priestly power is taken away from an excommunicate, not perpetually, but temporarily for his amendment. However it is taken away by canonical degradation as though by a life sentence.

---

[6] *Matthew* 19, 6

[b] A characteristically medieval use of the accommodated sense of Scripture.

*articulus 9. utrum liceat ab excommunicatis vel hæreticis seu peccatoribus communionem recipere et eorum missam audire**

AD NONUM sic proceditur:[1] 1. Videtur quod aliquis licite possit communionem recipere a sacerdotibus hæreticis vel excommunicatis vel etiam peccatoribus, et ab eis missam audire. Sicut enim Augustinus contra Petilianum dicit, *neque in homine bono, neque in homine malo aliquis Dei fugiat sacramenta.*[2] Sed sacerdotes, quamvis sint peccatores et hæretici vel excommunicati, verum conficiunt sacramentum. Ergo videtur quod non sit vitandum ab eis communionem accipere, vel eorum missam audire.

2. Præterea, corpus Christi verum figurativum est corporis mystici, sicut supra dictum est.[3] Sed a prædictis sacerdotibus verum corpus Christi consecratur. Ergo videtur quod illi qui sunt de corpore mystico possint eorum sacrificiis communicare.

3. Præterea, multa peccata sunt graviora quam fornicatio. Sed non est prohibitum audire missas sacerdotum aliter peccantium. Ergo etiam non debet esse prohibitum audire missas sacerdotum fornicariorum.

SED CONTRA est quod canon dicit, *Nullus missam audiat sacerdotis quem indubitanter concubinam novit habere*;[4] et Gregorius dicit quod *pater perfidus Arianum episcopum misit ad filium, ut de ejus manu sacrilegæ consecrationis communionem perciperet. Sed vir Deo deditus Ariano episcopo venienti exprobravit, ut debuit.*[5]

RESPONSIO: Dicendum quod, sicut supra dictum est,[6] sacerdotes, si sint hæretici, vel schismatici vel excommunicati vel etiam peccatores, quamvis habeant potestatem consecrandi Eucharistiam, non tamen ea recte utuntur, sed peccant utentes. Quicumque autem communicat alicui in peccato ipse particeps peccati efficitur. Unde et in II *Canonica Joannis* dicitur quod *qui dixerit ei, Ave,* scilicet hæretico, *communicat operibus illius malignis.*[7] Et ideo non licet a prædictis communionem accipere, aut eorum missam audire.

Differt tamen inter prædictas sectas: nam hæretici, et schismatici, et excommunicati, sunt per sententiam Ecclesiæ executione consecrandi privati. Et ideo peccat quicumque eorum missam audit, vel ab eis accipit sacramenta. Sed non omnes peccatores sunt per sententiam Ecclesiæ executione hujus potestatis privati. Et sic quamvis sint suspensi quantum ad se ex sententia divina, non tamen quantum ad alios ex sententia Ecclesiæ. Et ideo usque ad sententiam Ecclesiæ licet ab eis communionem accipere,

---

*Leonine: article 10

[1]cf 3a. 64, 9 ad 3. IV *Sent.* 13, 1, 3, iii. *Quodl.* XII, 11, 1

[2]*Epist. contra Petilianum* III, 9. PL 43, 563. Gratian, II, 1, 1, 36. RF 1, 372

*article 9. is it lawful to receive Communion from or assist at masses of heretical, schismatic, or sinful priests?**

THE NINTH POINT:[1] 1. Yes, so it seems. Because, as Augustine writes, *One should not shun God's sacrament be the man good or bad.*[2] And priests, whether sinners, heretics, excommunicates, effect a valid sacrament. It seems, therefore, that receiving Communion from them or hearing their mass is not to be avoided.

2. Again, Christ's true body is figurative of his mystical body, as has been said.[3] The priests in question consecrate the true body of Christ. Therefore those of the mystical body may communicate in their sacrifices.

3. Besides, there are many crimes graver than fornication. Yet it is not forbidden to hear the masses of priests who sin otherwise. Nor, therefore, of those who are fornicators.

ON THE OTHER HAND a canon lays down, *Let no man hear the mass of a priest whom he knows beyond doubt keeps a concubine.*[4] And Gregory tells of *a trustless father sent an Arian bishop to his son to receive at his hands communion of sacrilegious consecration, but when the bishop arrived the son, faithful to God, rebuked him, as was right.*[5]

REPLY: As we have said,[6] priests, whether heretics, schismatics, excommunicates, or even sinful, though they have the power of consecrating the Eucharist, do not rightly exercise their power, but sin in so doing. Now whoever communicates with another in sin becomes a sharer in the sin; thus we read in the second Canonical Epistle, *He who greets him, namely a heretic, shares his wicked work.*[7] And so it is not lawful to receive Communion from them or assist at their masses.

Still, they fall into different classes. For heretics, schismatics, and excommunicates, by sentence of the Church, have been deprived of the exercise of consecrating, so that whoever hears their mass or receives sacraments from them commits sin. Whereas not all sinners are debarred by sentence of the Church from exercising the power of consecrating. As for themselves they are suspended by divine sentence, but as for others not by the sentence of the Church. Consequently until the Church's sentence is pronounced, it is lawful to receive Communion from them and

---

[3] 3a. 67, 2; 73, 2; 80, 4
[4] Gratian, I, 32, 5. RF I, 117
[5] *Dialog.* III, 31. PL 77, 383. Gratian, II, I, I, 71. RF I, 383
[6] arts 5 ad I; 7 & 8
[7] II *John* II

et eorum missam audire. Unde super illud 1 *Cor.*, *Cum hujusmodi nec cibum sumere,*[8] dicit Glossa Augustini, *Hoc dicendo noluit hominem ab homine judicari ex arbitrio suspicionis, vel etiam extraordinario usurpato judicio, sed potius ex lege Dei, secundum ordinem Ecclesiæ, sive ultro confessum, sive accusatum et convictum.*[9]

1. Ad primum ergo dicendum quod in hoc quod refugimus audire missas talium sacerdotum, aut ab eis communionem recipere, non refugimus Dei sacramenta, sed potius ea veneramur (unde hostia a talibus sacerdotibus consecrata est adoranda, et si reservetur, licite potest sumi a sacerdote legitimo); sed refugimus culpam indigne ministrantium.

2. Ad secundum dicendum quod unitas corporis mystici est fructus corporis veri percepti. Illi autem qui indigne percipiunt vel ministrant, privantur fructu, ut supra dictum est.[10] Et ideo non est sumendum ex eorum dispensatione sacramentum ab eis qui sunt in unitate Ecclesiæ.

3. Ad tertium dicendum quod licet fornicatio non sit gravior cæteris peccatis, tamen ad eam proniores sunt homines propter carnis concupiscentiam. Et ideo specialiter hoc peccatum sacerdotibus prohibitum est ab Ecclesia, et ne aliquis audiat missam concubinarii sacerdotis. Sed hoc intelligendum est de notorio, vel *per sententiam* quæ fertur in convictum, vel *per confessionem in jure factam*, vel per evidentiam facti, quando non potest peccatum *aliqua tergiversatione celari.*[11]

articulus 10. *utrum liceat sacerdoti omnino a consecratione Eucharistiæ abstinere**

AD DECIMUM sic proceditur:[1] 1. Videtur quod liceat sacerdoti omnino a consecratione Eucharistiæ abstinere. Sicut enim ad officium sacerdotis pertinet Eucharistiam consecrare, ita etiam baptizare et in aliis sacramentis ministrare. Sed sacerdos non tenetur ministrare in aliis sacramentis, nisi propter curam animarum susceptam. Ergo videtur quod nec etiam teneatur Eucharistiam consecrare, si curam non habeat animarum.

2. Præterea, nullus tenetur facere quod sibi non licet; alioquin esset perplexus. Sed sacerdoti peccatori vel etiam excommunicato non licet Eucharistiam consecrare, ut supra dictum est.[2] Ergo videtur quod tales non teneantur ad celebrandum, et ita nec alii; alioquin ex sua culpa commodum reportarent.

3. Præterea, dignitas sacerdotalis non perditur per subsequentem infirmitatem; dicit enim Gelasius Papa, et habetur in *Decreto*, *Sicut præcepta canonica non patiuntur venire ad sacerdotium debiles corpore, ita si quis in eo*

*Leonine: article 5

[8]1 *Corinthians* 5, 11

[9]*Ordinaria.* Augustine, *Serm. ad Pop.* CCCLI, 4. PL 39, 547. Lombard. PL 191, 1575

[10]3a. 80, 4. art. 7 above

[11]*Decretals of Gregory* IX, III, 2, 10. RF II, 457

assist at their mass. Accordingly on the text, *With such a one do not eat*,[8] the Gloss from Augustine comments, *In saying this Paul was unwilling for a man to be judged by his fellow man on arbitrary suspicion or out of the ordinary by unwarranted judgement, but rather by God's law according to Church order, on his own confession or when convicted of the charge.*[9]

Hence: 1. By refusing to assist at the mass of such priests or receive communion from them, we do not shun God's sacraments, but rather honour them; accordingly a host consecrated by them is to be worshipped and, if reserved, may be lawfully consumed by a legitimate priest. What we shun is the fault of those who minister unworthily.

2. The unity of the mystical body is the fruit of the true body which is received. Those who unworthily receive or minister are deprived of the fruit, as we have said.[10] So then from them the sacrament is not to be received by those in the unity of faith.

3. Though fornication is not graver than other sins, yet men are more prone to it owing to the lust of the flesh. Accordingly this sin is particularly forbidden to priests by the Church, lest anyone assist at the mass of one living in concubinage. This, however, is to be understood of one who is notorious, either from being convicted and *sentenced*, or *by an acknowledgement of guilt in juridical form, or by plain evidence of the facts from which he cannot shuffle away.*[11]

*article 10. is it lawful for a priest to refrain altogether from consecrating the Eucharist?**

THE TENTH POINT:[1] 1. Yes, so it seems. For it is a priest's office to consecrate the Eucharist as it is to baptize and administer the other sacraments. Yet he is not bound to administer the other sacraments unless he has undertaken the care of souls. If he has not this charge it seems that he is not bound to consecrate the Eucharist.

2. Besides, no one is bound to do what he may not lawfully do: otherwise he would be caught in a trap.[a] Now it is not lawful for a priest who is in a state of sin or who is an excommunicate to consecrate the Eucharist, as we have agreed.[2] Therefore he is not bound, apparently, to consecrate. So too other priests in a like case, otherwise they could take advantage of their fault.

3. Also, the priestly dignity is not lost by subsequent weakness. Pope Gelasius writes, and is quoted in canon law, *As the canonical commands do not allow the feeble in body to the priesthood, so if anyone in that dignity*

[1]cf IV *Sent.* 13, 1, 2, i

[2]arts. 5 ad 1; 7 above

[a]*Perplexus*, entangled, involved in a dilemma of sinning whatever is done, or in a condition where all of the options are wrong.

fuerit constitutus, ac tunc fuerit sauciatus, amittere non potest quod tempore suæ sinceritatis accepit.[3] Contingit autem quandoque quod ordinati in sacerdotes incurrunt aliquos defectus, ex quibus a celebratione impediuntur, sicut est lepra vel morbus caducus, vel aliquid aliud hujusmodi. Non ergo videtur quod sacerdotes ad celebrandum teneantur.

SED CONTRA est quod dicit Ambrosius in quadam oratione, *Grave est quod ad mensam tuam mundo corde et manibus innocentibus non venimus; sed gravius est si dum peccata metuimus, etiam sacrificium non reddamus.*[4]

RESPONSIO: Dicendum quod quidam[5] dixerunt quod sacerdos potest omnino a consecratione licite abstinere, nisi teneatur ex cura sibi commissa celebrare, et pro populo sacramenta præbere. Sed hoc irrationabiliter dicitur, quia unusquisque tenetur uti gratia sibi data cum fuerit opportunum, secundum illud II ad *Cor.*, *Exhortamur ne in vacuum gratiam Dei recipiatis.*[6] Opportunitas autem sacrificium offerendi non solum attenditur per comparationem ad fideles Christi quibus oportet sacramenta ministrari, sed principaliter per comparationem ad Deum, cui consecratione hujus sacramenti sacrificium offertur. Unde sacerdoti, etiamsi non habeat curam animarum, non licet omnino a celebratione cessare; sed saltem videtur quod celebrare teneatur in præcipuis festis, et maxime in illis diebus in quibus fideles communicare consueverunt. Et hinc est quod II *Machab.*, contra quosdam sacerdotes dicitur quod *jam non circa altaris officia dediti erant, contempto templo et sacrificiis neglectis.*[7]

1. Ad primum ergo dicendum quod alia sacramenta perficiuntur in usu fidelium, et ideo in illis ministrare non tenetur nisi ille qui super fideles suscipit curam. Sed hoc sacramentum perficitur in consecratione Eucharistiæ, in qua sacrificium Deo offertur, ad quod sacerdos obligatur Deo ex ordine jam suscepto.

2. Ad secundum dicendum quod sacerdos peccator, si per sententiam Ecclesiæ sit executione ordinis privatus vel simpliciter vel ad tempus, redditus est impotens ad sacrificium offerendum; et ideo obligatio tollitur. Hoc autem cedit ei in detrimentum spiritualis fructus magis quam in emolumentum. Si vero non sit privatus potestate celebrandi, non solvitur obligatio; nec tamen perplexus est, quia potest de peccato pœnitere et celebrare.

3. Ad tertium dicendum quod debilitas vel ægritudo superveniens ordini sacerdotali ordinem non tollit; executionem tamen ordinis impedit

---

[3]Gelasius I, *Epist. fragm.* IX, Ad Palladium. Thiel 488. Gratian, I, 55, 12. RF I, 218
[4]Anselm, *Orat.* XXXIII. PL 158, 926
[5]cf Alexander of Hales, *Summa Theol.* IV, 50, 2. Bonaventure, *Sent.* IV, 12, 2, 2

becomes disabled, he cannot lose what he received when he was sound.[3] But it sometimes happens that the already ordained priests incur defects which prevent them from celebrating, such as leprosy or epilepsy, or the like. Consequently it does not seem that priests are bound to celebrate.

ON THE OTHER HAND Ambrose[b] says in a prayer, *It is a grave matter if we do not approach your altar with heart and hands clean and innocent, but it is graver still if while shunning sin we also fail to offer sacrifice.*[4]

REPLY: Some[5] have held that a priest may lawfully refrain altogether from consecrating unless he is bound by his charge to celebrate mass for the people and provide the sacraments. But the opinion is unreasonable. Everyone is bound to use the grace given him when opportunity serves, according to St Paul, *We exhort you that you receive not the grace of God in vain.*[6] For the opportunity of offering sacrifice is to be valued with reference not only to Christ's faithful, to whom the sacraments must be ministered, but also, and chiefly, to God to whom the sacrifice of this sacrament by consecration is offered. Accordingly it is not lawful for a priest, even if he does not have the care of souls, to cease altogether from celebrating; he seems to be bound to celebrate at least on the chief festival days, and especially when the faithful are accustomed to communicate. Hence it was complained against some priests, that *they were not now occupied about the offices of the altar, despising the Temple and neglecting the sacrifices.*[7]

Hence: 1. The other sacraments are accomplished in being used by the faithful. And so he alone is bound to minister them who has undertaken the care of souls. This sacrament, however, is accomplished in the consecration of the Eucharist in which a sacrifice is offered to God, and to this a priest is obliged on account of the Holy Orders he has received.

2. A sinful priest, if deprived by the Church's sentence of the exercise of his Orders, for life or for a period, is rendered incapable of offering sacrifice, consequently the obligation is removed. This indeed is to his loss of spiritual fruit rather than to his gain. If not so deprived, however, his obligation does not lapse. Nor is he caught between two evils, for he can repent of his sin and celebrate.

3. Weakness or sickness coming on after a priest's ordination does not deprive him of his Orders, but hinders him from exercising them with

---

[b]St Anselm of Canterbury, d. 1109.

[6] II *Corinthians* 6, 1

[7] II *Maccabees* 4, 14

quantum ad consecrationem Eucharistiæ, quandoque quidem propter impossibilitatem executionis, sicut si privetur oculis, aut digitis, aut usu linguæ; quandoque autem propter periculum, sicut patet de eo qui patitur morbum caducum, vel etiam quamcumque alienationem mentis; quandoque propter abominationem, sicut patet de leproso, qui non debet publice celebrare; potest tamen missam dicere occulte, nisi lepra adeo invaluerit, quod per corrosionem membrorum eum ad hoc reddiderit impotentem.

respect to the consecration of the Eucharist. Sometimes it renders this impossible, as when he loses his sight, or his fingers, or the use of his speech. Sometimes there is danger of accident, as in one suffering from epilepsy or who has lost his wits. Sometimes on account of distress to the congregation, thus a leper should not celebrate in public, though he can say mass privately, unless the leprosy has eaten away his limbs so far as to render him incapable.

Quæstio 83. de ritu hujus sacramenti

DEINDE CONSIDERANDUM EST de ritu hujus sacramenti, et circa hoc quæruntur sex:

1. utrum in celebratione hujus mysterii Christus immoletur;
2. de tempore celebrationis;
3. de loco et aliis quæ pertinent ad apparatum hujus celebrationis;
4. de his quæ in celebratione hujus mysterii dicuntur;
5. de his quæ circa celebrationem hujus sacramenti fiunt;
6. de defectibus qui circa celebrationem hujus sacramenti occurrunt.

articulus 1. *utrum in hoc sacramento Christus immoletur*

AD PRIMUM sic proceditur:[1] 1. Videtur quod in celebratione hujus sacramenti Christus non immoletur. Dicitur enim *Heb.* quod *Christus una oblatione consummavit in sempiternum sanctificatos.*[2] Sed illa oblatio fuit ejus immolatio. Christus ergo non immolatur in celebratione hujus sacramenti.

---

[1]cf 3a. 22, 3 ad 2; 73, 4. IV *Sent.* 12. *In Heb.* 10, *lect.* 1

[2]*Hebrews* 10, 14

[a]The first art. is the only one of directly theological interest; arts 2–6 are concerned with canonical and rubrical prescriptions and the liturgical words and actions observed in the main, despite a variety of local uses, by the Western Church at the time and for nearly seven centuries afterwards. Many are no longer in force, and some of the canonical appeals to the ordinances of early popes are to be treated with reserve. The discussions, which are characteristic of their period and evince more devotion to the liturgy as a present fact than informed appreciation of its historical development, may be read with profit, and not merely by a medievalist in an archæological spirit. Their length, compared with the brevity of the first discussion, which Cajetan passes over without commentary, may appear disproportionate in a work of theology. Idle to pretend that the author was sensitive to symmetry in such matters: indeed one may venture the observation that the size of an article is often in inverse ratio to its theological importance. Nevertheless the placing of the inquiry into the sacrifice of the mass under the title of and within the large setting of this Question is of a piece with his whole discourse, in which the sacrifice is neither isolated from the sacrament nor seen as a repetition of Calvary, but rather as its continuation by the liturgical action of the Church. He does not enter into theories of the essence of the sacrifice of the mass such as were developed, sometimes perhaps over-developed, by post-Tridentine writers. cf A. Michel, *Messe* V, in Dict. *Théol. Cath*, X, 1, 1143–1316. Paris, 1928.

[b]Sacrificed, *immoletur* in Latin text. *Immolo,* originally, to sprinkle a victim with sacrificial meal, *mola salsa,* and then, to bring as an offering or sacrifice; associated

Question 83. the ritual for this sacrament

NOW WE COME TO CONSIDER the sacramental rite. Here there are six points of inquiry:[a]

1. whether Christ is sacrificed in the celebration of this mystery;
2. on the time of celebrating;
3. on its place and accessories;
4. on the words used in the celebration of this mystery;
5. on the actions performed;
6. on defects which occur in celebrating this sacrament.

article 1. is Christ sacrificed in this sacrament?

THE FIRST POINT:[1b] 1. No, it would seem. For it is written in *Hebrews* that Christ *by a single offering has perfected for all time those who are sanctified.*[2] That offering was his sacrifice. Therefore he is not sacrificed in the celebration of this sacrament.

---

with *macto*, to slay, and applied to capital punishment. Now used only of sacrifice in which life is taken. The discourse refers later to the figurative immolations of Christ in the Old Testament. His real immolation was on Calvary: there he offered himself in his own natural body and shed his blood, *immolatio cruenta*; in the mass the immolation is the same though under the sacramental species and not in a bloody manner, *immolatio incruenta*. Perhaps it was to stress this real identity that St Thomas preferred the more poignant *immolatio* to *sacrificium*, but it seems better to avoid the term 'immolation' in a translation.

He treats sacrifice as an outward act of the virtue of religion in the single Question of four not lengthy articles (2a2æ. 85, 1–4). His commentary on the *Sentences* (III *Sent.* 9, 1, 1) and the *Contra Gentes* (*CG* III, 119–21) give it no more than passing consideration. The *Summa* draws a distinction between a simple offering, *oblatio*, and a sacrifice to God where something is done about the thing offered; *sacrificium* =*sacrum facere* (2a2æ. 85, 3 ad 3). Yet nowhere in his writings does he require as an essential condition that this should amount to its destruction, but that it is made sacred or in some sense set apart for God (cf Vol. 39 of this series, ed. K. O'Rourke, Appendix 4). Of course there is not any suggestion of Christ being killed in the mass.

He allows for St Augustine's wider definition of sacrifice, 'any work done in order that we may cleave to God in holy companionship' (*De Civ. Dei* X, 28. PL 41, 255). Hence every act of virtue shares in the nature of sacrifice. Indeed the very heart of sacrifice is the inward offering of self to God (2a2æ. 85, 3 & 4). St Thomas draws on St Augustine's thought to show how Christ's Passion, a supreme expression of love for God and man, worked our salvation in the manner of sacrifice, 3a. 48, 3: the art. closely underpins the present one.

2. Præterea, immolatio Christi facta est in cruce, in qua *tradidit semetipsum oblationem et hostiam Deo in odorem suavitatis.*[3] Sed in celebratione hujus mysterii Christus non crucifigitur. Ergo nec immolatur.

3. Præterea, sicut Augustinus dicit, *in immolatione Christi idem est sacerdos et hostia.*[4] Sed in celebratione hujus sacramenti, non est idem sacerdos et hostia. Ergo celebratio hujus sacramenti non est Christi immolatio.

SED CONTRA est quod Augustinus dicit, *Semel immolatus est in semetipso Christus, et tamen quotidie immolatur in sacramento.*[5]

RESPONSIO: Dicendum quod duplici ratione celebratio hujus sacramenti dicitur immolatio Christi. Primo quidem quia, sicut dicit Augustinus ad Simplicianum, *solent imagines earum rerum nominibus appellari quarum imagines sunt; sicut cum intuentes tabulam aut parietem pictum dicimus, Ille Cicero est, et ille Sallustius.*[6] Celebratio autem hujus sacramenti, sicut supra dictum est,[7] imago quædam est repræsentativa passionis Christi quæ est vera ejus immolatio. Unde Ambrosius dicit super illud *Heb.*, *Umbram enim*, etc., *In Christo semel oblata est hostia ad salutem sempiternam potens: quid ergo nos? nonne per singulos dies offerimus? sed ad recordationem mortis ejus.*[8]

Alio modo quantum ad effectum passionis. Unde in quadam dominicali oratione secreta dicitur, *Quoties hujus hostiæ commemoratio celebratur, opus nostræ redemptionis exercetur.*[9]

Quantum igitur ad primum modum, poterat dici Christus immolari etiam in figuris veteris Testamenti. Unde et *Apoc.* dicitur, *Quorum nomina non sunt scripta in libro vitæ Agni, qui occisus et ab origine mundi.*[10] Sed quantum ad secundum modum, proprium est huic sacramento quod in ejus celebratione Christus immoletur.

---

[3]*Ephesians* 5, 2
[4]*De Trin.* IV, 14. PL 42, 901
[5]Gratian, *Decretum* III, 2, 52, RF I, 1333. cf Augustine, *Epist.* XCVIII, ad Bonifacium. PL 33, 363
[6]*De divers. Quæst.* II, 3. PL 40, 143
[7]3a. 76, 2 ad 1; 79, 1
[8]From Chrysostom, *In Heb.* XVII. PG 63, 131. cf Ambrose, PL 17, 47. Rabanus Maurus, XXVII, on *Hebrews* 10, 1. PL 112, 780. Gratian, III, 2, 53. RF I, 1333
[9]Dominican Missal, 7th Sunday after Octave of Trinity
[10]*Revelation* 13, 8
[c]Though later on in the explanation it is allowed that Christ might be said to be sacrificed in the sacraments of the Old Law, e.g., the paschal lamb (3a. 73, 6), this first argument means more than that the mass is what we call a memorial service. *Imago* should be charged with its full sense, that which proceeds or issues forth

2. Moreover, Christ's sacrifice was made upon the cross; *He gave himself up for us, a fragrant offering and sacrifice to God.*[3] Now in the mass Christ is not crucified. Neither, then, is he sacrificed.

3. Again, *in Christ's sacrifice priest and victim are the same,* as Augustine points out.[4] Yet in the mass the priest and the victim are not the same. Therefore the celebration of this sacrament is not a sacrifice of Christ.

ON THE OTHER HAND Augustine says, *Once Christ was sacrificed in his very self, yet daily is he sacrificed in the sacrament.*[5]

REPLY: For two reasons is the celebration of this sacrament called the sacrifice of Christ. First,[c] because, as Augustine writes, *Images are called by the names of the things of which they are images, thus looking at a picture or fresco we say, That is Cicero, or, That is Sallust.*[6] Now, as we have said,[7] the celebration of this sacrament is a definite image representing Christ's Passion, which is his true sacrifice. Hence Ambrose writes on *Hebrews, In Christ was offered once a sacrifice potent for eternal salvation. What do we do? Is it not to offer it every day, yet for the recalling of his death?*[8]

Second,[d] in respect of the effect of Christ's Passion. By this sacrament we are made sharers of the fruit of the Lord's Passion. Hence in a Sunday secret prayer it is said, *Whenever the commemoration of this sacrifice is celebrated the work of our redemption is carried on.*[9]

As for the first reason, it could be said that Christ was sacrificed even in the figures of the Old Testament; *Whose names are written in the Book of Life of the Lamb, which was slain from the beginning of the world before the foundation of the world.*[10] Yet as for the second, it is peculiar to this sacrament that in its celebration Christ is the sacrifice.[e]

---

according to a likeness in nature and specific meaning, cf 1a. 35, 1 & 2; 93, 1 & 2. Also 3a. 25, 3. And the *exemplum* of ad 3 means a true exemplar cause, *exemplar effectivum,* cf 1a. 15, 1 & 3. See note *e* below. Here there is likeness to Christ with respect to the outward sign, *sacramentum,* but identity with respect to the inner reality, *res sacramenti.* For Christ's body is present in true fact, not merely figuratively, though it is untouched in the breaking of bread; 3a. 75, 1 & 7.

[d]The second argument, which is continuous with and not to be disjointed from the first, is that the sacrament-sacrifice carries on and applies the effects of the Passion of Christ (3a. 79, 1 & 2) by nourishing us spiritually and by configuring us to him in his sacrifice and reconciling us to God (3a. 49, 3 & 4; 82, 10).

[e]A sacrament is an effective sign by definition, 3a. 62, 1 ad 1. Its import is theologically more real than its outward show, its spiritual significance more than its bodily performance, or, in scholastic terms, its *esse intentionale* more than its *esse physicum.* The Eucharist as a sacrament is such a sign. And so also as a sacrifice. Even the sacrifice of Christ on the cross was a sign: the physical event of crucifixion was expressive of the offering to God in obedience and love, 3a. 48, 3. From and to

(Footnote contd. overleaf)

1. Ad primum ergo dicendum quod, sicut Ambrosius ibidem dicit, *una est hostia*, quam scilicet Christus obtulit, et nos offerimus, *et non multæ, quia semel oblatus est Christus.*[11] Hoc autem sacrificium exemplum est illius. *Sicut enim quod ubique offertur, unum est corpus, et non multa corpora, ita et unum sacrificium.*

2. Ad secundum dicendum quod sicut celebratio hujus sacramenti est imago repræsentativa passionis Christi, ita altare est repræsentativum crucis ipsius, in qua Christus in propria specie immolatus est.

3. Ad tertium dicendum quod per eamden rationem etiam sacerdos gerit imaginem Christi, in cujus persona et virtute verba pronuntiat ad consecrandum, ut ex supra dictis patet.[12] Et ita quodammodo idem est sacerdos et hostia.

articulus 2. utrum convenienter sit determinatum tempus celebrationis

AD SECUNDUM sic proceditur:[1] 1. Videtur quod inconvenienter sit determinatum tempus celebrationis hujus mysterii. Hoc enim sacramentum est repræsentativum dominicæ passionis.[2] Sed commemoratio dominicæ passionis fit in Ecclesia semel in anno; dicit enim Augustinus, *Quotiescumque Pascha celebratur, numquid toties Christus occiditur? Sed tamen anniversaria recordatio repræsentat quod olim factum est; et sic non facit moveri, tanquam videamus in cruce pendentem Dominum.*[3] Ergo hoc sacramentum non debet celebrari nisi semel in anno.

2. Præterea, passio Christi commemoratur in Ecclesia sexta feria ante Pascha, non autem in festo Natalis. Cum ergo hoc sacramentum sit commemorativum dominicæ passionis, videtur inconveniens esse quod in die Natalis ter celebretur hoc sacramentum, in Parasceve autem totaliter intermittatur.

---

this sacrifice the Eucharist is entirely derivative and relative. Given an appreciation, such as is found in patristic and liturgical texts, of the identity between the action of Christ and the action of the eucharistic sacrament-sacrifice, rather than of a correspondence between them in a series of like events, it seems unnecessary, if not anomalous, to seek to find in the mass a re-enactment of the historical fact of the Passion, whether by the consecratory separation of the body and the blood, or by Christ's humbling himself to be our spiritual food and drink, or even by his being imprisoned, as it were, in the sacramental species. The multiplication of masses adds nothing to Christ's sacrifice except to spread its effects to those who join in the offering, 3a. 79, 7. Statistics here have little bearing on theology.

---

[11]loc cit note 8
[12]3a. 82, 1 & 3
[1]cf IV *Sent.* 13, 1, 2, iii & iv
[2]art. 1
[3]*Enarr. in Psalm.* 21, 2, 1. PL 36, 171

Hence: 1. It is said in the same place that *there is but one victim*, namely offered by Christ and by us, *and not many, because Christ offered once, and that was the exemplar of our offering.* What is offered everywhere is one body, not many, so there is one sacrifice.[11f]

2. As the celebration of this sacrament[g] is an image representing Christ's Passion, so does the altar represent the cross on which Christ was sacrificed in his own proper form and figure.[h]

3. And for the same reason the priest also bears Christ's image, in whose person and by whose power he pronounces the words of consecration, as we have shown.[12] And so in a measure the priest and the victim are the same.

article 2.[a] has the time for celebrating this mystery been well fixed?

THE SECOND POINT:[1] 1. Apparently not. We have agreed[2] that the sacrament represents Christ's Passion. But the commemoration of this takes place in the Church but once a year. Augustine says, *Is not Christ slain as often as the Pasch is celebrated? Nevertheless the anniversary remembrance represents what was done in times past, and so does not move us as though we saw the Lord hanging on the cross.*[3] Therefore this sacrament ought not to be celebrated except once a year.

2. Again, Christ's Passion is commemorated on the Friday before Easter, not on Christmas Day. Since this sacrament commemorates the Lord's Passion it would seem unfitting for it to be celebrated three times on Christmas Day, whereas it is entirely omitted on Good Friday.

---

[f]Christ's sacrifice was offered once, *semel, hapex.* cf *Rom.* 6, 10. *Hebr.* 7, 27; 9, 28; 10, 10. 1 *Pet.* 3, 18. The mass is that one sacrifice, lasting in time, offered in a sacramental manner, and applied daily according to the New Covenant.

[g]Celebration of this sacrament: no special ritual moment is marked out and isolated, but, as the following arts 3–5 show, the whole tableau or scena of the eucharistic service as performed by the Church at one given period and in one region is taken as representing the Passion.

[h]i.e. not under the sacramental species.

[a]The remaining articles of the Question take the Romano-Frankish Rite in widespread though not uniform observance during the 13th century. St Thomas himself said mass according to the Dominican Use, which belonged to the same family, drawn up under the Master General, Humbert of Romans, and enacted into law in 1256. Cf J. A. Jungmann, *The Mass of the Roman Rite*, revision by C. R. Riepe, London, 1959, of *Missarum Sollemnia*, 4th ed., Vienna, 1959. Other rites are scarcely mentioned and there is little historical appreciation of the shaping of the liturgy. Characteristically medieval, too, is the dwelling on the symbolism of the liturgy in use. This was to be classically exemplified in Durandus, *Rationale Divinorum Officiorum*. William Durand, Bishop of Mende, d. 1296.

3. Præterea, in celebratione hujus sacramenti Ecclesia debet imitari institutionem Christi. Sed Christus consecravit hoc sacramentum hora serotina. Ergo videtur quod hora tali debeat hoc sacramentum celebrari.

4. Præterea, sicut habetur *de Consecrat.*, Leo Papa scribit Dioscoro Alexandrino episcopo, quod *in prima parte diei missas celebrare licet.*[4] Sed dies incipit a media nocte, ut supra dictum est.[5] Ergo videtur quod etiam post mediam noctem liceat celebrare.

5. Præterea, in quadam dominicali oratione secreta dicitur, *Concede nobis, Domine, quæsumus, hæc frequentare mysteria.*[6] Sed major erit frequentia, si etiam pluribus horis in die sacerdos celebret, ergo videtur quod non debeat prohiberi sacerdos pluries celebrare in die.

SED CONTRA est consuetudo quam servat Ecclesia secundum canonum statuta.

RESPONSIO: Dicendum quod, sicut dictum est,[7] in celebratione hujus mysterii attenditur repræsentatio dominicæ passionis, et participatio fructus ejus. Et secundum utrumque oportuit determinare tempus aptum celebrationi hujus sacramenti. Quia enim fructu dominicæ passionis quotidie indigemus propter quotidianos defectus, quotidie in Ecclesia regulariter hoc sacramentum offertur. Unde et Dominus nos petere docet, *Panem nostrum quotidianum da nobis hodie*:[8] quod exponens Augustinus dicit, *Si quotidianus est panis, cur post annum illum sumis, quemadmodum Græci in Oriente facere consueverunt? Accipe quotidie, ut quotidie tibi prosit.*[9] Quia vero dominica passio celebrata est a tertia hora usque ad nonam, ideo regulariter in illa parte diei solemniter hoc sacramentum in Ecclesiae celebratur.

1. Ad primum ergo dicendum quod in hoc sacramento recolitur passio Christi, secundum quod ejus effectus ad fideles derivatur, sed tempore passionis recolitur passio Christi, secundum hoc quod in ipso capite nostro fuit perfecta, quod quidem factum est semel; quotidie autem fructum dominicæ passionis fideles percipiunt: et ideo sola commemoratio fit semel in anno, hæc autem quotidie et propter fructum et propter jugem memoriam.

2. Ad secundum dicendum quod veniente veritate cessat figura. Hoc autem sacramentum est figura quædam et exemplum dominicæ passionis, sicut dictum est.[10] Et ideo in die quo ipsa passio Domini recolitur, prout realiter gesta est, non celebratur consecratio hujus sacramenti. Ne tamen Ecclesia ea etiam die sit sine fructu passionis per hoc sacramentum nobis

---

[4] Gratian, *Decretum* III, I, 51. RF I, 1307. Leo I, *Epist.* IX, 2. PL 54, 627

[5] 3a. 80, 8 ad 5

3. Besides, the Church's celebration of this sacrament ought to be modelled on Christ's institution. But he consecrated in the evening. Therefore it seems that this sacrament ought to be celebrated then.

4. Also, the *Decretum* quotes Pope Leo who writes to the Bishop of Alexandria that it is lawful to celebrate masses *in the first part of the day*.[4] We have agreed[5] that the day begins at midnight. So then it is lawful to celebrate in the middle of the night.

5. Also, it is said in a Sunday prayer, *Grant us, O Lord, we beseech thee, to frequent these mysteries*.[6] Now the frequency will be greater if the priest celebrates several times a day. It seems, therefore, that a priest ought not to be forbidden to celebrate several times a day.

ON THE OTHER HAND stands the custom observed by the Church according to canonical statutes.

REPLY: In the celebration of this mystery, as we have said,[7] we should take into consideration the representation of the Lord's Passion and the sharing of its fruits, and the time ought to be determined by each consideration. Now because we need the fruits owing to our daily defects, this sacrament is offered regularly every day by the Church. Hence our Lord teaches us to pray, *Give us this day our daily bread*:[8] this Augustine explains, *If it be a daily bread, why do you take it once a year, like the Greeks in the East? Take it daily that it may benefit you daily*.[9] And because our Lord's Passion was enacted from the third to the ninth hour, this sacrament is regularly solemnly celebrated in that part of the day.

Hence: 1. Inasmuch as its effect flows out to the faithful, Christ's Passion is gathered up in this sacrament, but at Passiontide his Passion is recalled as enacted in him who is our Lord. This was effected but once, whereas the faithful get the fruits of his Passion every day. Accordingly, the former is commemorated once a year, the latter daily, that we may share in its fruits and hold it in constant memory.[b]

2. When the reality comes its figure ceases. Now this sacrament is a figure and an example which portrays the Lord's Passion, as we have said,[10] and so on the day on which it is recalled as it really was accomplished, the consecration of this sacrament is not celebrated. Nevertheless, lest the Church be deprived on that day of the fruit of the Passion offered to

[6]Dominican Missal. Secret, 7th *Sun*. after Oct. of Trinity
[7]art. 1 above
[8]*Luke* 11, 3
[9]*Serm. suppos*. LXXXIV. PL 39, 1908
[10]body of art.
[b]cf art. 1 above.

exhibito, corpus Christi consecratum die præcedenti reservatur sumendum in illo die; non autem sanguis, propter periculum, et quia sanguis specialius est imago dominicæ passionis, ut supra dictum est.[11] Nec verum est quod quidam[12] dicunt quod per immissionem particulæ corporis Christi in vinum convertatur vinum in sanguinem. Hoc enim aliter fieri non potest quam per consecrationem factam sub debita forma verborum.

In die autem Nativitatis plures missæ celebrantur propter triplicem Christi nativitatem. Quarum una est æterna, quæ quantum ad nos est occulta; et ideo una missa cantatur in nocte, in cujus introitu dicitur, *Dominus dixit ad me, Filius meus es tu; ego hodie genui te.*[13] Alia autem est temporalis, sed spiritualis qua scilicet Christus oritur, *tanquam lucifer in cordibus*, ut dicitur II *Petr.*,[14] et propter hoc cantatur missa in aurora; in cujus introitu dicitur, *Lux fulgebit hodie super nos.*[15] Tertia est Christi nativitas temporalis et corporalis, secundum quam visibilis nobis processit ex utero virginali, carne indutus: et ob hoc cantatur tertia missa in clara luce, in cujus introitu dicitur, *Puer natus est nobis.*[16] Licet e converso possit dici quod nativitas æterna secundum se est in plena luce, et ob hoc in Evangelio tertiæ missæ fit mentio de nativitate æterna. Secundum autem nativitatem corporalem ad litteram natus est de nocte, in signum quod veniebat ad tenebras infirmitatis nostræ; unde et in missa nocturna dicitur Evangelium de corporali Christi nativitate.

Sic etiam in aliis diebus, in quibus occurrunt plura Christi beneficia vel recolenda, vel expetenda, plures missæ celebrantur in die, puta una pro festo, et alia pro jejunio vel pro mortuis.

3. Ad tertium dicendum quod, sicut dictum est superius.[17] Christus voluit ultimo hoc sacramentum discipulis suis tradere, ut fortius eorum cordibus imprimeretur; et ideo post cænam in fine diei hoc sacramentum consecravit, et discipulis suis tradidit. A nobis tamen celebratur hora dominicæ passionis, scilicet diebus festis in tertia, quando crucifixus est linguis Judæorum, ut dicitur *Marc.*,[18] et quando Spiritus Sanctus descendit super discipulos;[19] vel diebus profestis in sexta, quando crucifixus est manibus militum, ut habetur *Joan.*[20] vel diebus jejuniorum in nona quando voce magna clamans emisit spiritum, ut dicitur *Matt.*[21] Potest tamen tardari, maxime quando sunt ordines faciendi, et præcipue in sabbato sancto, tum propter prolixitatem officii, tum quia ordines pertinent ad

[11] 3a. 78, 3 ad 2
[12] cf Mabillon, *In Ord. Rom.* 12–13. PL 78, 893–903
[13] *Psalms* 2, 7. Introit, Midnight Mass, Christmas, Dominican Missal
[14] II *Peter* 1, 19
[15] Introit, Dawn Mass, Christmas. *Isaiah* 9, 2
[16] Introit, Forenoon Mass, Christmas. *Isaiah* 9, 6
[17] 3a. 73, 5

us by this sacrament, the body of Christ consecrated on the previous day is reserved to be received then; the blood, however, is not reserved, on account of danger, and because it is especially the image of the Lord's Passion, as we have observed.[11] Not that it is true, as some have held,[12c] that the wine is changed into blood when a particle of the body is dropped into it, because this cannot be done other than by the due form of words of consecration.

On Christmas Day, however, three masses are said on account of Christ's threefold birth. First, his eternal birth, which is hidden from our sight; accordingly one mass is sung at night, in which the Introit says, *The Lord said unto me, thou art my Son, this day I have begotten thee.*[13] Second, his spiritual birth in time, when Christ *rises like the morning star in our hearts.*[14] Accordingly the mass is sung at dawn with the Introit, *The light will shine on us to-day.*[15] Third, his bodily birth in time, whereby he came forth from the Virgin's womb and clothed with flesh became visible to us; accordingly the third mass is sung in broad daylight and the Introit says, *A child is born to us.*[16] Yet, it may be noted, his eternal birth of itself is in full light, and so the Gospel of the mass speaks of it. As regards his bodily birth, literally that was at night, a sign that he came to the darkness of our infirmity, and so the Gospel at midnight mass is about his bodily birth.

As for other days on which many of God's benefits have to be recalled or besought, several masses are said, for instance one for the feast and another for the fast or for the dead.

3. As already noted,[17] Christ willed to give this sacrament last of all to his disciples that it might be more deeply impressed in their hearts; and so it was after supper, at the close of day, that he consecrated and gave this sacrament. But we celebrate at the hour when he suffered, on feast-days at the hour of Terce[d] when he was crucified from the mouth of Jews,[18] and when the Holy Spirit came down upon the Apostles[19] or when no feast is kept, at the hour of Sext, when he was crucified at the hands of the soldiers[20] or on fast days, at the hour of None, when crying out with a low voice, he gave up the ghost.[21] However, mass can be postponed until later, especially when Orders have to be conferred, and especially on Holy Saturday, on account both of the length of the office and of Orders belong-

---

[18]*Mark* 15, 25
[19]*Acts* 2, 4
[20]*John* 19, 14
[21]*Matthew* 27, 50
[c]Amalarius of Metz, d. *c.* 850. Pseudo-Alcuin. Alcuin of York, d. 804.
[d]Terce, Sext, None; 'Little Hours' of the Divine Office.

diem dominicam, ut habetur in *Decreto.*[22] Possunt tamen missæ celebrari in prima parte diei propter aliquam necessitatem, ut dicitur *de Consecrat.*[23]

4. Ad quartum dicendum quod regulariter missa debet celebrari in die, et non in nocte, quia ipse Christus est præsens in hoc sacramento, qui dicit *Joan.*, *Me oportet operari opera ejus qui misit me, donec dies est: venit nox, quando nemo potest operari; quamdiu in mundo sum, lux sum mundi.*[24] Ita tamen quod principium diei accipiatur non a media nocte, nec etiam ab ortu solis, idest quando substantia solis apparet super terram, sed quando incipit apparere aurora; tunc enim quodammodo dicitur sol ortus, inquantum claritas radiorum ejus apparet. Unde et *Marc.* dicitur quod *mulieres venerunt ad monumentum orto jam sole,*[25] cum tamen venerunt, *cum adhuc tenebræ essent, ad monumentum,* ut dicitur *Joan.*[26] Sic enim hanc contrarietatem solvit Augustinus.[27] Specialiter tamen in nocte Natalis Domini missa celebratur propter hoc quod Dominus nocte natus est, ut dicitur *de Consecr.*[28] Et similiter etiam in sabbato sancto circa noctis principium, propter hoc quod Dominus nocte surrexit, idest cum adhuc tenebræ essent, ante manifestum solis ortum.

5. Ad quintum dicendum quod, sicut habetur *de Consecrat.*, ex decreto Alexandri II Papæ, *sufficit sacerdoti unam missam in die una celebrare, quia Christus semel passus est, et totum mundum redemit; et valde felix est, qui unam digne celebrare potest. Quidam tamen pro defunctis unam faciunt, alteram de die, si necesse sit. Qui vero pro pecunia aut adulationibus secularium, una die præsumunt plures celebrare missas, non æstimo evadere damnationem.*[29] Et *Extra.* dicit Innocentius III quod, *excepto die Nativitatis dominicæ, nisi causa necessitatis suadeat, sufficit sacerdoti semel in die unam missam solummodo celebrare.*[30]

articulus 3. *utrum oporteat hoc sacramentum celebrari in domo et vasis sacris*

AD TERTIUM sic proceditur:[1] 1. Videtur quod non oporteat hoc sacramentum celebrari in domo et vasis sacris. Hoc enim sacramentum est repræsentativum dominicæ passionis. Sed Christus non est passus in domo sed extra portam civitatis, secundum illud *Heb.*, *Jesus, ut sanctificaret per suum sanguinem populum, extra portam passus est.*[2] Ergo videtur quod hoc sacramentum non debeat celebrari in domo, sed magis sub dio.

2. Præterea, in celebratione hujus sacramenti debet Ecclesia imitari morem Christi et apostolorum. Sed domus in qua primo Christus hoc

[22]Gratian, *Decretum* I, 85, 4. RF I, 266
[23]ibid III, I, 51. RF I, 1307
[24]*John* 9, 4
[25]*Mark* 16, 2
[26]*John* 20, 1

ing to a Sunday, according to the *Decretum*.[22] There also it is said masses can be celebrated in the first part of the day on account of any necessity.[23]

4. Ordinarily mass ought to be said in daytime and not at night, for Christ, who is present in this sacrament, said, *I must work the works of him who sent me while it is day; night comes when no one can work. As long as I am in the world, I am the light of the world.*[24] Yet day should not be taken as starting from midnight, or from sunrise when the sun's orb appears above the horizon, but when the dawn begins to glow, for then the sun is risen when shines the brightness of its beams. Thus *Mark* says that the women *went to the tomb when the sun had risen*,[25] though as *John* relates *it was still dark*.[26] This discrepancy is explained by Augustine.[27] Exception is made on the night of Christmas because, as the *Decretum* says,[28] the Lord was born at night. And likewise on Holy Saturday about the beginning of night, since the Lord rose at night, that is when it was still dark, before the sunrise was manifest.[e]

5. Canon law states, from a decree of Pope Alexander II, *It is enough for a priest to celebrate one mass each day, for Christ suffered once and redeemed the whole world; indeed happy is a man who can celebrate one mass worthily. There are some who say one mass for the dead, and another of the day if need be. Yet I do not think those escape censure who presume to celebrate several masses daily either for money or for flattery by layfolk.*[29] Also Pope Innocent III said that *except on our Lord's birthday, unless necessity urges, it is enough for a priest to celebrate only once each day.*[30]

article 3. *ought this sacrament to be celebrated in a building and with sacred vessels?*

THE THIRD POINT:[1] 1. It seems not. For this sacrament is a representation of the Lord's Passion. But this took place not in a building, but outside the city gate; *Jesus suffered outside the gate in order to sanctify the people through his blood.*[2] Therefore it seems that this sacrament ought to be celebrated in the open air, not in a building.

2. Again, in the celebration of this sacrament the Church follows the practice of Christ and the Apostles. But the building in which Christ first

---

[27]*De Consensu Evangelist.* III, 24. PL 34, 1198
[28]Gratian, III, 1, 48. RF I, 1306
[29]Gratian, III, 1, 53. RF I, 1308. Alexander II, *Frag. Epist.* Mansi XIX, 979
[30]*Decretals of Gregory IX.* III, 41, 3. RF II, 636. cf PL 215, 781
[1]cf IV *Sent.* 13, 1, 2, v & vi; 24, 2, 2 ad 9
[2]*Hebrews* 13, 12
[e]Already in the 13th century the Holy Saturday was not a midnight vigil, but an evening service, later to be anticipated in the morning, then in our days restored to night.

sacramentum confecit non fuit consecrata, sed fuit quoddam commune cœnaculum a quodam patrefamilias præparatum, ut habetur *Luc.*[3] Legitur etiam *Act.* quod *apostoli erant perdurantes unanimiter in templo, et frangentes circa domos panem, et sumebant cibum cum exultatione.*[4] Ergo nec modo oportet domos esse consecratas in quibus hoc sacramentum celebratur.

3. Præterea, nihil frustra in Ecclesia fieri debet, quæ Spiritu Sancto gubernatur. Sed frustra videtur adhiberi consecratio ecclesiæ vel altari, et hujusmodi rebus inanimatis, quæ non sunt susceptivæ gratiæ vel spiritualis virtutis. Inconvenienter igitur hujusmodi consecrationes in Ecclesia fiunt.

4. Præterea, solum divina opera debent recoli cum quadam solemnitate, secundum illud *Psal.*, *In operibus manuum tuarum exultabo.*[5] Sed ecclesia vel altare opere humano consecratur, sicut et calix, et ministri, et alia hujusmodi: horum autem consecrationes non recoluntur celebriter in Ecclesia. Ergo neque consecratio ecclesiæ vel altaris cum solemnitate recoli debet.

5. Præterea, veritas debet respondere figuræ. Sed in veteri Testamento, quod gerebat figuram novi, non fiebat altare de lapidibus sectis: dicitur enim *Exod.*, *Altare de terra facietis mihi; quod si altare lapideum feceris mihi, non ædificabis illud de sectis lapidibus.*[6] *Exod.* etiam mandatur fieri altare *de lignis sethim vestitis ære* vel etiam *auro*, ut habetur *Exod.*[7] Ergo videtur inconvenienter observari in Ecclesia quod altare fiat solum de lapide.

6. Præterea, calix cum patena repræsentat sepulcrum Christi quod fuit excisum in petra, ut in Evangeliis habetur.[8] Ergo calix debet de petra fieri, et non solum de argento, vel auro, vel stanno.

7. Præterea, sicut aurum pretiosius est inter materias vasorum, ita panni serici pretiosiores sunt inter alios pannos. Ergo sicut calix fit de auro, ita pallæ altaris debent de serico fieri, et non solum de panno lineo.

8. Præterea, dispensatio sacramentorum et ordinatio eorundem ad ministros Ecclesiæ pertinet, sicut dispensatio rerum temporalium subjacet ordinationi principum secularium; unde et Apostolus dicit 1 *Cor.*, *Sic nos existimet homo ut ministros Christi et dispensatores mysteriorum Dei.*[9] Sed si circa dispensationem rerum temporalium aliquid fiat contra statuta principum habetur irritum. Ergo si hæc quæ dicta sunt convenienter sunt statuta per prælatos Ecclesiæ, videtur quod sine his corpus Christi confici non possit; et sic videtur sequi quod verba Christi non sint sufficientia ad hoc sacramentum conficiendum; quod est inconveniens. Non ergo videtur conveniens fuisse quod hæc circa celebrationem hujus sacramenti statuerentur.

---

[3] *Luke* 22, 11 [4] *Acts* 2, 46 [5] *Psalms* 91, 5
[6] *Exodus* 20, 24 [7] *Exodus* 27, 1. 25, 1

effected this sacrament was not consecrated, but an ordinary upper room prepared by a householder, as related in *Luke*.[3] We read also in *Acts* that the Apostles *day by day, attending the Temple together and breaking bread in their homes, . . . partook of food with glad and generous hearts.*[4] And so nowadays, there is no need of consecrated buildings in which this sacrament is celebrated.

3. Besides, nothing pointless should be done in the Church, which is governed by the Holy Ghost. Now it seems pointless that a church or an altar or suchlike inanimate things be consecrated for they are unable to receive grace or spiritual power, and, therefore, for such consecration to be the Church's practice.

4. Also, divine works alone ought to be consecrated with solemnity; *At the works of thy hand I will sing for joy.*[5] Now the consecration of a church or altar is the work of man, as also is a chalice or minister and the like. But the consecrations of these are not commemorated by the Church. Nor, therefore, should the consecration of a church or altar be recalled with solemnity.

5. Besides, the truth ought to match the figure. Now in the Old Testament the altar was not made of dressed stone; *An altar of earth you shall work for me, and if you make an altar of stone, you shall not build it of hewn stone.*[6] It is commanded also that it be made *of acacia wood, overlaid with bronze, or with pure gold.*[7] Therefore it seems improper for the Church to use exclusively altars made of stone.

6. Again, the chalice with the paten represent Christ's tomb, which was hewn out of the rock as related in the Gospels.[8] Therefore the chalice ought to be made of stone, not only of silver, or gold, or tin.

7. Also, as gold is the most precious material for vessels, so silk is for altar-cloths. Since chalices are of gold, so altar-cloths ought to be made of silk, not only of linen.

8. And again, sacramental ordinance and dispensation is for the Church's ministers, just as the dispensation of temporalities is subject to the secular authority; *This is how one should regard us, as servants of Christ and stewards of the mysteries of God.*[9] Now if anything be done against the statutes of the civil authorities, it is held to be void. Therefore if the rules of sacramental discipline are suitably laid down by the Church authorities, it seems that the body of Christ will not be consecrated unless they are observed. It seems to follow that Christ's words are not sufficient to effect this sacrament. But this is inadmissible. Consequently, it does not seem fitting that statutes should be imposed concerning the celebration of this sacrament.

---

[8]*Matthew* 27, 60. *Mark*, 15, 46. *Luke* 23, 53

[9]1 *Corinthians* 4, 1

SED CONTRA est quod ea quæ per Ecclesiam statuuntur ab ipso Christo ordinantur, qui dicit, *Ubicumque fuerint duo vel tres congregati in nomine meo, ibi sum in medio eorum.*[10]

RESPONSIO: Dicendum quod in his quæ circumstant hoc sacramentum duo considerantur: quorum unum pertinet ad repræsentationem eorum quæ circa dominicam passionem sunt acta; aliud autem pertinet ad reverentiam hujus sacramenti, in quo Christus secundum veritatem continetur, et non solum in figura. Unde et consecrationes adhibentur his rebus quæ veniunt in usum hujus sacramenti, tum propter sacramenti reverentiam, tum ad repræsentandum effectum sanctitatis quæ ex passione Christi provenit, secundum illud *Heb.*, *Jesus ut sanctificaret per suum sanguinem populum*, etc.[11]

1. Ad primum ergo dicendum quod regulariter hoc sacramentum celebrari debet in domo per quam significatur Ecclesia, secundum illud 1 *Tim.*, *Ut scias quomodo oporteat te in domo Dei conversari, quæ est Ecclesia Dei vivi.*[12] Extra Ecclesiam enim non est locus veri sacrificii, ut Augustinus dicit.[13] Et quia Ecclesia non erat concludenda sub finibus gentis Judaicæ, sed erat in universo mundo fundanda, ideo passio Christi non est celebrata intra civitatem Judæorum, sed sub dio, ut sic totus mundus se haberet ad passionem Christi ut domus: et tamen, ut dicitur *de Consecratione*, *in itinere positis si ecclesia defuerit, sub dio seu in tentorio, si tabula altaris consecrata cæteraque sacra mysteria ad id officium pertinentia ibi affuerint, missarum solemnia celebrari concedimus.*[14]

2. Ad secundum dicendum quod domus in qua hoc sacramentum celebratur Ecclesiam significat, et ecclesia nominatur; convenienter tamen consecratur, tum ad repræsentandam sanctificationem quam Ecclesia consecuta est per passionem Christi, tum etiam ad significandam sanctitatem quæ requiritur in his qui hoc sacramentum suscipere debent. Per altare autem significatur ipse Christus, de quo dicit Apostolus, *Per ipsum offerimus hostiam laudis Deo.*[15] Unde et consecratio altaris significat sanctitatem Christi, de qua dicitur, *Quod ex te nascetur sanctum, vocabitur Filius Dei.*[16] Unde *de Consecratione* dicitur, *Altaria placuit non solum unctione chrismatis, sed etiam sacerdotali benedictione sacrari.*[17] Et ideo regulariter non licet celebrare hoc sacramentum nisi in domibus consecratis. Unde, sicut habetur *de Consecratione nullus presbyter missas celebrare præsumat, nisi in consecratis ab episcopo locis.*[18] Propter quod etiam, quia pagani non sunt de Ecclesia, nec alii infideles, ideo in eadem distinctione, legitur, *Ecclesiam, in qua mortuorum cadavera infidelium sepeliuntur, sanctificare non licet, sed*

---

[10]*Matthew* 18, 20 [11]*Hebrews* 13, 12 [12]1 *Timothy* 3, 15
[13]Prosper of Aquitaine, *Sent.* 15. PL 51, 430

ON THE OTHER HAND, the Church's ordinances are Christ's own; he said, *Where two or three are gathered in my name, there am I in the midst of them.*[10]

REPLY: Two considerations are relevant to the surroundings of this sacrament. One regards the representation of the events of the Lord's Passion. the other the reverence owing to this sacrament, which holds Christ veritably, not just figuratively. Accordingly we consecrate those things made use of in this sacrament, both out of reverence for it, and to represent its effect of holiness, which flows from Christ's Passion; he suffered *in order to sanctify the people through his own blood.*[11]

Hence: 1. This sacrament ought to be celebrated as a rule in a building which signifies the Church, according to St Paul, *That you may know how we ought to behave in the household of God, which is the Church of the living God.*[12] As Augustine says, *Outside the Church then is no place for the true sacrifice.*[13] And because the Church was not to be confined within the boundaries of the Jewish people, but was to be established throughout the world, therefore Christ's Passion was not enacted within the city, but outside under the open sky, so that the whole world might serve as the house for Christ's Passion. Nevertheless it is stated in canon law, *If a church is not available, the solemn celebration of masses is allowed in the open air or in a tent, so long as the consecrated altar-table together with other requisites for the ceremony are there.*[14]

2. The building in which the sacrament is celebrated signifies the Church, and is called a church. It is fittingly consecrated, both to represent the holiness which the Church came to from Christ's Passion and to signify the holiness required in those who would receive this sacrament. By the altar Christ himself is signified, of whom it is said, *Through him let us offer a sacrifice of praise to God.*[15] Accordingly, its consecration signifies Christ's holiness, of whom it is said, *The child to be born will be called holy the son of God.*[16] Accordingly canon law says, *It has been decided for the altars not only to be anointed with chrism but also dedicated with a priestly blessing.*[17] And so normally it is not lawful to celebrate this sacrament outside a dedicated building. Hence the canon, *Let no priest presume to celebrate mass except in places consecrated by a bishop.*[18] On which account, furthermore, because pagans and other infidels are not within the Church, a canon rules, *It is not lawful to dedicate a church in which the bodies*

---

[14]Gratian, III, I, 30. RF I, 1302

[15]*Hebrews* 13, 15

[16]*Luke* I, 35

[17]Gratian, III, I, 32. RF I, 1302

[18]distinct cit 15. RF I, 1298

si apta videtur ad consecrandum, inde evulsis corporibus, et rasis parietibus vel tignis ejus loci reædificetur; sed si hæc consecrata prius fuerit, missas in ea celebrare licet, tamen si fideles fuerint qui in ea sepulti sunt.[19]

Propter necessitatem tamen potest hoc sacramentum peragi in domibus non consecratis vel violatis; sed tamen de consensu episcopi. Unde in eadem distinctione, *Missarum solemnia non ubique, sed in locis ab episcopo consecratis, vel ubi ipse permiserit, celebranda esse censemus.*[20] Non tamen sine altari portatili per episcopum consecrato. Unde in eadem dist. legitur, *Concedimus, si ecclesiæ fuerint incensæ vel combustæ, in capellis cum tabula consecrata missas celebrari.*[21] Quia enim sanctitas Christi fons est totius ecclesiasticæ sanctitatis, ideo in necessitate sufficit ad peragendum hoc sacramentum altare sanctificatum. Propter quod etiam nunquam ecclesia sine altari consecratur. Tamen sine ecclesia quandoque consecratur altare cum reliquiis sanctorum, quorum vita *abscondita est cum Christo in Deo.*[22] Unde in eadem distinctione legitur, *Placuit ut altaria in quibus nullum corpus aut reliquiæ martyrum conditæ probantur, ab episcopis, qui eisdem locis præsunt, si fieri potest, evertantur.*[23]

3. Ad tertium dicendum quod ecclesia, et altare, et alia hujusmodi inanimata consecrantur non quia sint gratiæ susceptiva, sed quia ex consecratione adipiscuntur quandam spiritualem virtutem, per quam apta redduntur divino cultui, ut scilicet homines devotionem quandam exinde percipiant, ut sint paratiores ad divina, nisi hoc propter irreverentiam impediatur. Unde et II *Machab.* dicitur, *Vere Dei virtus quædam est in loco; nam ipse qui habet in cælis habitationem, visitator et adjutor est loci illius.*[24] Et inde est quod hujusmodi ante consecrationem emundantur et exorcizantur, ut exinde virtus inimici pellatur. Et eadem ratione ecclesiæ quæ *sanguinis effusione, aut cujuscumque semine pollutæ fuerint*[25] reconciliantur, quia per peccatum ibi commissum apparet ibi aliqua operatio inimici. Propter quod etiam in eadem dist. legitur, *Ecclesias Arianorum, ubicumque inveneritis catholicas, eas divinis precibus et operibus absque ulla mora consecrate.*[26] Unde et quidam probabiliter dicunt quod per ingressum ecclesiæ consecratæ homo consequitur remissionem peccatorum venialium, sicut et per aspersionem aquæ benedictæ, inducentes quod in *Psal.* dicitur, *Benedixisti, Domine, terram tuam, remisisti iniquitatem plebis tuæ.*[27] Et ideo propter virtutem quæ ex consecratione ecclesiæ acquiritur, consecratio ecclesiæ non iteratur. Unde in eadem distinctione ex concilio Nicæno legitur, *Ecclesiis semel Deo consecratis non debet iterum consecratio adhiberi, nisi aut ab igne exustæ, aut sanguinis effusione, aut cujuscumque semine pollutæ fuerint; quia sicut infans a qualicumque sacerdote in nomine Patris,*

[19]distinct cit 28. RF I, 1301
[20]ibid 12. RF I, 1297
[21]ibid 30. RF I, 1301
[22]*Colossians* 3, 3

of unbelievers are buried, but if it seems suitable for consecration, let them be disinterred, and the beams and walls pulled down, and then let it be rebuilt. If, however, it has been already consecrated, and the faithful lie there, mass may be lawfully celebrated there.[19]

Nevertheless in a case of necessity the sacrament may be performed in non-consecrated or desecrated buildings, with the consent, however, of the bishop. Thus the canon, *We judge that masses are not to be celebrated anywhere, but in places consecrated by a bishop, or where he gives permission.*[20] Not, however, without a portable altar consecrated by the bishop. Thus canon law, *We permit that in churches which have been burnt masses may be celebrated in chapels with a consecrated altar.*[21] Because Christ's holiness is the fount of all the Church's holiness, in need a consecrated altar is enough for performing this sacrament. On this account a church is never consecrated without consecrating the altar. Sometimes, however, an altar is consecrated apart from a church, with the relics of saints, *whose life is hidden with Christ in God.*[22] Thus canon law, *It is our decision that altars in which no relics are enclosed, if possible, should be thrown down by the bishops with authority over such places.*[23]

3. The church, altar, and other like inanimate things are consecrated, not as though they were receptive of grace, but they acquire spiritual force by being adapted to divine worship, in that that men gather a certain devotion because of them, and are made open to difiine things, and not held back by irreverence. Hence it is written, *Truly there is a certain power of God in that place, for he that has his dwelling in the heavens is the visitor and protector of that place.*[24] So it is that such are blessed and cleansed and exorcized before they are dedicated to drive out the enemy's power. Those *defiled by blood or seed*[25] are reconciled, for by the sin committed there some machination of the enemy appears, accordingly *wherever you find churches of the Arians consecrate them without delay with devout prayers and rites.*[26] Hence, too, some say with probability that by entering a consecrated church we gain forgiveness of venial sins, as also by the sprinkling of holy water, citing the verse, *Lord thou wast favourable to thy land, thou didst forgive the iniquity of thy people.*[27] So, therefore, because of the virtue a church gathers by its consecration, this is never repeated. That is why in canon law *churches which have once been consecrated ought not to be reconsecrated unless they have been devastated by fire or defiled by the shedding of blood or of anyone's seed, because just as a child once baptized in*

[23]Gratian, distinct cit 26. RF 1, 1300

[24]II *Maccabees* 3, 38

[25]Gratian, distinct cit 20. RF 1, 1299

[26]ibid 21. RF 1, 1299

[27]*Psalms* 84, 2

et Filii et Spiritus Sancti semel baptizatus, non debet iterum baptizari, ita nec locus Deo dicatus est iterum consecrandus, nisi propter eas causas quas superius nominavimus; si tamen fidem sanctæ Trinitatis tenuerint qui consecraverunt,[28] alioquin qui sunt extra Ecclesiam, consecrare non possunt; sed, sicut in eadem distinctione legitur, *ecclesiæ vel altaria, quæ ambigua sunt de consecratione, consecrentur.*[29] Propter hoc etiam quod aliquam spiritualem virtutem adipiscuntur per consecrationem, in eadem distinctione statutum legitur, *Ligna ecclesiæ dedicata non debent ad aliud opus jungi, nisi ad aliam ecclesiam, vel igni comburenda, vel ad profectum in monasterio fratribus; in laicorum autem opera non debent admitti.*[30] Et ibidem legitur, *Altaris palla, cathedra, candelabrum et velum, si fuerint vetustate consumpta, incendio dentur; cineres quoque eorum in baptisterium inferantur, aut in pariete, aut in fossis pavimentorum jactentur, ne introeuntium pedibus inquinentur.*[31]

4. Ad quartum dicendum quod quia consecratio altaris repræsentat sanctitatem Christi, consecratio vero domus sanctitatem totius Ecclesiæ, ideo convenientius recolitur cum sanctitate et solemnitate consecratio ecclesiæ, vel altaris, quam aliorum quæ consecrantur. Propter quod etiam octo diebus solemnitas dedicationis agitur, ad significandam beatam resurrectionem Christi et membrorum Ecclesiæ. Nec est opus solius hominis consecratio ecclesiæ et altaris, cum habeat spiritualem virtutem. Unde *de Consecrat.* dicitur, *Solemnitates dedicationum ecclesiarum per singulos annos solemniter sunt celebrandæ. Quod autem octo diebus encænia sint celebranda, in libris Regum perlecta dedicatione templi reperies.*[32]

5. Ad quintum dicendum quod, sicut legitur *de Consecrat., altaria si non fuerint lapidea, chrismatis unctione non consecrentur.*[33] Quod quidem competit significationi hujus sacramenti, tum quia altare significat Christum, dicitur autem 1 *Cor., Petra autem erat Christus,*[34] tum etiam quia corpus Christi in sepulcro lapideo fuit reconditum. Competit etiam quoad usum sacramenti. Lapis enim et solidus est, et de facili potest inveniri ubique, quod non erat necessarium in veteri lege, ubi fiebat in uno loco altare. Quod autem mandatur altare fieri de terra, vel de lapidibus insectis, fuit ad idololatriam removendam.

6. Ad sextum dicendum quod sicut in distinctione eadem dicitur, *quondam sacerdotes non aureis, sed ligneis calicibus utebantur, Zephirinus autem Papa patenis vitreis missam celebrari constituit; deinde Urbanus omnia fecit argentea.*[35] Postmodum autem statutum est, *ut calix Domini cum patena, sive ex auro omnino, sive ex argento fiat, vel saltem stanneus calix habeatur. De ære aut ex aurichalco non fiat, quia ob vini virtutem æruginem parit, pariterque vomitum provocat. Nullus autem in ligneo seu vitreo calice*

[28]Gratian, ibid 20. RF 1, 1299. No reference to Nicæa discoverable, cf RF 1, 253–4

the name of the Father and the Son and the Holy Ghost ought not to be re-baptized, so neither ought a place once dedicated to God be reconsecrated, except owing to the causes mentioned, provided the consecrator holds faith in the Trinity.[28] In fact those outside the Church cannot consecrate. Yet, as we read in the same distinction, *Churches or altars of doubtful consecration are to be consecrated anew.*[29] Since these get special spiritual virtue from their consecration, we find it laid down that *the beams of a dedicated church should not be used for any other purpose, except it be for some other church; else they are to be burnt, or put to the use of the brethren of a monastery, but they should not be taken for secular works.*[30] Also that *altar cloths, chairs, candlesticks, and veiling, are to be given to the flames and the ashes placed in the baptistery or in the walls or in trenches beneath the flagstones so as not to be profaned by the feet of those who enter.*[31]

4. Since the consecration of the altar represents the holiness of Christ, that of the building the holiness of the whole Church, hence it is performed with greater solemnity than the consecration of other things. And so the dedication of a church is observed for eight days to signify the happy Resurrection of Christ and the members of the Church. Nor is the consecration a human work merely since it has spiritual power. Hence it is observed, *The solemnities of the dedication of churches are to be solemnly celebrated each year; that the festive commemoration should go on for eight days you will find in the Book of Kings.*[32]

5. As we read, *Altars, if not of stone are not to be consecrated with the anointing of chrism.*[33] This is in keeping with the signification of this sacrament, both because the altar signifies Christ, *The rock was Christ*,[34] and because his body was laid in a stone sepulchre. It is also in keeping with sacramental practice, because stone is solid and to be found everywhere, not a need under the Old Law where the altar was in a single place. As to the commandment to make the altar of earth or unhewn stone, it was enacted in order to remove idolatry.

6. The canons also relate that *formerly the priests used wooden chalices, not golden, but Pope Zephyrinus ordered the mass to be said with glass patens, and subsequently Pope Urban had everything made of silver.*[35a] Afterwards it was decided that *the Lord's chalice and paten should be entirely of gold, or of silver, or at least of tin. But it is not to be made of brass or copper, because the reaction to the wine produces verdigris, and causes vomiting. But*

[29]ibid 18. RF I, 1299
[30]ibid 38. RF I, 1303
[31]ibid 39. RF I, 1303
[32]ibid 17. RF I, 1298. I *Kings* 8, 66
[33]ibid 31. RF I, 1302
[34]I *Corinthians* 10, 4
[35]Gratian, ibid 44. RF I, 1305
[a]Pope Zephyrinus, d. 217. Blessed Urban II. d. 1099.

præsumat missam cantare,[36] quia scilicet lignum porosum est, et sanguis consecratus in eo remaneret; vitrum autem fragile est, et posset fractionis periculum imminere; et eadem ratio est de lapide. Et ideo propter reverentiam sacramenti statutum est ut ex prædictis materiis calix fiat.

7. Ad septimum dicendum quod ubi potuit sine periculo fieri, Ecclesia statuit circa hoc sacramentum id quod expressius repræsentat passionem Christi. Non erat autem tantum periculum circa corpus, quod ponitur in corporali, sicut circa sanguinem, qui continetur in calice. Et ideo licet calix non fiat de petra, corporale tamen fit de panno lineo, quo corpus Christi fuit involutum. Unde in epistola Silvestri Papæ, in eadem distinctione legitur, *Consulto omnium statuimus ut sacrificium altaris non in serico panno, aut intincto quisquam celebrare præsumat, sed in panno lineo ab episcopo consecrato; sicut corpus Christi in sindone linea et munda sepultum fuit.*[37] Competit etiam pannus lineus propter sui munditiam, ad significandam conscientiæ puritatem, et propter multiplicem laborem quo talis pannus præparatur, ad significandam Christi passionem.

8. Ad octavum dicendum quod dispensatio sacramentorum pertinet ad ministros Ecclesiæ; sed consecratio eorum est ab ipso Deo. Et ideo ministri Ecclesiæ non habent aliquid statuere circa formam consecrationis, sed circa usum sacramenti et modum celebrandi. Et ideo si sacerdos verba consecrationis proferat super materia debita cum intentione consecrandi, absque omnibus prædictis scilicet domo et altari, calice et corporali consecratis, et cæteris hujusmodi per Ecclesiam institutis, consecrat quidem in rei veritate corpus Christi; peccat tamen graviter, ritum Ecclesiæ non servans.

articulus 4. *utrum convenienter ordinentur ea quæ circa hoc sacramentum dicuntur*

AD QUARTUM sic proceditur:[1] 1. Videtur quod inconvenienter ordinentur ea quæ circa hoc sacramentum dicuntur. Hoc enim sacramentum verbis Christi consecratur, ut Ambrosius dicit.[2] Non ergo debent aliqua alia in hoc sacramento dici quam verba Christi.

2. Præterea, verba et facta Christi nobis per Evangelium innotescunt. Sed quædam dicuntur circa consecrationem hujus sacramenti quæ in Evangeliis non ponuntur: non enim legitur in evangelio quod Christus in consecratione hujus sacramenti oculos ad cœlum levaverit; similiter etiam in evangeliis dicitur, *Accipite et comedite,*[3] nec ponitur *omnes,* cum in celebratione hujus sacramenti dicatur, *Elevatis oculis in cœlum,* et iterum, *Accipite et manducate ex hoc omnes.* Inconvenienter ergo hujusmodi verba dicuntur in celebratione hujus sacramenti.

---

[37]Sylvester, cf Council of Rome (324), Mansi II, 616. Gratian, distinct cit 46. RF I, 1306

[36]Gratian, district cit 45. RF I, 1306

no one is to presume to sing mass with wooden or glass chalice,[36] because as the wood is porous the consecrated blood would soak into it, while glass is brittle and there might also be danger of a breakage, and the same for stone. Accordingly out of reverence for the sacrament it has been laid down that the chalice should be made of the suitable metal, as indicated.

7. Where it can be done without risk the Church orders that to be done concerning this sacrament which more expressively represents Christ's Passion. There is less risk with respect to the body placed on the corporal than with the blood in the chalice. Though the cup is not made of stone, yet the corporal is made of linen, and in this Christ's body was wrapped. Thus canon law incorporates a letter of Pope Sylvester,[b] *Taking counsel of all we declare that no one should presume to celebrate mass upon a cloth of silk or dyed material, but upon linen consecrated by a bishop, since Christ's body was buried in a clean linen shroud.*[37] Linen is befitting to denote purity of conscience, and to denote Christ's Passion because of the manifold labour with which it is prepared.

8. The dispensing of the sacraments is for the Church's ministers, but their consecrating is from God himself. And so the Church's ministers decide regarding the application of the sacrament and the mode of celebrating it, but not concerning the form of consecration. And therefore if a priest pronounces the words of consecration on the proper matter with the intention of consecrating without all the canonical accessories—without church, altar, consecrated chalice and corporal—he consecrates Christ's body really and truly, nevertheless he sins seriously in not observing the Church's rite.

article 4. are the sacramental prayers well framed?

THE FOURTH POINT:[1] 1. Apparently not. Ambrose says[2] that the sacrament is consecrated by the words of Christ. Consequently no other words are to be pronounced than those.

2. Also, Christ's deeds and words are made known to us through the Gospel. But in consecrating this sacrament words are used which are not set down in the Gospel. There we read that Christ lifting his eyes to heaven, said, *Take and eat,*[3] whereas in celebrating the sacrament we say, *Lifting up his eyes to heaven*, and, *Take all of you and eat this*. Such additional words, then, are out of place in consecrating this sacrament.

---

[1]cf IV *Sent.* 1, 1, 5, i ad 2; 15, 4, 3, i. *In* I *Tim.* 2, *lect.* 1
[2]*De Sacram.* IV, 4. PL 16, 459
[3]*Matthew* 26, 26. I *Corinthians* 11, 24
[b]St Sylvester I, d. 335.

3. Præterea, omnia sacramenta ordinantur ad salutem omnium fidelium. Sed in celebratione aliorum sacramentorum non fit communis oratio pro salute fidelium defunctorum. Ergo inconvenienter fit in hoc sacramento.

4. Præterea, baptismus dicitur specialiter fidei sacramentum. Ea ergo quæ pertinent ad instructionem fidei, magis debent circa baptismum tradi quam circa hoc sacramentum, sicut doctrina apostolica et evangelica.

5. Præterea, in omni sacramento exigitur devotio fidelium. Non ergo magis in hoc sacramento quam in aliis deberet excitari devotio fidelium per laudes divinas et per admonitiones, puta cum dicitur, *Sursum corda.*

6. Præterea, minister hujus sacramenti est sacerdos, ut dictum est.[4] Omnia ergo quæ in hoc sacramento dicuntur, a sacerdote dici deberent, et non quædam a ministris, quædam a choro.

7. Præterea, hoc sacramentum per certitudinem operatur virtus divina. Superflue ergo sacerdos petit hujus sacramenti perfectionem, cum dicit, *Quam oblationem tu, Deus, in omnibus*, etc.

8. Præterea, sacrificium novæ legis multo est excellentius quam sacrificium antiquorum patrum. Inconvenienter ergo sacerdos petit quod hoc sacrificium habeatur sicut sacrificium Abel, Abrahæ et Melchisedech.

9. Præterea, corpus Christi sicut non incipit esse in hoc sacramento per loci mutationem, ut supra dictum est,[5] ita etiam nec esse desinit. Inconvenienter ergo sacerdos petit, *Jube hæc perferri per manus sancti angeli tui in sublime altare tuum.*

SED CONTRA est quod dicitur *de Consec., Jacobus frater Domini secundum carnem cui primum credita est Jerosolymitana Ecclesia, et Basilius Cæsariensis episcopus ediderunt missæ celebrationem*;[6] ex quorum auctoritate patet convenienter singula circa hoc dici.

RESPONSIO: Dicendum quod quia in hoc sacramento tantum mysterium nostræ salutis comprehenditur, ideo præ cæteris sacramentis cum majori solemnitate agitur. Et quia scriptum est *Eccles., Custodi pedem tuum ingrediens domum Domini*:[7] et *Eccl., Ante orationem præpara animam tuam*,[8] ideo ante celebrationem hujus mysterii primo quidem præmittitur præparatio quædam ad digne agenda ea quæ sequuntur. Cujus præparationis prima pars est laus divina, quæ fit in introitu, secundum illud *Psal., Sacrificium laudis honorificabit me, et illic iter quo ostendam illi salutare Dei*;[9] et sumitur hoc ut pluries de psalmis, vel saltem cum psalmo

[4] 3a. 82, 1
[5] 3a. 75, 2
[6] Gratian, *Decretum* III, I, 47. RF I, 1306
[7] *Ecclesiastes* 4, 17
[8] *Ecclesiasticus* 18, 23
[9] *Psalms* 49, 23
[a] The Liturgy of St James, extant in Greek and Syriac, has many correspondences

3. Also, all the sacraments are planned for the salvation of the faithful. But in the celebration of the other sacraments there is no common prayer for the salvation of the faithful departed. Therefore it is unfitting in this sacrament.

4. Also, Baptism is called especially the sacrament of faith. With Baptism rather than with this sacrament should not the instruction be in the faith, as in the Epistles and Gospels?

5. Also, the devotion of the faithful is required in every sacrament. It ought not be roused more in this sacrament than in the others by divine praises and admonitions, as when it is said, *Lift up your hearts.*

6. Also, as we have agreed,[4] the minister of the sacrament is a priest. Therefore all the words ought to be uttered by the priest, and not some by the server or choir.

7. Also, divine power effects this sacrament infallibly. Superfluously, then, the priest prays for its accomplishment, *Which oblation do thou, O God*, etc.

8. Also, the sacrifice of the New Law is more excellent than that of the Patriarchs. Therefore, it is unfitting for the priest to pray that it may be as acceptable as the sacrifice of Abel, Abraham and Melchizedek.

9. Also, Christ's body does not begin to be in this sacrament by a change of place, as we have agreed.[5] So likewise it does not cease to be in a place. And so it is odd for the priest to pray, *Bid it be borne by the hands of your holy angels unto thine altar on high.*

ON THE OTHER HAND it is stated in the *Decretum* that James, the brother of the Lord according to the flesh, and Basil, Bishop of Cæsarea, edited the rite of celebrating mass.[6a] From this authority it is clear that the words used are suitable.

REPLY: Because in this sacrament the whole mystery of our salvation is comprised, therefore it is performed with greater solemnity than the other sacraments. And because it is written, *Be on your guard when you go to the Temple*,[7] and, *Before your prayers prepare your soul*,[8] a certain preparation precedes the celebration of this sacrament in order that we may perform it worthily. The first part of this preparation is divine praise, which is done in the Introit, according to the psalm, *The sacrifice of praise shall glorify me, and that is the way by which I will show him the salvation of God.*[9] This praise is for the most part taken from the *Psalms*, or at least is sung with a

---

with the liturgy known to St Cyril of Jerusalem, d. 386. The Liturgy of St Basil, d. 370, still used in the Eastern Church on certain days in place of the Ordinary Liturgy of St John Chrysostom.

cantatur, quia, ut Dionysius dicit, *Psalmi comprehendunt per modum laudis quidquid in sacra Scriptura continetur.*[10] Secunda pars continet commemorationem præsentis miseriæ, dum misericordia petitur, dicendo, *Kyrie eleison*, ter quidem pro persona Patris, ter autem pro persona Filii, cum dicitur, *Christe eleison*, et ter pro persona Spiritus Sancti, cum subditur, *Kyrie eleison*, contra triplicem miseriam, ignorantiæ, culpæ et pœnæ; vel ad significandum quod omnes personæ sunt in se invicem. Tertia autem pars commemorat cœlestem gloriam ad quam tendimus post præsentem vitam et miseriam, dicendo *Gloria in excelsis Deo*; quod cantatur in festis, in quibus commemoratur cœlestis gloria; intermittitur autem in officiis luctuosis, quæ ad commemorationem miseriæ pertinent. Quarta autem pars continet orationem quam sacerdos pro populo facit, ut digni habeantur tantis mysteriis.

Secundo autem præmittitur instructio fidelis populi, quia hoc sacramentum est mysterium fidei, ut supra habitum est.[11] Quæ quidem instructio dispositive quidem fit per doctrinam prophetarum et Apostolorum, quæ in Ecclesia legitur per lectores et subdiaconos; post quam lectionem cantatur a choro graduale quod significat profectum vitæ, et alleluia quod significat spiritualem exultationem vel tractus in officiis luctuosis qui significat spiritualem gemitum; hæc enim consequi debent in populo ex prædicta doctrina. Perfecte autem populus instruitur per doctrinam Christi in Evangelio contentam, quæ a summis ministris legitur, scilicet a diaconibus; et quia Christo credimus tanquam divinæ veritati, secundum illud *Joan.*, *Si veritatem dico vobis, quare non creditis mihi?*[12] Lecto Evangelio, Symbolum fidei cantatur, in quo populus ostendit se per fidem Christi doctrinæ assentire. Cantatur autem hoc Symbolum in festis de quibus fit aliqua mentio in Symbolo, sicut in festis Christi, et beatæ Virginis, et Apostolorum qui hanc fidem fundaverunt, et aliis hujusmodi.

Sic igitur populo præparato et instructo consequenter acceditur ad celebrationem mysterii, quod quidem et offertur ut sacrificium, et consecratur et sumitur ut sacramentum. Unde primo peragitur oblatio; secundo consecratio materiæ oblatæ; tertio ejusdem perceptio.

Circa oblationem vero duo aguntur: scilicet laus populi in cantu offertorii, per quod significatur lætitia offerentium, et oratio sacerdotis, qui petit ut oblatio populi sit Deo accepta. Unde et I *Paralip.* dixit David, *Ego in simplicitate cordis mei lætus obtuli universa hæc, et populum tuum, qui hic repertus est, vidi cum ingenti gaudio tibi offerre donaria;* et postea orat dicens, *Domine Deus, custodi hanc voluntatem.*[13]

Deinde circa consecrationem, quæ supernaturali virtute agitur, primo excitatur populus ad devotionem in præfatione; unde et monetur *sursum*

[10]*De Eccles. Hier.* 3. PG 3, 429

psalm, because as Dionysius says, *The Psalms have whatever is contained in holy Scriptures in the way of praise.*[10] The second part calls to mind our present misery and so we beg for mercy in the threefold *Kyrie*, because of our threefold misery of ignorance, fault, and punishment, and also to signify that the three Persons are within one another.[b] The third part calls to mind heavenly glory, the goal of our present life of misery, *Glory be to God on high*. This is sung on feast days, and is omitted in those sorrowful offices which recall our unhappy state. The fourth part contains the collect which the priest makes for the people that they be made worthy of such great mysteries.

Next comes the instruction of the faithful, because, as we have said,[11] this sacrament is the mystery of faith. It is given dispositively by the teaching of the Prophets and Apostles, read in the Church by lectors and subdeacons. After this the choir sings the Gradual, which signifies progress in life, and the Alleluia, which signifies exultation of the spirit, or the Tract in sorrowful offices, which signifies sighing of the spirit, all these feelings ought to arise from the aforesaid instruction. Then the people are fully instructed in the teachings of Christ in the Gospel, which is read by the higher ministers, namely the deacons. And because we believe in Christ as the divine truth, according to *John*, *If I tell the truth, why do you not believe me*?[12] the Gospel having been read, the Creed is sung, by which the people show they assent to Christ's teaching. It is sung on feast days of which mention is made therein, namely of Christ and the blessed Virgin and the Apostles, who laid the foundations of this faith, and on other like days.

So then, the people being instructed and prepared, the celebration of the mysteries is next proceeded to. This is both offered as a sacrifice and consecrated and received as a sacrament. So first the offertory, second, the consecration of the matter offered, third, the Communion.

Concerning the offering, two things are done, namely the people's praise in singing the Offertory expressing the joy of the offerers, and the priest's prayer that the offering be made acceptable to God. As David said, *In the simplicity of my heart I have offered up those things: and I have seen with great joy thy people which are here present offer thee their offerings.* To which he adds the prayer, *O Lord God, keep this will.*[13]

Second, respecting the consecration done by supernatural power, first the people are roused to devotion in the Preface, so they are told to *lift up*

---

[11] 3a. 78, 3
[12] *John* 8, 46
[13] I *Chronicles* 29, 17
[b] The interpenetration of the three Persons of the Trinity, *circumincessio*, *perichōrēsis* 1a. 42, 5.

corda habere ad Dominum, et ideo, finita præfatione, populus devote laudat divinitatem Christi, cum angelis dicens: *Sanctus, Sanctus, Sanctus*, et humanitatem cum pueris dicens, *Benedictus qui venit*, etc. Deinde sacerdos secreto commemorat, primo quidem pro quibus hoc sacrificium offertur, scilicet pro universali Ecclesia, et *pro his qui in sublimitate sunt constituti*, 1 *Tim.*,[14] et specialiter quosdam qui offerunt, vel pro quibus offertur. Secundo commemorat sanctos quorum patrocinia implorat pro prædictis, cum dicit, *Communicantes et memoriam venerantes*, etc. Tertio petitionem concludit, cum dicit, *Ut hæc oblatio sit illis pro quibus offertur salutaris*.

Deinde accedit ad ipsam consecrationem, in qua primo petit consecrationis effectum, cum dicit, *Quam oblationem tu, Deus*, etc. Secundo consecrationem peragit per verba Salvatoris, cum dicit, *Qui pridie*, etc. Tertio excusat præsumptionem per obedientiam ad mandatum Christi, cum dicit, *Unde et memores*, etc. Quarto petit hoc sacrificium peractum esse Deo acceptum, cum dicit, *Supra quæ propitio*, etc. Quinto petit hujus sacrificii et sacramenti effectum, primo quidem quantum ad ipsos sumentes, cum dicit, *Supplices te rogamus;* secundo quantum ad mortuos, qui jam sumere non possunt, cum dicit, *Memento etiam, Domine*, etc.; tertio specialiter quantum ad ipsos sacerdotes offerentes, cum dicit, *Nobis quoque peccatoribus*, etc.

Deinde agitur de perceptione sacramenti, et primo præparatur populus ad percipiendum, primo quidem per orationem communem totius populi, quæ est oratio dominica in qua petimus panem quotidianum nobis dari, et etiam privatam, quam specialiter sacerdos pro populo offert, cum dicit, *Libera nos, quæsumus, Domine*, etc. Secundo præparatur populus per pacem, quæ datur dicendo, *Agnus Dei*, est enim hoc sacramentum unitatis et pacis, ut supra dictum est.[15] In missis tamen defunctorum in quibus sacrificium offertur non pro pace præsenti, sed pro requie mortuorum, pax intermittitur. Deinde sequitur perceptio sacramenti, primo percipiente sacerdote, et postmodum aliis dante, quia, ut Dionysius dicit, *ille qui aliis divina tradit, primo debet ipse particeps esse.*[16]

Ultimo autem tota missæ celebratio in gratiarum actione terminatur, populo exultante pro sumptione mysterii, quod significat cantus post communionem, et sacerdote per orationem gratias offerente, sicut et Christus celebrata cœna cum discipulis, hymnum dixit, ut dicitur *Matt.*[17]

1. Ad primum ergo dicendum quod consecratio solis verbis Christi conficitur; alia vero necesse est addere ad præparationem populi sumentis, sicut dictum est.[18]

2. Ad secundum dicendum quod, sicut dicitur *Joan.*,[19] multa sunt a

---

[14] 1 *Timothy* 2, 2

[15] 3a. 67, 2; 73, 3 ad 3; 4; 79, 1

their hearts to God. Then they devoutly praise Christ's godhead saying with the angels, *Holy, Holy, Holy,* and his humanity, saying with the children, *Blessed is he that cometh.* Next the priest quietly recalls, first, those for whom the sacrifice is offered, namely the universal Church and *those in high places,*[14] and especially for those who offer or for whom the mass is offered; next the saints, for whom he invokes their patronage for the above, when he says *Communicating with and honouring the memory,* etc. Third, he concludes with the petition, *Wherefore that this offering be salutary to them for whom it is offered.*

Then he comes to the Consecration, in which he first asks for its effect to be achieved, *which oblation do thou, O God,* etc. Next, he performs it, using our Saviour's words after he says, *Whom the day before,* etc. Thirdly, in obeying Christ's command he excuses himself from presumption, saying, *Wherefore calling to mind,* etc. Fourthly, he asks that the sacrifice gone through may find favour with God when he says, *Look down upon them propitiously,* etc. Fifthly, he begs for the effect of this sacrifice and sacrament, begging with the partakers, *We humbly beseech thee*; then for the dead who can no longer receive it, *Be mindful also, O Lord,* etc., ending with the priests themselves, *And to us sinners,* etc.

Then follows the act of receiving the sacrament. First, the people are prepared for it. To begin with by the common prayer of them all, the Lord's Prayer, in which we ask, *Give us this day our daily bread*; and also by private prayer, which the priest puts up specially for the people, *Deliver us we beseech thee, O Lord,* etc. Then by the kiss of peace, given in saying, *Lamb of God,* for this is the sacrament of unity and peace, as we have seen.[15] In masses for the dead, however, it is omitted, for these are offered for their repose, not our present peace. Next the actual reception of the sacrament, the priest receiving first and afterwards giving it to others, as Dionysius says, *He who delivers divine things to others ought first to share in them himself.*[16]

Finally the whole celebration of mass ends with the thanksgiving, with the people rejoicing at receiving the mystery, signified by the singing, and the priest returning thanks in the prayer, following Christ's example at the Last Supper with his disciples, *When they had sung a hymn they went out.*[17]

Hence: 1. The consecration is effected by the words alone. Others often are added, as we have said,[18] to prepare the people for receiving it.

2. As stated in the last chapter of *John*[19], our Lord did and said many

---

[16] *De Ecclest. Hierar.* 3. PG 3, 445

[17] *Matthew* 26, 30

[18] body of art.

[19] *John* 21, 25

Domino facta vel dicta, quæ Evangelistæ non scripserunt, inter quæ fuit hoc quod Dominus in cœna oculos levavit in cœlum; quod tamen Ecclesia ex traditione apostolorum habuit.[20] Rationabile enim videtur ut qui in suscitatione Lazari, ut habetur *Joan.*,[21] et in oratione quam pro discipulis fecit, *Joan.*,[22] oculos levavit ad Patrem, in hujus sacramenti institutione multo magis hoc fecerit, tanquam in re potiori. Quod autem dicitur, *Manducate*, et non, *comedite*, non differt quantum ad sensum, nec multum refert quid dicatur, præsertim cum verba illa non sint de forma, ut supra dictum est.[23] Quod autem additur, *omnes*, intelligitur in verbis Evangelii, licet non exprimatur, quia ipse dixerat *Joan.*, *Nisi manducaveritis carnem Filii hominis, non habetitis vitam in vobis*,[24] et quia porrigendo calicem dixit, *Bibite ex hoc omnes.*[25]

3. Ad tertium dicendum quod Eucharistia est sacramentum totius ecclesiasticæ unitatis; et ideo specialiter in hoc sacramento, magis quam in aliis, debet fieri mentio de omnibus quæ pertinent ad salutem totius Ecclesiæ.

4. Ad quartum dicendum quod instructio fidei est duplex. Una quæ fit noviter imbuendis, scilicet catechumenis, et talis instructio fit circa baptismum. Alia autem est instructio qua instruitur fidelis populus, qui communicat huic mysterio; et talis instructio fit in hoc sacramento, et tamen ab hac instructione non repelluntur etiam catechumeni et infideles. Unde dicitur *de Consecrat.*, *Episcopus nullum prohibeat ingredi in ecclesiam, et audire verbum Dei, sive gentilem, sive hæreticum, sive Judæum, usque ad missam catechumenorum*,[26] in qua scilicet continetur instructio fidei.

5. Ad quintum dicendum quod in hoc sacramento et major devotio requiritur quam in aliis sacramentis, propter hoc quod in hoc sacramento totus Christus continetur, et etiam communior, quia in hoc sacramento requiritur devotio totius populi christiani, pro quo sacrificium offertur, et non solum percipientium sacramentum, sicut in aliis sacramentis. Et ideo, ut Cyprianus dicit, *sacerdos præfatione præmissa parat fratrum mentes dicendo, Sursum corda, ut dum respondet plebs, Habemus ad Dominum, admoneatur nihil aliud se quam Deum cogitare debere.*[27]

6. Ad sextum dicendum quod in hoc sacramento, sicut dictum est,[28] tanguntur ea quæ pertinent ad totam Ecclesiam. Et ideo quædam dicuntur a choro, quæ pertinent ad populum, quoram quædam chorus totaliter prosequitur, quæ scilicet toti populo inspirantur; quædam vero populus prosequitur, sacerdote inchoante, qui personam Dei gerit; in signum quod talia pervenerunt ad populum ex revelatione divina, sicut fides et gloria cœlestis; et ideo sacerdos inchoat Symbolum fidei, et *Gloria in excelsis Deo*.

---

[20]cf *Decretals of Gregory IX*, III, 41, 6. RF II, 637

[21]*John* 11, 41

[22]*John* 17, 1

[23]3a. 78, 1 ad 2 & 4

things which are not recorded by the Evangelists; among them is his lifting up his eyes to heaven at the Last Supper, which nevertheless the Church has by tradition from the Apostles.[20c] It seems reasonable he who lifted up his eyes to the Father in raising Lazarus[21] and in the prayer he made for his disciples,[22] had more cause to do so in instituting this sacrament which is of greater importance. The use of the word *comedite* instead of *manducate* does not signify; they have the same sense, and anyway are not part of the sacramental form, as we have seen.[23] The word *all* is implied in the Gospel, though it is not explicit, for the Lord said, *Unless you eat the flesh of the Son of man you have no life in you*,[24] and, in giving the cup, *Drink of this all of you.*[25]

3. The Eucharist is the sacrament of unity for the entire Church, and therefore in this sacrament especially, more than in the others, reference should be made to all that relates to salvation in the universal Church.

4. The instruction of faith is twofold. One for those receiving it for the first time, namely catechumens. And this is given for Baptism. The other is that for the faithful who take part in this mystery, and this is given by this sacrament. Nevertheless unbelievers and catechumens are not excluded. Thus canon law, *Let a bishop forbid no one to enter a church and hear the word of God, whether gentile, heretic, or Jew, until the mass of the catechumens begins*,[26] which contains the instruction of faith.

5. This sacrament calls for devotion deeper than do the other sacraments, because it contains the whole Christ. Moreover the devotion should be more communal, namely of the entire people, since it is offered for them, not only of the recipients of the sacrament, as with the other sacraments. Hence Cyprian writes, *The priest, in the Preface, disposes the souls of the brethren by saying, Lift up your heart, and when the people answer, We have lifted them up to the Lord, let them remember that they are to think of nothing else but God.*[27]

6. As we have said,[28] this sacrament touches all relating to the whole Church. Consequently some things relating to the people are sung by the choir; some words are also sung, as though inspiring them all, whereas others are started by the priest acting in the person of God and taken up by the people, to show that these blessings of faith and heavenly glory come to them from divine revelation; accordingly the priest intones the *Gloria*

---

[24] *John* 6, 54
[25] *Matthew* 26, 27
[26] Gratian, III, I, 67. RF I, 1312
[27] *De Orat. Dom.* 31. PL 4, 557
[28] ad 3 above
[c] cf miraculous multiplication of loaves, *Matt.* 14, 19.

Quædam vero dicuntur per ministros, sicut doctrina veteris et novi Testamenti, in signum quod per ministros a Deo missos est doctrina hæc populis annuntiata. Quædam vero sacerdos solus prosequitur, quæ scilicet ad proprium officium sacerdotis pertinent, ut scilicet *dona et preces offerat pro populo*, sicut dicitur *Heb.*[29] In his tamen quædam dicit publice, scilicet quæ pertinent et ad sacerdotem et ad populum, sicut sunt orationes communes; quædam vero pertinent ad solum sacerdotem, sicut oblatio et consecratio; et ideo quæ circa hæc sunt dicenda, occulte a sacerdote dicuntur. In utrisque tamen excitat attentionem populi, dicendo, *Dominus vobiscum*, et expectat assensum dicentium, *Amen.* Et ideo etiam in his quæ secrete dicuntur, publice præmittit, *Dominus vobiscum*, et subjungit, *Per omnia sæcula sæculorum*; vel secreta aliqua sacerdos dicit in signum quod circa Christi passionem discipuli nonnisi occulte confitebantur Christum.

7. Ad septimum dicendum quod efficacia verborum sacramentalium impediri potest per intentionem sacerdotis. Nec tamen est inconveniens quod a Deo petamus id quod certissime scimus ipsum facturum, sicut Christus petit suam clarificationem.[30] Non tamen videtur ibi sacerdos orare ut consecratio impleatur, sed ut nobis fiat fructuosa: unde signanter dicit, *Ut nobis corpus et sanguis fiat;* et hoc significant verba quæ præmittit, dicens, *Hanc oblationem facere digneris benedictam*, secundum Augustinum, idest *per quam benedicamur*, scilicit per gratiam; *adscriptam*, idest *per quam in cœlo adscribamur; ratam*, idest *per quam de visceribus Christi trajiciamur, vel in visceribus Christi censeamur per incorporationem; rationabilem*, idest *per quam a bestiali sensu exuamur; acceptabilem*, *ut qui nobis ipsis displicemus, per hanc acceptabiles ejus unico Filio simus.*[31]

8. Ad octavum dicendum quod licet hoc sacrificium* ex seipso præferatur omnibus antiquis sacrificiis, tamen sacrificia antiquorum fuerunt Deo acceptissima ex eorum devotione. Petit ergo sacerdos ut sic hoc sacrificium acceptetur a Deo ex devotione offerentium, sicut illa accepta fuerunt Deo.

9. Ad nonum dicendum quod sacerdos non petit neque quod species sacramentales deferantur in cœlum, neque corpus Christi verum, quod ibi esse non desinit; sed petit hoc pro corpore mystico, quod scilicet in hoc sacramento significatur, ut scilicet orationes sacerdotis et populi angelus assistens divinis mysteriis Deo repræsentet, secundum illud *Apoc.*, *Ascendit fumus incensorum de oblationibus sanctorum de manu angeli.*[32] Sublime autem altare Dei dicitur vel ipsa Ecclesia triumphans, in quam transferri petimus, vel ipse Deus, cujus participationem petimus; de hoc enim altari dicitur *Exod.*, *Non ascendes ad altare meum per gradus*,[33] idest

*Piana: *sacramentum*

in excelsis Deo and *Credo*. Other words are said by the ministers, such as the teaching of the Old and New Testament, to acknowledge that they were announced to the peoples by ministers sent by God. Other words which the priest alone recites belong to his proper office; *that he might offer up gifts and sacrifices for the people.*[29] Some he says aloud, such as the prayers common to him and the people; others are for him alone, such as the offertory and consecration, consequently they are said in a low voice. Nevertheless he calls the people's attention by saying aloud, *The Lord be with you*, and awaits their assenting *Amen*. Even the words he recites under his breath, in token of the disciples only hiddenly acknowledging Christ at his Passion, he starts by speaking up, *The Lord be with you*, and ends, *For ever and ever, world without end.*

7. The efficacy of the sacramental words can be obstructed by the priest's intention. Nor is there anything odd in our asking from God what we know he will do; thus Christ prayed that he might be glorified.[30] However, the priest in this case does not pray that the consecration might be effected, but that it may be fruitful to us. Hence the point of the words *that it may become for us the body and blood*. So also the words, *Deign to make this oblation blessed*, that is to say, according to Augustine, *that we may be blessed*, namely by grace; *enrolled*, namely *in heaven*; *ratified*, that is *incorporated with Christ*; *reasonable*, that is *divested of carnal grossness*; *acceptable*, that is *that we who in ourselves are unpleasing may be made acceptable to his only Son.*[31]

8. Though this sacrifice of itself ranks above the ancient sacrifices, yet these were very acceptable to God on account of the devotion of men of old. Accordingly the priest asks that this sacrifice may be accepted by God, as the others were, because of the devotion of those who offer it.

9. The priest does not pray that the sacramental species may be borne up to heaven, nor Christ's true body, for it does not cease to be there. He prays for the mystical body, which is signified by this sacrament, namely, that the angel standing by the divine mysteries may present to God the prayers of priest and people; *The smoke of the incense rose with the prayers of the saints from the hand of the angel before God.*[32] The *sublime altar of God* refers either to the Church Triumphant, whereto we pray to be transported, or to God himself in whom we ask to share; of this *Exodus* speaks, *You shall not go up by steps to my altar,*[33] that is, according to a gloss, *You*

---

[29] *Hebrews* 5, 1
[30] *John* 17, 1–5
[31] Paschasius Radbertus, *De Corp. et Sang. Dom.* 12. PL 120, 1812
[32] *Revelation* 8, 4
[33] *Exodus* 20, 26

in Trinitate gradus non facies.[34] Vel per angelum intelligitur ipse Christus, qui est *magni consilii Angelus*,[35] qui corpus suum mysticum Deo Patri conjungit et Ecclesiæ triumphantis. Et propter hoc etiam missa nominatur, quia per angelum sacerdos preces ad Deum mittit, sicut populus per sacerdotem, vel quia Christus est hostia nobis missa a Deo: unde et in fine missæ diaconus in festivis diebus populum licentiat, dicens, *Ite missa est*, scilicet hostia ad Deum per angelum, ut scilicet sit Deo accepta.

articulus 5. utrum ea quæ in celebratione hujus sacramenti aguntur sint convenientia

AD QUINTUM sic proceditur:[1] 1. Videtur quod ea quæ in celebratione hujus sacramenti aguntur non sint convenientia. Hoc enim sacramentum ad novum Testamentum pertinet, ut ex forma ipsius apparet. In novo autem Testamento non sunt observandæ cæremoniæ veteris Testamenti, ad quas pertinebat quod sacerdos et ministri aqua lavabantur quando accedebant ad offerendum; legitur enim *Exod.*, *Lavabunt Aaron, et filii ejus manus suas ac pedes, quando ingressuri sunt tabernaculum testimonii, et quando accessuri sunt ad altare.*[2] Non est ergo conveniens quod sacerdos lavet manus suas inter missarum solemnia.

2. Præterea, ibidem Dominus mandavit quod sacerdos* adoleret incensum suave fragrans super altare quod erat ante propitiatorium;[3] quod etiam pertinebat ad cæremonias veteris Testamenti. Inconvenienter ergo in missa sacerdos thurificatione utitur.

3. Præterea, ea quæ in sacramentis Ecclesiæ aguntur non sunt iteranda. Inconvenienter igitur sacerdos multoties iterat crucesignationes super hoc sacramentum.

4. Præterea, Apostolus dicit *Heb.*, *Sine ulla contradictione, quod minus est a majori benedicitur.*[4] Sed Christus, qui est in hoc sacramento post consecrationem, est multo major sacerdote. Inconvenienter igitur sacerdos post consecrationem benedicit hoc sacramentum, cruce signando.

5. Præterea, in sacramento Ecclesiæ nihil debet fieri quod ridiculosum videatur. Videtur autem ridiculosum gesticulationes facere, ad quas pertinere videtur quod sacerdos quandoque brachia extendit, manus jungit, digitos complicat, et seipsum inclinat. Ergo hæc non debent fieri in hoc sacramento.

6. Præterea, ridiculosum etiam videtur quod sacerdos multoties se ad populum vertit, et multoties populum salutat. Non ergo debent hæc fieri in celebratione hujus sacramenti.

7. Præterea, Apostolus pro inconvenienti habet quod Christus divisus sit.[5] Sed post consecrationem Christus est in hoc sacramento. Inconvenienter ergo hostia frangitus a sacerdote.

*Piana: Aaron

shall not step up to the Trinity.[34] Or by the angel is meant Christ himself. who is the *Angel of Great Counsel*,[35] and unites his mystical body with God the Father and the Church Triumphant. And from this the mass gets its name. For the priest sends (*mittit*) his prayers through the angel, as the people do through the priest. Or else because Christ is the victim sent (*missa*) to us from God. Accordingly on feasts the deacon dismisses the people with the words, *Ite missa est*, that is the victim has been sent to God through the angel so that it may be accepted by him.

article 5. are the actions performed in celebrating this sacrament fitting?

THE FIFTH POINT:[1] 1. It seems not. From its form it is apparent that this sacrament belongs to the New Testament, under which the ceremonies of the Old Law are not to be observed, such as that the priests and ministers washed with water when they approached the sacrifice: thus *Aaron and his sons shall wash their hands and their feet when they go into the tent of meeting, or when they come near to the altar to minister.*[2] It is not fitting, therefore, for the priest to wash his hands in solemnizing mass.

2. Moreover, the Lord commanded the priest to burn sweet-smelling incense before the altar.[3] This also was part of the ceremonies of the Old Law. Therefore it is not fitting for a priest to use incense at mass.

3. Besides, repetitions should be avoided in administering the sacraments of the Church. And so the priest improperly repeats the sign of the cross many times in this sacrament.

4. Also, St Paul says that *it is beyond dispute that the inferior is blessed by the superior.*[4] But Christ, present in the sacrament after consecration, is much superior to a priest. Therefore, it is unseemly for the priest to bless this sacrament with the sign of the cross after the consecration.

5. Then also, nothing which appears ridiculous ought to be done in the Church's sacrament. And such seem the gestures used by a priest, sometimes stretching out his arms, joining his hands, joining together his fingers, and bowing down. They ought not to be done in this sacrament.

6. So as well for him to turn round frequently to the people and greet them. Such actions ought not to take place in celebrating this sacrament.

7. Again, as something inadmissible St Paul asks, *Is Christ divided?*[5] Yet after the consecration Christ is present in the sacrament. Therefore it is objectionable for the host to be broken by the priest.

---

[34]Interlinear Gloss

[35]*Isaiah* 9, 6. Septuagint

[1]cf IV *Sent.* 12

[2]*Exodus* 30, 19

[3]*Exodus* 30, 7

[4]*Hebrews* 7, 7

[5]1 *Corinthians* 1, 13

8. Præterea, ea quæ in hoc sacramento aguntur passionem Christi repræsentant. Sed in passione Christi corpus fuit divisum in locis quinque vulnerum. Ergo corpus Christi in quinque partes frangi deberet magis quam in tres.

9. Præterea, totum corpus Christi in hoc sacramento seorsum consecratur a sanguine. Inconvenienter ergo una pars ejus sanguini miscetur.

10. Præterea, sicut corpus Christi proponitur in hoc sacramento ut cibus, ita et sanguis Christi ut potus. Sed sumptioni corporis Christi non adjungitur in celebratione missæ alius corporalis cibus. Inconvenienter igitur sacerdos post sumptionem sanguinis Christi vinum non consecratum sumit.

11. Præterea, veritas debet respondere figuræ. Sed de agno paschali, qui fuit figura hujus sacramenti, mandatur quod non remaneret ex eo quidquam usque mane.[6] Inconvenienter igitur hostiæ consecratæ reservantur, et non statim sumuntur.

12. Præterea, sacerdos pluraliter loquitur audientibus, cum dicit, *Dominus vobiscum*, et, *Gratias agamus*. Sed inconveniens videtur pluraliter loqui uni soli, maxime minori. Ergo inconveniens videtur quod sacerdos uno tantum ministro præsente celebret missam. Sic igitur videtur quod inconvenienter aliqua agantur in celebratione hujus sacramenti.

SED IN CONTRARIUM est Ecclesiæ consuetudo, quæ errare non potest, utpote a Spiritu Sancto instructa.

RESPONSIO: Dicendum quod, sicut supra dictum est,[7] in sacramentis dupliciter aliquid significatur, scilicet verbis et factis, ad hoc quod sit perfectior significatio. Significantur autem verbis in celebratione hujus sacramenti quædam pertinentia ad passionem Christi, quæ repræsentatur in hoc sacramento, vel etiam ad corpus mysticum, quod significatur in hoc sacramento; et quædam pertinentia ad usum hujus sacramenti, qui debet esse cum devotione et reverentia. Et ideo in celebratione hujus mysterii quædam aguntur ad repræsentandam passionem Christi, vel etiam dispositionem corporis mystici; et quædam aguntur pertinentia ad devotionem et usum hujus sacramenti.

1. Ad primum ergo dicendum quod ablutio manuum fit in celebratione missæ propter reverentiam hujus sacramenti, et hoc dupliciter. Primo quidem quia aliqua pretiosa tractare non consuevimus nisi manibus ablutis; unde indecens videtur quod ad tantum sacramentum aliquis accedat manibus etiam corporaliter inquinatis. Secundo propter significationem, quia, ut Dionysius dicit,[8] extremitatum ablutio significat emundationem etiam a minimis peccatis, secundum illud *Joan.*, *Qui lotus est, non indiget nisi ut pedes lavet.*[9] Et talis emundatio requiritur ab eo qui accedit ad hoc sacra-

8. Again, the ritual actions represent Christ's Passion, during which his body was parted in the places of the five wounds. Therefore Christ's body ought to be broken into five parts rather than into three.

9. Also, Christ's entire body is consecrated apart from the blood. Consequently a particle is unfittingly mixed with the blood.

10. Also, as Christ's body is set before us as food so is his blood as drink. But no other bodily food is added in the mass to the eating of the body. And so it is out of place for the priest to drink unconsecrated wine after taking the chalice.

11. Also, truth and its figure should match. But concerning the paschal lamb, which was the figure of this sacrament, it was commanded that *you shall let none of it remain until morning*.[6] It is improper, then, for consecrated hosts to be reserved, and not consumed at once.

12. Also, the priest addresses in the plural those who are hearing mass, *The Lord be with you*, and, *Let us return thanks*. But it is out of keeping to address one individual in the plural, especially an inferior. Consequently it is out of keeping for a priest to celebrate mass with only a single server present. So it seems that some rubrics lack propriety.

ON THE CONTRARY is the Church's custom, and the Church, guided by the Holy Ghost, cannot make a mistake.

REPLY: As we have said,[7] the sacraments signify something in a twofold manner, by words and by actions. For the celebration of this sacrament words are used to signify things relating to Christ's Passion, which it represents, and to his mystical body,[a] which it signifies, and to its reception, which ought to be devout and reverent. Accordingly, some actions of the mass are for representing Christ's Passion or also the disposing of the mystical body, and some are to further the taking of this sacrament with devotion.

Hence: 1. The washing of hands in mass is done out of reverence, and for two reasons. First, we are not wont to handle precious objects except with clean hands; it seems not decent for anyone to approach the sacrament with hands that are in fact dirty. Second, its signification: Dionysius says[8] that washing the tips of the fingers denotes cleansing even from the smallest sins, according to *John*, *He that is washed needs not but wash his feet*.[9] Such

---

[6]*Exodus* 12, 10
[7]3a. 60, 5 & 6
[8]*De Eccles. Hier.* 3. PG 3, 440
[9]*John* 13, 10
[a]Mystical body, cf 3a. 8, on Christ's grace as head of the Church.

mentum; quod etiam significatur per confessionem, quæ fit ante introitum missæ. Et hoc idem significabat ablutio sacerdotum in veteri lege, ut ibidem Dionysius dicit.[10] Nec tamen Ecclesia hoc servat tanquam cæremoniale veteris legis præceptum, sed quasi ab Ecclesia institutum, sicut quiddam secundum se conveniens, et ideo non eodem modo observatur sicut tunc: prætermittitur enim pedum ablutio, et servatur ablutio manuum, quæ potest fieri magis in promptu, et quæ sufficit ad significandam perfectam mundationem: cum enim manus sit *organum organorum*, ut dicitur *de Anima*,[11] omnia opera attribuuntur manibus: unde in *Psalmo*, dicitur, *Lavabo inter innocentes manus meas.*[12]

2. Ad secundum dicendum quod etiam thurificatione non utimur quasi cæremoniali præcepto legis, sed sicut Ecclesiæ statuto; unde non eodem modo utimur sicut in lege veteri erat statutum. Pertinet autem ad duo. Primo quidem ad reverentiam hujus sacramenti, ut scilicet per bonum odorem depellatur, si quid corporaliter pravi odoris in loco fuerit, quod posset provocare horrorem. Secundo pertinet ad repræsentandum effectum gratiæ, qua, sicut bono odore Christus plenus fuit, secundum illud *Gen.*, *Ecce odor filii mei, sicut odor agri pleni;*[13] et a Christo derivatur ad fideles officio ministrorum, secundum illud II *Cor.*, *Odorem notitiæ suæ spargit per nos in omni loco*;[14] et ideo, undique thurificato altari, per quod Christus designatur, thurificantur omnes per ordinem.

3. Ad tertium dicendum quod sacerdos in celebratione missæ utitur crucesignatione ad exprimendam passionem Christi, quæ ad crucem est terminata. Est autem passio Christi quibusdam quasi gradibus peracta. Nam primo fuit Christi traditio, quæ facta est a Deo, Juda et Judæis; quod significat trina crucesignatio super illa verba, *Hæc dona, hæc munera, hæc sancta sacrificia illibata.*

Secundo fuit Christi venditio: est autem venditus sacerdotibus, scribis et pharisæis: ad quod significandum fit iterum trina crucesignatio super illa verba, *Benedictam, adscriptam, ratam;* vel ad ostendendum pretium venditionis, scilicet triginta denarios. Additur autem et duplex crux super illa verba, *Ut nobis corpus et sanguis*, etc., ad designandam personam Judæ venditoris et Christi venditi.

Tertio autem fuit præsignatio passionis Christi facta in cœna; ad quod designandum fiunt tertio duæ cruces, una in consecratione corporis, alia in consecratione sanguinis; ubi utrobique dicitur, *benedixit.*

Quarto autem fuit ipsa passio Christi; unde ad repræsentandum quinque plagas Christi fit quarto quintuplex crucesignatio super illa verba, *Hostiam puram, hostiam sanctam, hostiam immaculatam, panem sanctum vitæ æternæ et calicem salutis perpetuæ.*

---

[10]loc cit note 8

cleansing is required of him who approaches this sacrament, and it is signified by the confession which is made before the Introit. It was signified by the washing of the priest under the Old Law, as Dionysius observes.[10] However, the Church observes the practice because it is seemly in itself, and therefore instituted by the Church, not because it was a ceremonial prescribed by the Old Law. Accordingly it is not observed in the same way as it was then. The foot-washing is omitted, and the hand-washing is kept, because this can more readily be done, and is enough to signify perfect cleaning. Since, as Aristotle says, *The hand is the organ of organs*,[11] all our works are attributed to the hands. Hence the *Psalm, I wash my hands in innocence and go about thy altar, O Lord.*[12]

2. Even our manner of thurifying is not the same, for we use incense as commanded by the Church, not by a ceremonial precept of the Old Law. It has two functions, first, to show reverence towards this sacrament, by its agreeable scent dispelling any bad smell about the place; second, to show the effect of grace, wherewith Christ was filled: *See the smell of my son is as the smell of a field at harvest.*[13] From Christ it spreads to the faithful through his ministers; who *through us spreads the fragrance of the knowledge of him everywhere.*[14] So when the altar, which signifies Christ, has been censed, then afterwards all are censed in turn.

3. In celebrating mass the priest makes use of the sign of the cross to signify Christ's Passion which was ended on the cross. Now Christ's Passion was accomplished in stages. First, his being handed over, which was done by God, by Judas, and by the Jews; and this is signified by the triple sign of the cross at the words, *These gifts, these presents, these holy unspotted sacrifices.*

Second, his being sold to the priests, to the scribes and the Pharisees, and to signifying this the threefold sign of the cross is repeated at the words, *blessed, enrolled, ratified*, or else to signify the price, namely, thirty pence. And a double cross is added at the words, *that it may become for us the body and the blood*, to signify the person of Judas the seller, and of Christ who was sold.

Third, too, for foreshadowing of the Passion at the Last Supper. And to signify this two crosses are used at the consecration, one for the body, the other for the blood, each time saying, *He blessed.*

Fourth, the Passion itself. And to represent Christ's five wounds there is a fivefold signing at the words, *a pure victim, a holy victim, a spotless victim, the holy bread of eternal life and the cup of everlasting* salvation.

---

[11]Aristotle, *De Anima* III, 8. 432a1
[12]*Psalms* 25, 6
[13]*Genesis* 27, 27
[14]II *Corinthians* 2, 14

Quinto repræsentatur extensio corporis et effusio sanguinis, et fructus passionis per trinam crucesignationem quæ fit super illis verbis, *Corpus et sanguinem sumpserimus, omni benedictione*, etc.

Sexto repræsentatur triplex oratio quam fecit in cruce; unam pro persecutoribus, cum dixit, *Pater, ignosce illis*;[15] secundam pro liberatione a morte, cum dixit, *Deus meus, Deus meus, utquid dereliquisti me?*[16] tertia pertinet ad adeptionem gloriæ cum dixit, *Pater, in manus tuas commendo spiritum meum;*[17] et ad significandum fit trina crucesignatio super illa verba, *Sanctificas, vivificas, benedicis*, etc.

Septimo repræsentantur tres horæ quibus pependit in cruce, scilicet a sexta usque ad horam nonam; et ad hoc significandum fit iterum trina crucesignatio ad illa verba, *Per ipsum, et cum ipso, et in ipso.*

Octavo autem repræsentatur separatio animæ a corpore per duas cruces subsequentes extra calicem factas.

Nono autem repræsentatur resurrectio tertia die facta per tres cruces, quæ fiunt ad illa verba, *Pax Domini sit semper vobiscum.*

Potest autem brevius dici quod consecratio hujus sacramenti, et acceptatio hujus sacrificii, et fructus ipsius procedit ex virtute crucis Christi et ideo ubicumque fit mentio de aliquo horum, sacerdos crucesignatione utitur.

4. Ad quartum dicendum quod sacerdos post consecrationem non utitur crucesignatione ad benedicendum et consecrandum, sed solum ad commemorandum virtutem crucis, et modum passionis Christi, ut ex dictis patet.[18]

5. Ad quintum dicendum quod ea quæ sacerdos in missa facit non sunt ridiculosæ gesticulationes, fiunt enim ad aliquid repræsentandum. Quod enim sacerdos brachia extendit post consecrationem, significat extensionem brachiorum Christi in cruce. Levat etiam manus orando, ad designandum quod oratio ejus dirigitur pro populo ad Deum, secundum illud *Thren.*, *Levemus corda nostra cum manibus ad Dominum in cœlos*:[19] et *Exod.* dicitur quod *cum levaret Moyses manus vincebat Israel.*[20] Quod autem manus interdum jungit et se inclinat est suppliciter et humiliter orantis, et designat humilitatem et obedientiam Christi, ex qua passus est. Digitos autem jungit post consecrationem, scilicet pollicem cum indice, quibus corpus Christi consecratum tetigerat, ut si qua particula digitis adhæserit, non dispergatur; quod pertinet ad reverentiam sacramenti.

6. Ad sextum dicendum quod quinquies se sacerdos vertit ad populum, ad significandum quod Dominus die resurrectionis quinquies se manifestavit, ut supra dictum est in tractatu de resurrectione Christi.[21] Salutat

[15] *Luke* 23, 34
[16] *Matthew* 27, 46
[17] *Luke* 23, 46
[18] ad 3 above
[19] *Lamentations* 3, 41

Fifth, the outstretching of Christ's body and the shedding of his blood and the fruits of the Passion are signified by the triple signing at the words, *as many as shall receive the body and the blood may be filled with every blessing*, etc.

Sixth, the representation of Christ's threefold prayer on the cross, one for his persecutors, *Father, forgive them*;[15] the second for deliverance from death, *My God, my God, why hast thou forsaken me?*[16] the third referring to his entrance into glory, *Father, into thy hands I commend my spirit.*[17] And so there is a triple signing at the words, *Thou dost sanctify, quicken, bless*, etc.

Seventh, the three hours he hung on the cross, namely from the sixth to the ninth hour, are represented in the triple signing at the words, *through him, and with him, and in him.*

Eighth, the parting of his soul from his body is signified by the two signs of the cross made later over the chalice.

Ninth, resurrection on the third day is represented by the three crosses at the words, *May the peace of the Lord be always with you.*

More briefly we may say that the consecration of this sacrament, the acceptance of this sacrifice, and its fruits, proceed from the power of Christ's cross, and accordingly whenever mention is made of any of these the priest uses the sign of the cross.

4. The priest makes the sign of the cross after the consecration, not for the purpose of blessing or consecrating, but only for calling to mind the virtue of the cross and the manner of Christ's suffering, as is evident from what has been said.[18]

5. The priest's actions in mass are not ridiculous gestures; all are done to represent something. That he stretches out his arms after the consecration is to signify Christ's stretching out his arms on the cross. He lifts up his hands to pray to point out that his prayer is directed to God; according to *Jeremiah*, *Let us lift up our hearts and hands to God in heaven*,[19] and *Exodus*, *When Moses lifted up his hands Israel prevailed.*[20] That at times he joins his hands and bows down, praying earnestly and humbly, designates Christ's humility and obedience with which he suffered. He closes his thumb and index finger after the consecration, because he has touched the consecrated body of Christ, to avoid any adhering particles being scattered. This he does out of reverence for the sacrament.

6. Five times the priest turns round to the people to mark that our Lord manifested himself five times on the day of his resurrection, as we have recalled.[21] The priest greets the people seven times, five times in turning

---

[20] *Exodus* 17, 11

[21] 3a. 55, 3

autem septies populum scilicet quinque vicibus, quibus se convertit ad populum, et bis, quando se non convertit, scilicet cum ante præfationem dicit, *Dominus vobiscum*, et cum dicit, *Pax Domini sit semper vobiscum*, ad designandam septiformem gratiam Spiritus Sancti. Episcopus autem celebrans in festis in prima salutatione dicit, *Pax vobis*,[22] quod post resurrectionem discipulis dixit Dominus, cujus personam repræsentat præcipue episcopus.

7. Ad septimum dicendum quod fractio hostiæ tria significat. Primo quidem ipsam divisionem corporis Christi, quæ facta est in passione. Secundo distinctionem corporis mystici secundum diversos status. Tertio distributionem gratiarum procedentium ex passione Christi, ut Dionysius dicit;[23] unde talis fractio non inducit divisionem Christi.

8. Ad octavum dicendum quod, sicut Sergius Papa dicit, et habetur *de Consecr., triforme est corpus Domini*:[24] *pars oblata in calicem missa corpus Christi, quod jam resurrexit, monstrat*, scilicet ipsum Christum, et beatam Virginem, vel si qui alii sancti cum corporibus jam sunt in gloria; *pars comesta ambulantes adhuc super terram*, quia scilicet viventes in terra sacramento uniuntur, et passionibus conteruntur, sicut et panis comestus conteritur dentibus; *pars in altari usque ad finem missæ remanens est corpus jacens in sepulcro, quia usque in finem seculi corpora sanctorum in sepulcris erunt*; quorum tamen animæ sunt vel in purgatorio, vel in cœlo. Hic tamen ritus non servatur modo, ut scilicet una pars servetur usque in finem missæ, propter periculum; manet tamen eadem significatio partium, quam quidam metrice expresserunt dicentes:

Hostia dividitur in partes, tincta beatos
Plene, sicca notat vivos, servata sepultos.[25]

Quidam[26] tamen dicunt quod pars in calicem missa significat eos qui vivunt in hoc mundo; pars autem extra calicem servata significat plene beatos, scilicet quantum ad animam et corpus; pars autem comesta significat cæteros.

9. Ad nonum dicendum quod per calicem duo possunt significari. Uno modo ipsa passio Christi, quæ repræsentatur in hoc sacramento, et secundum hoc per partem in calicem missam significantur illi qui adhuc sunt participes passionum Christi. Alio modo potest significari fruitio beata, quæ etiam in hoc sacramento præfiguratur; et ideo illi quorum corpora jam sunt in plena beatitudine, significantur per partem in calicem missam. Et est notandum quod pars in calicem missa non debet populo dari in

---

[22] *Luke* 24, 36. *John* 20, 19–26
[23] *De Eccles. Hier.* 3. PG 3, 444

round to them and twice without turning round, namely when he says *The Lord be with you*, before the Preface, and again when he says, *May the peace of the Lord be always with you*, and this is to represent the sevenfold gift of the Holy Spirit. When a bishop celebrates on festival days, in his first greeting he uses the words of our Lord, whose person he chiefly represents, to the disciples, *Peace be to you.*[22]

7. The breaking of the host signifies three things, first, the rending of Christ's body in the Passion; second, the distinction of his mystical body according to its various states; third, the distribution of the graces which flow from Christ's Passion, as Dionysius notes.[23] Hence it does not introduce division unto Christ.

8. As Pope Sergius[b] says, and he is quoted in the *Decretum*,[24] *The Lord's body is threefold, the part offered and put into the chalice points to Christ's risen body*, namely Christ himself and the blessed Virgin and the other saints, if there be any, already in bodily glory. *The part consumed indicates those still walking on earth*, because while living upon the earth they are united by the sacrament, and are bruised by the passions as the bread eaten is bruised by the teeth. *The part reserved on the altar until the close of mass is his body hidden in the tomb, because the bodies of the saints will be in their graves until the end of the world*, though their souls will be in heaven or in purgatory. However, this practice of leaving one particle on the altar until the end of mass is no longer kept on account of danger, nevertheless the same meaning is preserved, which has been expressed in verse:

The host divided, the host dipped mark the blest,
The part undipped the living, the part reserved the rest.[25]

Yet it may be added that others hold that[26] the part put in the chalice represents those still living in this world, the part kept outside those fully blessed in soul and body, while the part consumed represents the remainder.

9. The chalice can signify two things. First, Christ's Passion itself which is represented by this sacrament, and accordingly the particle put in the chalice, signifies those who are still sharers in Christ's sufferings. Second, it can signify the bliss of the blessed, which likewise is foreshadowed in this sacrament: accordingly the particle put in the chalice signifies those whose bodies are already in full happiness. Note that this particle ought not to

---

[24]cf Pseudo-Hugh of St Victor, PL 176, 145. Gratian, III, 2, 22. RF I, 1321
[25]To be found in Albert, *Sent.* IV, 13
[26]William of Auxerre, *Summa Aurea* IV, 3. cf Baldwin of Canterbury, PL 204, 771. Innocent III, PL 217, 907
[b]St Sergius, d. 701.

supplementum communionis, quia panem intinctum non porrexit Christus nisi Judæ proditori.

10. Ad decimum dicendum quod vinum ratione suæ humiditatis est ablutivum, et ideo sumitur post susceptionem hujus sacramenti ad abluendum os, ne aliquæ reliquiæ remaneant, quod pertinet ad reverentiam sacramenti. Unde *Extra.* dicitur, *Semper sacerdos vino os perfundere debet, postquam totum percepit Eucharistiæ sacramentum, nisi cum eodem die aliam missam debuerit celebrare, ne si forte vinum perfusionis acciperet, celebrationem aliam impediret*;[27] et eadem ratione perfundit vino digitos, quibus corpus Christi tetigerat.

11. Ad undecimum dicendum quod veritas quantum ad aliquid debet respondere figuræ, quia scilicet non debet pars hostiæ consecratæ, de qua sacerdos et ministri vel etiam populus communicat, in crastinum reservari. Unde, ut habetur *de Consecr.*, Clemens I Papa statuit quod *tanta holocausta in altari offerantur, quanta populo sufficere debeant; quod si remanserint, in crastinum non reserventur, sed cum timore et tremore clericorum diligentia consumantur.*[28] Quia tamen hoc sacramentum quotidie sumendum est, non autem agnus paschalis quotidie sumebatur, ideo oportet alias hostias consecratas pro infirmis conservare. Unde in eadem distinctione legitur, *Presbyter Eucharistiam semper habeat paratam, ut quando quis infirmatus fuerit, statim eum communicet, ne sine communione moriatur.*[29]

12. Ad duodecimum dicendum quod in solemni celebratione missæ plures debent adesse. Unde Soter Papa dicit, ut habetur *de Consecr.*, *Hoc quoque statutum est, ut nullus presbyterorum missarum solemnia celebrare præsumat, nisi duobus præsentibus, sibique respondentibus, ipse tertius habeatur; quia cum pluraliter ab eo dicitur, Dominus vobiscum, et illud in secretis, Orate pro me, aptissime convenit ut ipsius respondeatur salutationi.*[30] Unde et ad majorem solemnitatem ibidem statutum legitur quod episcopus cum pluribus missarum solemnia peragat.[31] In missis tamen privatis sufficit unum habere ministrum, qui gerit personam totius populi catholici, ex cujus persona sacerdoti pluraliter respondet.

articulus 6. utrum possit sufficienter occurri defectibus circa celebrationem hujus sacramenti occurrentibus statuta Ecclesiæ observando

AD SEXTUM sic proceditur:[1] 1. Videtur quod non possit sufficienter occurri defectibus qui circa celebrationem hujus sacramenti occurrunt statuta Ecclesiæ observando. Contingit enim quandoque quod sacerdos ante consecrationem, vel post moritur, vel alienatur, vel aliqua alia infirmitate

---

[27] *Extravagantes.* cf *Decretals of Gregory IX*, III, 2, 23. RF II, 636

[28] Gratian, *Decretum* III, 2, 23. RF I, 1301. Pseudo-Clement I, Mansi I, 125. cf Isidore Mercator, False Decretals. PL 130, 38

be given to supplement the Communion given to the people, because Christ gave dipped bread only to Judas, the betrayer.

10. Because of its wetness wine is capable of washing. Consequently it is used for rinsing the mouth after receiving Communion: this belongs to reverence for the sacrament. Accordingly the *Decretals* lay down, *The priest should always cleanse his mouth with wine after he receives the complete sacrament, except when he has to celebrate another mass on the same day, lest from the strength of the wine he be prevented from doing so.*[27] For the same reason wine is poured over his fingers which have touched Christ's body.

11. The truth should correspond to the figure in some respect and so part of the host consecrated, of which the priest, ministers, or the people also communicate, ought not to be reserved until the day following. Hence Pope Clement ordered that *as many hosts are to be offered on the altar as shall serve the people; should any be left over they are not to be reserved until the morrow, but let the clergy carefully consume them with fear and trembling.*[28] Yet since this sacrament is to be received daily, whereas the paschal lamb was not, other hosts should be reserved for the sick. Hence we read in the same place, *Let the priest always have the Eucharist ready, so that when anyone fall sick Communion may be taken to him at once lest he die without it.*[29]

12. Several persons ought to be present at the solemn celebration of the mass. Pope Soter[c] lays down and the *Decretum* repeats him, *It has been ordained that no priest is to presume to celebrate solemn mass unless two others are present answering him, while he himself makes a third, because when he says in the plural, The Lord be with you, and again in the secret prayers, Pray for me, it is most manifestly fitting that they should reply to his greeting.*[30] Hence for greater solemnity it is decreed that a bishop is to solemnize mass with several assistants.[31] Nevertheless one server suffices in private masses; he takes the place of the whole Catholic people, on whose behalf he answers the priest in the plural.

article 6. does the observance of the rules of the Church sufficiently meet defects arising in the celebration of this sacrament?

THE SIXTH POINT:[1] 1. Apparently not. For it sometimes happens that before or after the consecration the priest dies or goes mad, or is stopped by some infirmity from receiving the sacrament and completing the mass. And so the Church ordinance that the consecrating priest should receive Communion, cannot be kept.

---

[29]Gratian, op cit 93. RF 1, 1351

[30]Mansi 1, 692. Gratian, op cit 61. RF 1, 1311

[31]Gratian, op cit 59. RF 1, 1310

[1]cf IV *Sent.* 11 & 13

[c]St Soter or Salvator, d. 174.

impeditur, ne sacramentum sumere possit, et missam perficere. Ergo videtur quod non possit impleri statutum Ecclesiæ quo præcipitur quod sacerdos consecrans suo sacrificio communicet.

2. Præterea, contingit quandoque quod sacerdos ante consecrationem vel post recolit se aliquid comedisse vel bibisse, vel etiam alicui peccato mortali subjacere, vel etiam excommunicationi, cujus prius memoriam non habebat. Necesse est ergo quod ille qui est in tali articulo constitutus peccet mortaliter contra statutum Ecclesiæ faciens, sive sumat, sive non sumat.

3. Præterea, contingit quandoque quod in calicem musca vel aranea, vel aliquod animal venenosum cadit post consecrationem, vel etiam cognoscit sacerdos calici venenum esse immissum ab aliquo malevolo causa occidendi ipsum; in quo casu si sumat, videtur mortaliter peccare se occidendo, vel Deum tentando: similiter si non sumat, peccat contra statutum Ecclesiæ faciens. Ergo videtur esse perplexus et subjectus necessitati peccandi, quod est inconveniens.

4. Præterea, contingit quandoque quod per negligentiam ministri aut aqua non ponitur in calice, aut etiam nec vinum, et hoc sacerdos advertit. Ergo in hoc etiam casu videtur esse perplexus, sive sumat corpus sine sanguine, quasi imperfectum faciens sacrificium, sive non sumat nec corpus nec sanguinem.

5. Præterea contingit quandoque quod sacerdos non recolit se dixisse verba consecrationis, vel etiam alia quæ in celebratione hujus sacramenti dicuntur. Videtur ergo peccare in hoc casu, sive reiteret verba super eandem materiam, quæ forte jam dixerat, sive utatur pane et vino non consecratis, quasi consecratis.

6. Præterea, contingit quandoque propter frigus, quod sacerdoti dilabitur hostia in calicem, sive ante fractionem, sive post. In hoc ergo casu non poterit sacerdos ritum Ecclesiæ implere vel de ipsa fractione, vel etiam de hoc quod sola tertia pars mittatur in calicem.

7. Præterea, contingit quandoque quod per negligentiam sacerdotis sanguis Christi effunditur, vel etiam quod sacerdos sacramentum sumptum vomit, aut etiam quod hostiæ consecratæ tamdiu conservantur ut putrefiant, vel etiam a muribus corrodantur, vel etiam qualitercumque perdantur; in quibus casibus non videtur posse huic sacramento debita reverentia exhiberi secundum Ecclesiæ statuta. Non videtur ergo quod his defectibus seu periculis occurri possit, salvis Ecclesiæ statutis.

SED CONTRA est quod sicut Deus, ita Ecclesia non præcipit aliquid impossibile.

RESPONSIO: Dicendum quod periculis seu defectibus circa hoc sacramentum contingentibus dupliciter potest occurri: uno modo præveniendo, ne

2. Besides, it sometimes happens that before the consecration the priest remembers what he had forgotten when beginning mass, that he has taken some food or drink, or that he is burdened with a mortal sin, or that he is under excommunication. Therefore in such a dilemma he must necessarily commit a mortal sin by breaking the Church rules whether he receives or not.

3. Moreover, it sometimes happens that a fly or spider or some venomous creature falls into the chalice after the consecration, or even that the priest comes to know that poison has been put in it by an enemy in order to murder him. In which case, if he drinks it, he would seem to sin gravely by killing himself or by tempting God,[a] and if he does not drink he would sin by breaking the rules of the Church. Consequently he is in a dilemma and must needs sin whatever he does, which is awkward.

4. And, it sometimes happens that by the server's negligence water is not poured into the chalice or even wine. When the priest discovers this, he is faced with a dilemma, for he sins whether he receives the body without the blood, thus effecting an incomplete sacrament, or whether he receives neither.

5. Also, it sometimes happens that the priest cannot recall having said the words of consecration or other words pronounced in the celebration of this sacrament. In this case he seems to sin, whether he repeats the words possibly already said over the same matter, or whether he uses as consecrated, bread and wine which are not consecrated.

6. Again, it sometimes happens that because of the cold the host slips from the priest's hands into the chalice either after or before the breaking. Then he will be unable to comply with the Church's rite either as to the breaking or as to putting the third particle in the chalice.

7. Also, it happens sometimes that by the priest's carelessness the blood of Christ is spilt, or that he vomits the sacrament received, or else that the consecrated hosts are kept so long that they decay, or are nibbled by mice, or are lost in some manner or another. In such cases it does not seem possible for due reverence to be shown this sacrament according to the Church's rules. It does not seem, then, that these can meet the defects or dangers arising.

ON THE OTHER HAND the Church, like God, does not command the impossible.

REPLY: Defects or mishaps incidental to this sacrament can be met with in two ways. First, by preventing them so that they do not occur. Second,

---

[a]Tempting God, 2a2æ. 97.

scilicet periculum accidat; alio modo subsequendo, ut scilicet id quod accidit emendetur, vel adhibendo remedium, vel saltem per pœnitentiam ejus qui negligenter egit circa hoc sacramentum.

1. Ad primum ergo dicendum quod si sacerdos morte aut infirmitate gravi occupetur ante consecrationem corporis et sanguinis Domini, non oportet ut per alium suppleatur. Si vero, incœpta consecratione, hoc acciderit, puta consecrato corpore ante consecrationem sanguinis, vel etiam consecrato utroque, debet missæ celebritas per alium expleri. Unde, ut habetur in *Decret.*, in Toletano concilio legitur,[2] *Censuimus convenire ut cum a sacerdotibus missarum tempore mysteria sacra consecrantur, si ægritudinis accidat cujuslibet eventus, quo cœptum nequeant explere mysterium, sit liberum episcopo vel presbytero alteri consecrationem exequi incœpti officii. Non enim aliud competit ad supplementum initiatis mysteriis, quam aut incipientis aut subsequentis benedictio completa sacerdotis; quia nec perfecta videri possunt, nisi perfecto ordine compleantur. Cum enim simus omnes unum in Christo, nihil contrarium diversitas personarum format, ubi efficaciam prosperitatis unitas fidei repræsentat. Ne tamen quod naturæ languoris causa consulitur, in præsumptionis perniciem convertatur. Nullus absque patenti proventu molestiæ minister vel sacerdos, cum cœperit, imperfecta officia præsumat omnino relinquere. Si quis hoc temerarie præsumpserit, excommunicationis sententiam sustinebit.*

2. Ad secundum dicendum quod ubi difficultas occurrit, semper est accipiendum illud quod habet minus de periculo. Maxime autem periculosum circa hoc sacramentum est quod est contra perfectionem hujus sacramenti, quia hoc est immane sacrilegium; minus autem est illud quod pertinet ad qualitatem sumentis. Et ideo si sacerdos post consecrationem incœptam recordetur se aliquid comedisse vel bibisse, nihilominus debet perficere sacrificium, et sumere sacramentum; similiter si recordetur se peccatum aliquod commisisse, debet pænitere cum proposito confitendi et satisfaciendi; et sic non indigne sed fructuose sumet sacramentum; et eadem ratio est si meminerit se excommunicationi cuicumque subjacere; debet enim assumere propositum humiliter absolutionem petendi; et sic per invisibilem Pontificem Jesum Christum absolutionem consequetur quantum ad hunc actum, quod peragat divina mysteria. Si vero ante consecrationem alicujus prædictorum sit memor, tutius reputarem, maxime in casu manducationis et excommunicationis, quod missam incœptam desereret, nisi grave scandalum timeretur.

3. Ad tertium dicendum quod si musca vel aranea in calicem ante consecrationem ceciderit, aut etiam venenum deprehenderit esse immissum,

---

[2]Gratian II, 7, 1, 16. RF I, 573. Toledo VII, 2 (646). Mansi X, 767

by dealing with them in such a manner that what has happened amiss is put right, by applying the remedy or at least by the repentance of him who has acted negligently regarding the sacrament.

Hence: 1. If the priest is overtaken by death or grave illness before the consecration there is no need for it to be completed by another. If this happens after the consecration, for instance when the host but not the blood has been consecrated, or even after both have been consecrated, then the celebration of the mass ought to be completed by another. Hence canon law cites a council of Toledo,[2] *We consider it to be fitting that when the sacred mysteries are consecrated by priests during the time of mass, if any sickness supervenes in consequence of which they cannot finish the mystery begun, let it be free for a bishop or priest to finish the office. For nothing else is fitting to complete the mysteries begun unless the consecration be completed either by the priest who began it or by one who follows him, for they cannot be complete unless performed in perfect order. Since we are all one in Christ the diversity of person is no obstacle, where the unity of faith makes it opportune. Yet let not this course we propose for cases of sickness be converted to the wickedness of presumption, and let no minister or priest dare to leave the divine office unfinished unless he be clearly prevented from continuing. If anyone shall have rashly presumed to do so, he will incur the sentence of excommunication.*[2]

2. When a difficulty is met the less dangerous course should be always followed.[b] The greatest danger regarding this sacrament is whatever threatens its completion, for that is a great sacrilege, while that danger is less which regards the condition of the recipient. Accordingly, if after the consecration the priest recalls that he has eaten or drunk something, he ought nevertheless to complete the sacrifice and receive the sacrament. Likewise if he recalls a sin he has committed, he ought to repent and intend to confess and make satisfaction; then he will not receive the sacrament unworthily, but fruitfully. The same applies if he remembers that he is under some excommunication; he ought to resolve humbly to seek absolution, and so he will receive absolution from the invisible high priest, Jesus Christ, for his action of completing the divine mysteries. If indeed he calls to mind any of the above before the consecration, it would be safer for him to stop the mass begun, especially if he has broken his fast or is under excommunication, unless giving grave scandal might be feared.[c]

3. If a fly or spider fall into the chalice before the consecration, or if it

---

[b]i.e. in administering the sacraments. The 'safety first' of Tutiorism is not a first principle for a decision respecting moral conduct.

[c]Scandal, a sin directly against the outward act of charity called *beneficentia*, 2a2æ. 43.

debet effundi, et abluto calice, denuo aliud vinum poni consecrandum. Si vero aliquid horum post consecrationem acciderit, debet animal caute capi et diligenter lavari, et comburi, et ablutio cum cineribus in sacrarium mitti. Si vero venenum ibi deprehenderit immissum, nullo modo debet sumere, nec alii dare, ne calix vitæ vertatur in mortem, sed debet diligenter in aliquo vasculo ad hoc apto cum reliquiis conservari; et ne sacramentum remaneat imperfectum, debet aliud vinum apponere in calicem, et denuo resumere a consecratione sanguinis, et sacrificium perficere.

4. Ad quartum dicendum quod si sacerdos ante consecrationem sanguinis, et post consecrationem corporis percipiat aut vinum aut aquam non esse in calice, debet statim apponere et consecrare. Si vero post consecrationis verba perceperit quod aqua desit, debet nihilominus procedere, quia impositio aquæ, ut supra dictum est,[3] non est de necessitate sacramenti: debet tamen puniri ille ex cujus negligentia hoc contingit. Nullo autem modo debet aqua vino jam consecrato misceri, quia sequeretur corruptio sacramenti pro aliqua parte, ut supra dictum est.[4] Si vero percipiat post verba consecrationis quod vinum non fuerit positum in calice, si quidem hoc percipiat ante sumptionem corporis, debet, deposita aqua si ibi fuerit, imponere vinum cum aqua, et resumere a verbis consecrationis sanguinis. Si vero hoc perceperit post sumptionem corporis, aliam hostiam apponere debet iterum consecrandam simul cum sanguine; quod ideo dico, quia si diceret sola verba consecrationis sanguinis, non servaretur debitus ordo consecrandi; et, sicut dicitur in prædicto cap. Toletani concilli, *perfecta videri non possunt sacrificia, nisi perfecto ordine compleantur.*[5] Si vero inciperet a consecratione sanguinis, et repeteret omnia verba consequentia, non competeret, nisi adesset hostia consecrata, cum in verbis illis occurrant quædam dicenda et fienda, non solum circa sanguinem, sed etiam circa corpus; et debet in fine iterum sumere hostiam consecratam et sanguinem, non obstante etiam si prius sumpserit aquam quæ erat in calice, quia præceptum de perfectione vel de perceptione hujus sacramenti majoris est ponderis quam præceptum quod hoc sacramentum a jejunis sumatur, ut supra dictum est.[6]

5. Ad quintum dicendum quod licet sacerdos non recolat se dixisse aliqua eorum quæ dicere debuit, non tamen debet ex hoc mente perturbari; non enim qui multa dicit recolit omnia quæ dixit; nisi forte aliquid in dicendo apprehenderit sub ratione jam dicti; sic enim aliquid efficitur memorabile. Unde si aliquis attente cogitet illud quod dicit, non tamen cogitet se dicere illud, non multum postea recolit se dixisse; sic enim fit

---

[3]3a. 74, 7
[4]3a. 77, 8
[5]loc cit note 2

be discovered that the wine is poisoned, the wine ought to be poured out, and after cleansing the chalice fresh wine should be served for consecrating. If anything of the sort happens after the consecration, the insect ought to be cautiously caught, throughly washed, and burnt, and the ablutions and ashes together poured into the piscina. If it be discovered that the wine is poisoned, on no account should the priest receive it or give it to others, lest the cup of life be changed into death, but it should be put carefully aside in a suitable vessel and kept with the relics. And lest the sacrament remain incomplete, other wine is to be put into the chalice, the mass resumed from the consecration of the blood, and the sacrifice completed.

4. If before the consecration of the blood and after the consecration of the body the priest detects that either the wine or the water are not in the chalice, then he ought to add them and consecrate. If after the words of consecration he discovers the water is absent, he ought notwithstanding to go straight on, because the addition of the water is not necessary for the sacrament, as we have seen,[3] though the person responsible for the neglect should be punished. On no account should water be mixed with the consecrated wine, for corruption in part of the sacrament would result, as we have seen.[4] But if after the consecration the priest perceives that no wine has been put in the chalice, and if he detect it before receiving the body, then putting the water aside, he ought to pour in wine with water, and begin from the words of the consecration of the blood. But if he notice it after receiving the body, he ought to take a new host to be consecrated together with the blood. I say this because if he were to say only the words of consecrating the blood the proper order of consecration would not be observed; as laid down by a council of Toledo, *sacrifices are not perfectly achieved if they are not completed in perfect order.*[5] If he were to begin from the consecration of the blood and to repeat the canon of the mass, it would not suffice unless a consecrated host were present, since things to be said and done there refer to the body, not only to the blood, and at the close he ought to consume the consecrated host and the blood, even if he had already taken the water which was in the chalice, because the precept of completing is of greater weight than the precept of fasting, as we have seen.[6]

5. Although the priest may not recollect having said some of the words he should have said, he ought not to be troubled in mind on that account. For a man who speaks many words does not recall all that he has said, unless perhaps in speaking about something he appreciates that he has said it before, and so this is impressed on his memory. And so if a man attends to what he is saying, without adverting to the fact he is uttering some particular words, shortly afterwards he recalls that he has uttered them; any-

[6]ad 2 above. 3a. 80, 8

aliquid objectum memoriæ inquantum accipitur sub ratione præteriti, sicut dicitur in lib. *de Memoria.*[7] Si tamen sacerdoti probabiliter constet se aliqua omisisse, si quidem non sunt de necessitate sacramenti, non existimo quod propter hoc debeat resumere, immutando ordinem sacrificii, sed debet ulterius procedere; si vero certificetur se omisisse aliquid eorum quæ sunt de necessitate sacramenti, scilicet formam consecrationis, cum forma consecrationis sit de necessitate sacramenti, sicut et materia, idem videtur faciendum, quod dictum est,[8] in defectu materiæ, ut scilicet resumatur a forma consecrationis, et cætera per ordinem reiterentur, ne mutetur ordo sacrificii.

6. Ad sextum dicendum quod fractio hostiæ consecratæ, et quod una sola pars mittatur in calicem, respicit corpus mysticum, sicut admixtio aquæ significat populum, et ideo horum prætermissio non facit imperfectionem sacrificii, ut propter hoc sit necesse aliquid reiterare circa celebrationem hujus sacramenti.

7. Ad septimum dicendum quod, sicut legitur *de Cons.*, ex decreto Pii I Papæ, *si per negligentiam aliquid de sanguine stillaverit in tabulam quæ terræ adhæret, lingua lambetur, et tabula radetur. Si vero non fuerit tabula, terra radetur, et igni consumetur, et cinis intra altare condetur, et sacerdos quadraginta diebus pœniteat. Si autem super altare stillaverit calix sorbeat minister stillam, et tribus diebus pœniteat. Si super linteum altaris, et ad aliud stilla pervenerit, quatuor diebus pœniteat; si usque ad tertium, novem diebus pœniteat; si usque ad quartum, viginti diebus pœniteat; et linteamina quæ stilla tetigerit, tribus vicibus lavet minister calice subtus posito; et aqua ablutionis sumatur, et juxta altare recondatur.*[9] Posset etiam sumi in potum a ministro, nisi propter abominationem dimitteretur. Quidam autem ulterius partem illam linteaminum incidunt et comburunt, et cinerem in altari, vel sacrario reponunt.

Subditur autem ibid. ex Pœnitentiali Bedæ Presbyteri, *Si quis per ebrietatem vel voracitatem Eucharistiam evomuerit, quadraginta diebus pœniteat, si laicus est; clerici vel monachi, seu diaconi et presbyteri septuaginta diebus pœniteant; episcopus nonaginta. Si autem infirmitatis causa evomuerint, septem diebus pœniteant.*[10] Et in eadem dist. legitur ex concilio Aurelianensi,* *Qui non bene custodierit sacramentum, et mus, vel aliquod aliud animal illud comederit, quadraginta diebus pœniteat; qui autem perdiderit illud in Ecclesia, aut pars ejus ceciderit, et non inventa fuerit, triginta diebus pœniteat.*[11] Et eadem pœnitentia videtur dignus sacerdos per cujus

---

*Piana: *Arelatensi*, Arles (IV)

[7]Aristotle. *De Memoria et Reminiscentia* I. 449b24

[8]ad 4 above

[9]Gratian, III, 2, 27. RF I, 1323. Pseudo-Theodore, *Pœnitentiale* 51. PL 99, 950

thing becomes an object of memory precisely as being in the past, as Aristotle remarks.[7] But if the priest is fairly sure that the words he omitted are not necessarily part of the sacrament, I think that he ought not repeat them by changing the order of the sacrifice, but that he ought to go on. If however it is certain that he left out words necessary for the sacrament, namely the form of consecration, this is as necessary for the sacrament as the matter is, and so the same course ought to be followed as with a defect of matter,[8] namely he should begin again from the form of consecration, and repeat it in due sequence, lest the order of the sacrifice be changed.

6. The breaking of the consecrated host and the putting of only one particle into the chalice refers to the mystical body, as the mixing with water refers to the people. Therefore the omission of either causes not such imperfection in the sacrifice as to call for going back to them in the celebration of this sacrament.

7. According to canon law based on a decree of Pope Pius I,[d] *If by carelessness a drop of blood fall on a board of the floor let it be licked up and the board scraped. But if it be the ground let it be scraped up and burnt and the ashes put inside the altar. And let the priest do penance for forty days. If a drop fall on the altar from the chalice, let the minister suck it up, and do penance for three days. If on the altar cloth and it penetrates to the second altar cloth, let him do four days' penance, if to the third, then nine days' penance, if to the fourth, twenty days' penance. And let the altar linens be washed three times by the priest, holding the chalice below, then let the water be taken and put by the altar.*[9] It might even be drunk by the minister unless it might be rejected because of nausea. Some priests go further and cut that part of the linen, which they burn and put the ashes in the altar or sacrarium.

The *Decretum* continues with a quotation from the Penitential of Bede the Priest,[e] *If owing to drunkenness or gluttony, anyone vomits up the Eucharist let him do forty days' penance if he be a layman, but let clerics and monks, deacons and priests do seventy days' penance, and a bishop, ninety days. If they vomit from sickness, then seven days.*[10] In the same place we read from a synod at Orleans,[f] *Those who do not safely preserve the sacrament, and a mouse or other animal eat it, must do forty days' penance; he also who loses it in church or lets fall a part which is not found, shall do thirty days' penance.*[11] And the priest who from neglect allows the hosts to

[10]Gratian, op cit 28. RF I, 1328. Bede, *De Remediis Pecc., De Ebrietate*. PL 94, 573
[11]Gratian, op cit 94. RF I, 1352. cf Pseudo-Theodore, *Pœnitentiale* 55. PL 99, 951
[d]St Pius I, d. *c.* 154.
[e]The Venerable Bede, d. 735.
[f]Orleans III, anno 538.

negligentiam hostiæ consecratæ putrefiunt. Prædictis autem diebus debet pœnitens jejunare, et a communione cessare. Pensatis tamen conditionibus negotii et personæ, potest minui vel addi ad pœnitentiam prædictam. Hoc tamen observandum est quod ubicumque species integræ inveniuntur sunt reverenter conservandæ vel etiam sumendæ; quia manentibus speciebus manet ibi corpus Christi, ut supra dictum est.[12] Ea vero in quibus inveniuntur, si commode fieri potest, sunt comburenda, cinere in sacrario recondito, sicut de rasura tabulæ dictum est.[13]

---

[12] 3a. 76, 6 ad 3; 77, 4 & 5

go mouldy seems to deserve the same penance. And on those days the one doing penance ought to fast and abstain from Communion. However, having weighed the circumstances of the fact and the person concerned, these penances may be lessened or increased. It must be observed that wherever the species are found to be entire, they must be reverently kept or consumed, because so long as they be entire the body of Christ is there, as we have stated.[12] If it can be done conveniently, the things in which they are found are to be burnt, and the ashes put in the sacrarium, as was said about the floor scrapings.[13]

---

[13]ad 7 above

Glossary

accident: in logic a predicate that is not essentially implied in the subject. In natural philosophy, one of the nine categories of being other than substance, of which relation, quality, and quantity are the most noteworthy. The appearances or species of bread and wine are treated as accidents, though in fact they are empirical objects, not precisely in a metaphysical category of being.

causality: the operation of an efficient or final cause and the influence of a material and formal cause. Sacramental causality is commonly ranged under efficient causality: efficient cause or agent, the producer of an effect, whether as a principal cause (which may be a secondary cause deriving its power of acting from a first cause, this power, however, being its own) or an instrumental cause (which acts in virtue of the causality of a principal cause). A sacrament acts as an instrumental cause, *signum effectivum.* Yet other causality is present, notably final and exemplar. See below.

cause: a real principle on which the existence of something depends. The four causes: efficient cause or the agent; final cause or its end and purpose; formal cause, its inner shaping meaning; material cause, that in which it is produced. To these should be added the exemplar cause, a blend of the efficient, final and formal cause: this idea in the mind of the maker is to be remarked in the working of the sacraments by which we are configured to Christ. Also noted is the 'meritorious' and 'satisfactory' cause, by which Christ's merits and satisfaction are communicated to us.

concomitance: the doctrine that the whole Christ is present in the Blessed Sacrament in each of the consecrated elements by virtue not directly of the words of consecration, but of his being there in a sacramental manner yet substantially as he really is.

exemplar cause: the original and formative idea in the producer of an effect.

Gloss, the; a gloss: the former refers to the *Glossa Ordinaria*, the work of Anselm of Laon (d. 1117) and his school, but containing parts traceable to Walafrid Strabo (d. 849); the latter to other scriptural glosses, e.g. 'Interlinear' and Lombard's.

image: a representative sign configured to the original from which it derives.

intention: the determinate purpose of a minister in applying the matter and form of a sacrament, and more generally the opening out of knowing and loving to a real object, and also the whole relativeness of sacraments and sacrifices to the reality they express.

sacramentum & res sacramenti: the outward sign & the inward grace. In the Eucharist the *res* is Christ himself.

sign: a strong word in sacramental theology, especially when it is an image-sign, reflecting, leading to, causing, and even holding the reality signified.

sin: peccatum or more precisely *culpa*, fault, a morally bad act by commission or omission, which leaves a state or condition of vice, *vitium*. The distinction between mortal and venial sin refers, not to the type or kind of the fault, but rather to the degree of the commitment, mortal sin being so deep and deliberate as to deprive us of the habit of charity, of the condition of being in love with God, while venial conflicts with the activity of loving God.

species: in this volume has the original meaning of external appearance to the senses; the sacramental species are the bread and wine before consecration, and their sensible form which remains afterwards. It is not used here as an epistemological concept or as a class-term for a definite nature.

substance: the ultimate reality of which the nature is not to exist in another as in a subject, unlike a modifying accident which is grounded in it.

usus: though sometimes bearing the sense of utilization of a means, *uti*, as contrasted to realization of an end, *frui*, the term in this volume rather means application or the actual performance of a work in the order of execution as contrasted with its being resolved in the order of intention.

Index

A

B

C

D

E

F

G

H

I

J

K

L

M

N

O

P

R

S

T

U

V

W

Z

VOLUMES

General Editor: THOMAS GILBY, O.P.

PRIMA PARS

1 Christian Theology (1a. 1) Thomas Gilby, O.P.
2 Existence and Nature of God (1a. 2–11) Timothy McDermott, O.P.
3 Knowing and Naming God (1a. 12–13) Herbert McCabe, O.P.
4 Knowledge in God (1a. 14–18) Thomas Gornall, S.J.
5 God's Will and Providence (1a. 19–26) Thomas Gilby, O.P.
6 The Trinity (1a. 27–32) Ceslaus Velecky, O.P.
7 Father, Son, and Holy Ghost (1a. 33–43) T. C. O'Brien
8 Creation, Variety, and Evil (1a. 44–9) Thomas Gilby, O.P.
9 Angels (1a. 50–64) Kenelm Foster, O.P.
10 Cosmogony (1a. 65–74) W. A. Wallace, O.P.
11 Man (1a. 75–83) Timothy Suttor
12 Human Intelligence (1a. 84–9) P. T. Durbin
13 Man Made to God's Image (1a. 90–102) Edmund Hill, O.P.
14 Divine Government (1a. 103–9) T. C. O'Brien
15 The World Order (1a. 110–19) M. J. Charlesworth

PRIMA SECUNDÆ

16 Purpose and Happiness (1a2æ. 1–5) Thomas Gilby, O.P.
17 Psychology of Human Acts (1a2æ. 6–17) Thomas Gilby, O.P.
18 Principles of Morality (1a2æ. 18–21) Thomas Gilby, O.P.
19 The Emotions (1a2æ. 22–30) Eric D'Arcy
20 Pleasure (1a2æ. 31–9) Eric D'Arcy
21 Fear and Anger (1a2æ. 40–8) J. P. Reid, O.P.
22 Dispositions (1a2æ. 49–54) Anthony Kenny
23 Virtue (1a2æ. 55–67) W. D. Hughes, O.P.
24 The Gifts of the Spirit (1a2æ. 68–70) Edward D. O'Connor, C.S.C.
25 Sin (1a2æ. 71–80) John Fearon, O.P.
26 Original Sin (1a2æ. 81–5) T. C. O'Brien
27 Effects of Sin, Stain and Guilt (1a2æ. 86–9) T. C. O'Brien
28 Law and Political Theory (1a2æ. 90–7) Thomas Gilby, O.P.
30 The Gospel of Grace (1a2æ. 106–14) Cornelius Ernst, O.P.

SECUNDA SECUNDÆ

31 Faith (2a2æ. 1–7) T. C. O'Brien
32 Consequences of Faith (2a2æ. 8–16) Thomas Gilby, O.P.

33 Hope (2a2æ. 17–22) W. J. Hill, O.P.
34 Charity (2a2æ. 23–33) R. J. Batten, O.P.
35 Consequences of Charity (2a2æ. 34–46) Thomas R. Heath, O.P.
36 Prudence (2a2æ. 47–56) Thomas Gilby, O.P.
37 Justice (2a2æ. 57–62) Thomas Gilby, O.P.
38 Injustice (2a2æ. 63–79) Marcus Lefebure, O.P.
39 Religion and Worship (2a2æ. 80–91) Kevin O'Rourke, O.P.
40 Superstition and Irreverence (2a2æ. 92–100) T. F. O'Meara, O.P. and M. J. Duffy, O.P.
41 Virtues of Justice in the Human Community (2a2æ. 101–22) T. C. O'Brien
42 Courage (2a2æ. 123–40) Anthony Ross, O.P. and P. G. Walsh
43 Temperance (2a2æ. 141–54) Thomas Gilby, O.P.
44 Well-tempered Passion (2a2æ. 155–70) Thomas Gilby, O.P.
45 Prophecy and other Charisms (2a2æ. 171–8) Roland Potter, O.P.
46 Action and Contemplation (2a2æ. 179–82) J. R. Aumann, O.P.
47 The Pastoral and Religious Lives (2a2æ. 183–9) J. R. Aumann, O.P.

TERTIA PARS

48 The Incarnate Word (3a. 1–6) R. J. Hennessey, O.P.
49 The Grace of Christ (3a. 7–15) Liam Walsh, O.P.
50 The One Mediator (3a. 16–26) Colman O'Neill, O.P.
51 Our Lady (3a. 27–30) Thomas R. Heath, O.P.
52 The Childhood of Christ (3a. 31–7) Roland D. Potter, O.P.
53 The Life of Christ (3a. 38–45) S. R. Parsons, O.P.
54 The Passion of Christ (3a. 46–52) T. A. R. Murphy, O.P.
55 The Resurrection of the Lord (3a. 53–9) C. Thomas Moore, O.P.
56 The Sacraments (3a. 60–5) David Bourke
57 Baptism and Confirmation (3a. 66–72) J. J. Cunningham, O.P.
58 The Eucharistic Presence (3a. 73–8) Abp. William Barden, O.P.
59 Holy Communion (3a. 79–83) Thomas Gilby, O.P.
60 The Sacrament of Penance (3a. 84–90) R. R. Masterson, O.P. and T. C. O'Brien

20950752R10131

Made in the USA
Middletown, DE
13 June 2015